# RHETORIC AND HUMAN UNDERSTANDING

## ANN GILL
### *Colorado State University*

WAVELAND
PRESS, INC.
Prospect Heights, Illinois

## Consulting Editor

Robert E. Denton, Jr.

For information about this book, write or call:

Waveland Press, Inc.
P.O. Box 400
Prospect Heights, Illinois 60070
(847) 634-0081

# Table of Contents

iii

## Part Four    Challenges to the Rational Paradigm    171

# Acknowledgements

This text is the product not only of other texts but of countless conversations about rhetoric and human understanding. My debt is particularly large to those individuals who were my teachers. Professor Ted Johnson's oral renditions of passages from *Preface to Plato* and *House Made of Dawn* captured my imagination and kindled my love for words. The late Professor Gordon Hostettler taught me not only rhetoric but respect for knowledge. Professor Sonja Foss, by both tutelage and example, made me a writer. The late O. William Gill bequeathed to me the values of fairness and tolerance and the habit of reading, and Carol Gill set standards I can only hope to reach of generosity, hard work, and intellectual curiosity. From Nell Brown Propst, I learned the power of the spoken word, and from discussions and arguments with Stephen Lewis came the energy for this book. Perhaps most of all, however, I owe this text to all the conversations I have had with students in the Department of Speech Communication at Colorado State University, for whom this book was written and to whom it is dedicated. In truth, it was they who were teaching me.

Finally, my appreciation to those who participated in the production of this text. It was markedly improved by the careful and insightful editing of Carol Rowe and G. Jack Gravlee. I owe much to Rich Hausmann and Ronnie Molina, who helped in locating sources, and even more to the patience of Jeff Browne.

# Introduction

The study of rhetoric dominates contemporary scholarship, not only in the humanities and social sciences but in some natural sciences as well, as scholars ranging from philosophers to physicists to computer scientists investigate the effects of particular human uses of signs. Topics from this scholarship, including the individual and societal creation of meaning, are central to our lives and to the search for self. However, much of the scholarly conversation is very abstract, and it involves a specialized vocabulary. As a result, the material is inaccessible to those not steeped in the scholarship of contemporary linguistics, philosophy, rhetoric, and other disciplines. This text is an attempt to review the scholarly conversation about rhetoric and signs in a way that is useful even to those unfamiliar with the taxonomy of these disciplines and of "postmodernism"—the term itself indicating the taxonomic difficulties presented by the scholarly literature. The review begins with signs, moves through various rhetorical understandings, and ends with a challenge to readers to develop their own unique rhetorical perspectives.

The human animal is a signifying animal, set apart from other creatures by the complex and wide-ranging systems of signs that can be used to comprehend experience, to contemplate that which lies beyond experience, to communicate with other humans, and to create a meaningful existence. The various aspects of human signification are reviewed in Part One.

To create a context for understanding contemporary human rhetorical experience, Part Two describes the rhetorical experience of humans in early, nonliterate societies. These chapters review

1

speculation about mythological or primal minds and the experience and understanding of humans who lived in such oral societies. By understanding something about the rhetorical reality inhabited by such people, contemporary humans are better able to gauge the influence of rhetoric and the patterns of meaning it creates.

In Part Three, various influences on the modern Western mind and rhetorical experience are reviewed: literacy; communication technologies; logic and argumentation; and conceptions of certainty and truth. These influences on contemporary Western human experience help to explain the common-sense reality likely experienced by many readers of this book, a reality sometimes characterized as the "rational paradigm."

Many contemporary discussions of rhetoric are cast as challenges to this so-called rational paradigm. These scholars call into question common-sense assumptions about reality and the role of human signification in the experience of reality. In Part Four, views on language and rhetoric from the structural and poststructural movements illustrate this fundamental challenge to rationality as does the postmodern project. In addition, challenges to dominant societal understandings are illustrated by demands that various discourses be given a voice. These challenges to the rational paradigm demonstrate the rhetorical nature of that which humans frequently deem to be reality.

Thus, the goal of this text is to introduce basic concepts of human signification, to explain both primal and contemporary rhetorical experience, and to offer challenges to common-sense understandings. The form of the text is intended to encourage an extended dialogue with those scholars who have theorized and written about rhetoric and signs. Thus, you are invited to join the conversation concerning rhetoric. As a participant in that conversation, you have an obligation to play an active role; ideas presented in this and other texts should not be accepted uncritically. Think about various ideas. Develop refutations to challenge those with which you disagree. After such critical examination, discard those you find wanting. But also challenge yourself. Be open to new ways of thinking about yourself, your world, and your experience as a rhetorical human being. Accept responsibility for contributing to this lively and fascinating conversation. Only by such active participation in the conversation can you begin to develop your own rhetorical point of view and personal strategies necessary for living in a rhetorical reality.

Although the text eschews sexist language, direct quotations are faithful to the original language, in respect for the conventions of the time and to demonstrate the pervasive use of such language.

# Part One

# The Signifying Animal

Attempts to identify the trait that makes humans distinct from other animals include Aristotle's claim that humans are the rational animal and Ernst Cassirer's suggestion that humans are symbol-using animals. The human characteristic directly related both to the rational and symbolic nature of humans is the ability to use sophisticated systems of arbitrary signs. Although all living creatures communicate, none seems to have developed the breadth or variety of signs nor, specifically, the linguistic capacity that humans display. Development of language changes a human infant into a fully communicative person. At base, this development involves mastery of the ability to symbolize, to use signs to signify one thing by means of another. Once this ability is developed, the human capacity for creativity, invention, reason, and expression can be realized. Part One reviews signs and symbols as well as the human creations that result from the ability to signify—language, rhetoric, and meaning.

# Chapter One

# Signs and Symbols

Many of us devote a portion of our lives to the quest for self-knowledge. Who are we? What is our relationship to the world around us? Such questions are at the heart of philosophical inquiry, which struggles with questions about truth and knowledge. Certainly, these questions are among the main concerns of ancient Greek philosophers, who laid the foundation for modern Western philosophy. In one of Plato's dialogues, Socrates says to Phaedrus:

> I can't as yet "know myself," as the inscription at Delphi enjoins, and so long as that ignorance remains it seems to me ridiculous to inquire into extraneous matters. Consequently I . . . direct my inquiries, as I have just said, rather to myself, to discover whether I really am a more complex creature and more puffed up with pride than Typhon, or a simpler, gentler being whom heaven has blessed with a quiet, un-Typhonic nature.[1]

These questions continue to occupy philosophers in present times, although focus of the inquiry has moved from metaphysical speculation to inquiry into language and other sign systems. To understand humans, a study of human capabilities and creations is helpful. That study begins with the identification of perhaps the most significant attribute of humans—their amazingly sophisticated ability to use signs and symbols.

## Symbols—The Definition of a Human Being

One concern of Western thinkers, at least since the ancient Greeks, has been the nature of human beings and their distinction from other living creatures. This search for a defining characteristic has led to the consideration of human language and the capabilities that language ability gives to human beings. Language allows humans to communicate with each other, to think, and to reason. In each of the following attempts to "define" the human being, the ability to use language plays a central role.

## Aristotle

The human ability to use language led Aristotle to distinguish humans by defining them as rational animals. In the introduction to *Metaphysics*, he writes:

> All men by nature desire to know. An indication of this is the delight we take in our senses; for even apart from their usefulness they are loved for themselves; and above all others the sense of sight. For not only with a view to action, but even when we are not going to do anything, we prefer seeing (one might say) to everything else. The reason is that this, most of all the senses, makes us know and brings to light many differences between things.[2]

Aristotle's definition of the human being as a rational animal has some appeal. In all the animal world, no other species seems to devote significant amounts of time to thinking about questions of meaning or being; apparently no other species sets out to define itself or is given to wondering about its place in the cosmos. Aristotle notes, "The animals other than man live by appearances and memories, and have but little of connected experience; but the human race lives also by art and reasonings."[3] The capacity for rational thought, in Aristotle's view, is that which sets humans apart.

## Ernst Cassirer

Ernst Cassirer, a German philosopher who fled to the United States prior to World War II, was not content with Aristotle's definition of a human being, thinking it begged the question of a unique human characteristic. Cassirer suggests we must search beyond Aristotle's claim that we are rational animals; he proposes instead to identify the particular human ability which *results* in rationality, the ability which allows humans to think and to create new things. His definition of the human being involves the specific human capacity whereby reason and creativity are possible. Cassirer claims that a human being is an *animal symbolicum*—the symbol-using animal.[4]

Cassirer's notion of a symbol, which he identifies as the distinguishing characteristic of humans, involves three aspects: 1) a symbol is a sense datum, that is, a material stimulus of human sensation; 2) the symbol stands for something other than itself; 3) and the relationship between the symbol and that for which it stands is conventional and not natural. The types of stimuli which can operate as symbols are numerous. In spoken language, the sounds we make operate as symbols. Those sounds allow humans to distinguish between the two words which both are spelled "lead" in the following sentence: The scientific evidence about *lead* in gasoline may *lead* one to concur that newer automobiles should use only unleaded gasoline. Furthermore, the different sounds made when the Reverend Martin Luther King, Jr., said "I have a dream" and those made when Clint Eastwood's character, "Dirty Harry," said "Make my day" are what create very different meaning when audiences hear those two statements.

Marks on paper or other surfaces also operate as symbols. As you read this book, you are able to understand the marks, to interpret them as words in a language you speak; they have meaning for you. The process of learning to read is one of becoming aware of the meaning of these marks. Some oral societies, when introduced to writing, have referred to it as "making paper talk." Of course, letters are not the only marks that operate as symbols. Drawings on cave walls may represent seasons, myths and legends, family genealogy, or an individual's story. Some marks are useful in that they may be recognized by speakers of many languages. Male and female figures frequently are used on restroom doors in airports, and the circle with a slash through it is recognized as a negation of whatever it pictures, such as the "no smoking" sign.

Gestures also may operate as symbols. Extending the index and middle finger, spread apart, meant "peace" in the 1960s, particularly when flashed during anti-war demonstrations. The same gesture meant "victory" to soldiers returning from World War II. When George Bush traveled to Australia in early 1992, he flashed the sign to demonstrating Aussies, apparently unaware the gesture had a vulgar meaning in Australian society. When a hitchhiker extends a thumb, she indicates she wants a ride. When a stranger smiles, it may be an indication that he would welcome conversation.

Smells also can operate as symbols. As more states outlaw smoking in public places during the 1990s, the smell of smoke in an airport or a restaurant may indicate that the local government has an unenlightened attitude towards public health. When I was a child, the smell of baking bread when I entered my home after school symbolized that this was my mother's day off from her job as an evening-shift nurse.

Not every sense datum is a symbol, however. The second criterion is that the stimulus must stand for something other than itself. That is, a person who perceives a stimulus must gain some meaning from it that goes beyond the stimulus itself, or the person creating the sense datum must intend it as such. For example, a car sitting in front of a house may be noticed, and intended, for nothing beyond itself. If so, it is not operating as a symbol. However, if the interpreter notices the car, notices that it is a Mercedes, and thinks, "I didn't realize that my neighbor was wealthy," the car has become a symbol of wealth. Some stimuli are nearly always symbolic, having relatively little importance in themselves. The sounds and marks of language, number systems, and objects such as an abacus are such sense data. Every stimuli has the potential to operate as a symbol. Things may be intended as symbols by the one using the symbol. In our culture, people frequently wear rings to symbolize their marital status. Certain dress or haircuts are intended to symbolize membership in groups or rebellion from the dominant cultural values. When an individual wishes to be left alone on an airplane trip, she buries her nose in a book, avoids eye contact with the person sitting next to her, and sits so her legs and shoulders are pointed toward the window. On the other hand, things may be interpreted symbolically, no matter what the intention, by the one perceiving the symbol. A person from out of town may dress in red, unaware that the color symbolizes gang membership to inner-city youth. Although the sound of a cock crowing may indicate the start of a new day to a farm family, likely the cock did not intend to send that particular message. The fact that humans can use and interpret symbols makes every sense datum ripe with potential meanings. Indeed, the world is awash in potential symbols.

The final criterion for a symbol is that the relationship between a symbol and its meaning is conventional, not natural. A saw naturally causes a certain sound. However, the sounds of the word *table* bear no natural relationship to the object in your kitchen upon which you set plates for supper. To a person speaking another language, the sounds or marks of *table* are meaningless. A Spanish speaker associates the object beneath his supper plate with the sounds or marks of *la mesa*. Any stimulus used symbolically has a conventional relationship with its referent. In a research report, the author may establish that $x$ will represent men and $y$, women. These relationships are merely conventional; there is no natural connection between the stimulus and the referent.

Some sense data bear a natural relationship to their referents. For example, spots on the skin may be an indication that the person is suffering from measles. This relationship is not conventional but natural. A student of Cassirer's and a well-known philosopher in her own right, Susanne Langer makes this distinction between symbols and what she calls "signs":

> [A] significant sound, gesture, thing, event (e.g. a flash, an image), may be either a *sign* or a *symbol.*
>
> A sign indicates the existence—past, present, or future—of a thing, event, or condition. Wet streets are a sign that it has rained. A patter on the roof is a sign that it is raining. A fall of the barometer or a ring round the moon is a sign that it is going to rain. In an unirrigated place, abundant verdure is a sign that it often rains there. . . .
>
> All the examples here adduced are *natural signs.* A natural sign is a part of a greater event, or of a complex condition, and to an experienced observer it signifies the rest of that situation of which it is a notable feature. It is a *symptom* of a state of affairs. . . .
>
> Symbols are not proxy for their objects, but are *vehicles for the conception of objects.* . . . In talking *about* things we have conceptions of them, not the things themselves; and *it is the conceptions, not the things, that symbols directly "mean."* . . . The fundamental difference between signs and symbols is this difference of association, and consequently of their *use* by the third party to the meaning function, the subject; signs *announce* their objects to him, whereas symbols *lead him to conceive* their objects.[5]

Animals respond to what Langer calls "signs." An increased volume of wind may be a sign of rain, and raccoons may scurry for shelter. Mercury rising or falling in a graduated glass tube is a symbol of weather change; it must be interpreted by a human to be understood.

Rather than living in the physical world of mere sensation and memory of sensation, as animals seem to do, Cassirer argues that humans live in a different plane of reality; our responses are not organic and direct, as are theirs, but symbolic.[6] What this means is that sounds, sights, and smells come to represent things other than themselves—things such as ideas, feelings, other objects, and so on. This process of representation, of creating meaning, is the essence of being human, according to Cassirer. Although humans may react to natural signs, they also are separated from the natural world by their symbols. Cassirer explains:

> No longer in a merely physical universe, man lives in a symbolic universe. Language, myth, art, and religion are parts of this universe. They are the varied threads which weave the symbolic net, the tangled web of human experience. . . . No longer can man confront reality immediately; he cannot see it, as it were, face to face. Physical reality seems to recede in proportion as

man's symbolic activity advances. Instead of dealing with the
things themselves man is in a sense constantly conversing with
himself. He has so enveloped himself in linguistic forms, in
artistic images, in mythical symbols or religious rites that he
cannot see or know anything except by the interposition of this
artificial medium.[7]

Yet this artificial medium, symbolization, opens to humans the life of
the mind, the world of dreams and possibility, the expressiveness of art,
and the potential for religion and belief. Therefore, Cassirer's claim is
that the capacity to use symbols is that which defines the human being.

## Alfred Korzybski

Cassirer's definition has set the tone for much scholarship about
communication in the twentieth century. Another writer making a
similar distinction is Alfred Korzybski. Korzybski was associated with
the General Semantics movement, popular in the United States during
the 1940s and 1950s. Korzybski distinguished between *chemical
binders*, *space binders*, and *time binders*. All life forms, according to
Korzybski, have the natural ability to make chemical changes; hence,
apple trees, buffalo, and residents of Des Moines, Iowa, all are chemical
binders. The ability to move by self-locomotion, however, distinguishes
humans and animals from other life forms; they are space binders. The
difference between humans and animals, a difference based on the
ability to use symbols, is that humans can anticipate and imagine the
future as well as remember and learn from the past. Humans, alone,
are time binders, according to Korzybski. A human can read a book
about a culture that existed in the 1500s. On the basis of that reading,
she can recreate a tool, a household product, or a style of clothing;
furthermore, she can put off doing it today, instead making plans for
such tasks over the course of the next two years. That is, in Korzybski's
taxonomy, binding time.[8]

## Kenneth Burke

Perhaps the most poetic definition of a human being is that of Kenneth
Burke, a prolific literary critic and rhetorician who suggests that the
human capacity to use symbols gives us the ability to intend, the
capacity to create meaning:

> *Man is*
> *the symbol-using (symbol-making, symbol-misusing) animal*
> *inventor of the negative (or moralized by the negative)*
> *separated from his natural condition by instruments of his*

> *own making*
> *goaded by the spirit of hierarchy (or moved by the sense of*
> *order)*
> *and rotten with perfection.*[9]

Understanding Burke's definition requires a digression into symbolic potential, for symbols allow us to do many things. Anatol Rapoport lists three: 1) symbols make possible the transmission of experience by language alone; 2) symbols allow humans to imagine the possible; and 3) symbols allow humans to transmit and believe false messages.[10]

We often take for granted the ability to use language to communicate experience. I have never visited Barrow, Alaska. However, my husband and two of his brothers have lived there. From their stories, from pictures, and from things I have read, I know what the Arctic Ocean looks like when frozen. I know that a man's beard becomes covered with frost and icicles when he walks to the store in December. I know that the sun does not rise above the horizon during the winter and that, if you do not have indoor plumbing, you must walk to the public high school for a shower. I know that "Joe-the-water-boy" used to deliver desalinated ocean water in a truck with a broken window, wearing only a T-shirt and pants, and somehow he did not freeze, and I know that jet planes land on a runway of snow and ice. Furthermore, I am able to quote the words of Isocrates, although he died centuries before I was born. I also know what my friend Barbara is doing in Milwaukee although I haven't seen her since 1980. These, along with most of the things I claim to know, I know not as a result of direct experience but because of language, of symbols.

Many things in our lives extend our individual experience by means of symbols. The Vietnam War was the first war brought to noncombatants by television; some refer to it as the first war fought in our living rooms. During the first night of the Gulf War, Saddam Hussein could watch CNN and get a firsthand account of the bombing of Baghdad. A person driving down an interstate highway in Los Angeles can talk by phone to someone on an airplane. A professor can explain the meaning of the latest Supreme Court ruling on free speech to a class in Corvallis, Oregon. A child can tell her father about her first day at school. Friends living in different states can "chat" with each other by typing on a keyboard. Life without symbols is difficult to imagine. Your only "knowledge" would be the raw data of your individual sense experience. You would have no ability to dream or plan; you would not learn from the past; you would experience only those things directly in your sight or which you hear, taste, touch, or smell.

Humans also use symbols to imagine the possible. Our imaginations lead to great inventions, from potato chips to computer chips. The ability to imagine results in E.T. riding across a huge screen perched on the handlebar of a bicycle, a young girl visualizing herself as Chief Justice on the U.S. Supreme Court, a painter explaining that this shade of blue is too intense for the exterior trim on a house. You can imagine what you will look like when you are older, what you might do next weekend, what job you would like when you finish your degree. Dreaming is a wonderful, enlightening, liberating human activity, made possible by symbols.

Symbols not only liberate humans but also may be used for ill, as symbols allow us to transmit and believe false messages. To have the capacity to use symbols is to have the capacity for deceit. A child tells his mother that he was not the one who broke her vase. Richard Nixon told the American public that he had no knowledge of the Watergate break-in. Transmission of false messages can cause enormous damage, which in part explains the societal value for telling the truth. Imagine the trauma to a family who is informed, falsely and maliciously, that a son or daughter was killed in a traffic accident. Courts recognize the harm that can result to a person's reputation by the publication of false reports, allowing such plaintiffs to collect damage awards in successful defamation lawsuits.

The same symbolic nature that allows the transmission of false messages also allows individuals to believe such messages. Thus, large numbers of individuals can be manipulated by a few, as every dictator who seizes control of a country's media knows. Individuals can develop hatreds and superstitions as a result of their symbolic capacity, believing a religious leader who tells them they are the superior race. Others spend lives in emotional pain because, as children, they were told they were stupid, ugly, or worthless.

The ability to use symbols is essential to any system of values. Humans have the potential for immoral behavior by means of, and as a result of, their symbolizing activities. This is what Kenneth Burke refers to when he defines humans as "symbol-using (symbol-making, symbol-misusing) animals." The particular symbolic concept that allows human activity to be either moral or immoral, according to Burke, is the negative. Burke suggests that humans have "invented" the concept of the negative, for he finds no negatives in nature. To search for the negative in nature would be, he claims, as silly as to search for the square root of "minus-one."[11] Both concepts are symbolic only. Any object in nature simply exists. A human, however, can occupy herself indefinitely with enumerating what the object is not: "This horse is not a cow, nor is it a star, nor a plant, nor my classmate, nor a flavor of ice cream." The concept of negation is of enormous significance to humans, as it is necessary for rational decision making. To choose involves accepting one alternative while negating all others.

When the people of a country go to the polls, not only do they choose a leader but they *do not* choose any other candidate running for that office. To choose to behave in a certain fashion involves deciding *against* the other possibilities. The negative is central to human morality, as it is necessary for "a thou-shalt-not."[12] This is why Burke says the human being is the "inventor of the negative (or moralized by the negative)."

The result of symbolic ability is that humans have access to the natural world only through language or other symbol systems. This state of affairs, which Cassirer also discusses, leads Burke to say that a human being is "separated from his natural condition by instruments of his own making."

In addition, symbol systems allow humans to make distinctions, create hierarchies, and strive for success—the pinnacle of hierarchies. In any human activity, we rank things according to better and worse, with best being the top of any given hierarchy. In high school, students form cliques, and some cliques are more popular or farther up the hierarchy. On a sports team, the starters are at the top of the hierarchy; in a classroom, the "A" students are at the top of the hierarchy; in academia, the full professors with national reputations are at the top of the hierarchy. As humans strive to be at the top of the hierarchies most important to them, they are, in Burke's words, "goaded by the spirit of hierarchy (or moved by the sense of order) and rotten with perfection," that is, the human drive for perfection is an all-consuming motive.

Whether the particular human capacity described above is called symbol using or the ability to bind time, the ideal of an arbitrary symbol is, for many scholars, the key to understanding human beings. Not all scholars, however, are content merely to distinguish the symbolic from the nonsymbolic. A related thrust of scholarly inquiry into particular human capacities is discussed as "signification."

## Signs

Langer distinguished symbols from signs based on whether the sign or symbol and its object are associated on a one-to-one basis. For her, symbols are not merely names for objects but are vehicles for the conception of objects. Meaning is the conception rather than the object. Yet much scholarship concerning language uses the term *sign* rather than *symbol*. This use of the term refers to a category broader than symbols, for these scholars refer to all human signifying activity as the operation of signs, only a portion of which are, for them, symbolic. Although the terminology is consistent with Langer's, the scholarship on signs draws on the writings of C. S. (Charles Sanders) Peirce and Ferdinand de Saussure, two very different individuals. Peirce, a brilliant philosopher who was denied tenure at Johns Hopkins University, wrote copiously about the theory of signs. In contrast, Saussure, a Swiss linguist, was a very successful professor who wrote little; his lectures are available to modern scholars only through student notes.

## C. S. Peirce

Peirce, who sometimes is referred to as the greatest American philosopher, wrote on semiotics in the late nineteenth and early twentieth centuries. Many of his ideas were developed in his correspondence with Victoria Lady Welby, who also wrote about signs. Among other things, Peirce describes the process of sign interpretation—identifying and cataloging an amazing variety of signs. He lays out ten trichotomies for classifying signs, yielding the potential for over 59,000 different classes of signs.[13] Although this incredibly complicated scheme has not influenced scholars significantly, his basic system is the foundation for most modern scholarship on signs. This influence has widened as his writings have become available; a large portion of what Peirce wrote was not published before his death.

In Peirce's various writings, he gives several definitions of a sign, including: "A sign is an object which stands for another to some mind"[14] and "A sign stands *for* something *to* the idea which it produces, or modifies."[15] Thus a sign is a sense datum; it has some "material quality" which is the character of the sign. For example, printed words involve black ink in a certain shape; spoken words involve particular sounds; and so on. The sign also must have some connection to the thing it signifies. Peirce does not mean that the sign necessarily has a natural relationship to its objects. It may or may not. Instead, he means that it has *some* relationship—either natural, such as the weathercock has to the wind direction, or conventional, such as words have to their referents. Peirce does not believe that signs are purely arbitrary; an object or fact prompts someone to use a particular sign(s). He calls this second characteristic of signs their "pure demonstrative application." Although, at a fundamental level, the word *rainbow* has only a conventional relationship to that which it signifies, the relationship between *rainbow* and certain patterns of light visible after a rain is not arbitrary for anyone who speaks English. Finally a sign becomes a sign only when it is regarded as such. If something is not a sign to a particular mind, then it is nothing more than the material quality, such as black marks on paper. A mind "must conceive" the marks, or whatever material qualities, "to be connected with its object so that it is possible to reason from the sign to the thing." He goes on: "Thus our mere sensations are only the material quality of our ideas considered as signs. Our ideas have also a causal connection with the things that they represent without which there would be no real knowledge."[16]

Peirce makes an attempt to distinguish between signs and symbols when listing categories of thought, which he felt was his major contribution to philosophy. Signs are representations "whose relation to their objects consists in a correspondence in fact." *Symbols* are representations "whose relation to their objects is an imputed character, which are the same as *general signs*."[17] This distinction comes from his tripartite distinction between symbols or arbitrary signs and two types of motivated signs—icons and indices. Thus, his notion of a symbol is very similar to Langer and Cassirer, for symbols bear only conventional relationships to their objects. He calls symbols "arbitrary signs," as the relationship between the sign and its object is a function of the "interpretant," that is, a subsequent thought. (The subsequent thought is so named because it plays the role of an interpreter.[18]) Linguistic signs are symbols in Peirce's taxonomy.

Peirce calls *indices* and *icons* "degenerate" signs, as the relationship between the sign and the object is, to some degree, independent of the interpretant. Icons refer to objects by virtue of the actual characteristics of the icon; an icon bears some similarity to the object it represents. The streak made by a lead pencil, says Peirce, represents a geometrical line and so is classified as an icon. He also classifies diagrams as icons of relationships and maps as icons of certain territory. In the iconic relationship, the sign bears some resemblance to the object. An index, on the other hand, refers to an object by virtue of being affected by the object. For example, a stop sign with a bullet hole is a sign of the gunshot that caused the hole.[19] Similarly, smoke is a sign of fire, and wet pavement is a sign of rain. His point is that neither icons nor indices are completely arbitrary as regards their relationship to their referent.[20]

## Ferdinand de Saussure

Saussure, frequently credited as the "father" of modern linguistics, discusses signs and symbols somewhat differently than do Peirce and Langer. For Saussure, the linguistic sign is the standard example of a sign. By restricting his discussion to linguistic signs, Saussure uses the term *sign* to refer to what Peirce and Langer acknowledge as a *symbol*. He also expands the notion of sign to include more than the material stimulus.

For Saussure, a linguistic sign is a two-part psychological entity, formed of the *concept* and the *sound-image*. The sound-image is not the physical sound made when a person speaks. Instead, it is the "psychological imprint" of that sound, the sensation of the sound.[21] For example, the sensation created when a person utters the word *ocean* is the sound-image portion of that particular linguistic sign. Saussure is careful to point out that the sound-image is not phonic but "incorporeal," constituted by distinctions between itself and other sound-images rather than its material substance.[22]

The mental construct which corresponds to that sound-image is the concept. The concept of *ocean* is the mental image one associates with the sensation of that utterance. The two—sound-image and concept—together are the sign. Thus, the sensation of the sound made when saying "running" and the mental construct one has for that term constitute a sign. After explaining both the sound-image and the concept, Saussure discards the term *sound-image* for *signifier*, and replaces *concept* with *signified*. The signified is the intelligible aspects of the sign; the signifier is the sensible or perceptible aspects.[23]

Saussure claims that other scholars use the word *symbol* to mean the portion of the linguistic sign which he calls the sound-image or signifier.[24] He suggests that the sign more accurately consists of both the signifier and the signified. Thus, his notion of a sign focuses not on the material stimulus so much as the sensation created by the stimulus, and he adds to the notion of a sign the mental construct associated with that sensation. His position on the arbitrary nature of signs is discussed in chapter two.

## Taxonomy

To avoid confusing terminology throughout this text, the definitions used by a number of scholars discussed in this chapter are combined in the following manner, which attempts to avoid as much damage as possible to the ideas of any scholar. First, *signs* are any material or stimuli which have meaning for human beings. *Symbols* are a subset of signs and are those stimuli or materials that have a purely conventional relationship with their object. All symbols are signs, but not all signs are symbols. Just as spots are a sign of measles if interpreted thusly, so the weathercock is a sign that the wind is blowing in a particular direction. Both the spots and the weathercock are an *index*, as they are "affected" by the object—measles cause spots and the wind affects the direction of the weathercock. An *icon* is a sign which resembles, in some way, an object. The international figures of men and women on restroom doors are icons, as is a crucifix. Neither an icon nor an index bears a purely conventional relationship to its referent, as do the sounds of language.

All signs—symbols, icons, indices—indeed involve not only the signifier and signified, as discussed by Saussure, but an interpretant as well. To avoid confusion, and in keeping with common-sense usage, *sign*, *symbol*, *icon*, and *index* are used to refer to the signifier. A signifier, however, is a sign only because of the signified and the interpretant.

## Summary

Although humans are poorly adapted for survival without these sign systems, the ability to use signs can result in extreme damage to your own life and to the lives of others. In one of the ancient Greek tragedies, Creon and his niece, Antigone, are locked in conflict. A terrible civil war is raging in Thebes, and Antigone's two brothers, who fought on opposite sides in the war, have killed each other in battle. Creon, the king of Thebes, is a political pragmatist who understands the public's need for certainty. He has one brother buried with state honors while leaving the body of the other unburied, to rot on the battlefield, as a symbol of the justice of one cause. Creon chose the "unjust" side arbitrarily, merely wanting to end the war. He decreed that anyone who tried to bury that body would be put to death. Antigone, who is betrothed to Creon's son, defies his order, as her religious beliefs compel her to bury her brother, so that his soul will be at rest. The bitter battle between the practical and the ideal symbolized by Creon and Antigone results in Antigone's death.

History is replete with similar symbolic deaths. People have died for saluting the wrong flag, praying to the wrong god, or loving the wrong person. The lives of two Americans were ruined when, following their Olympic triumph, they raised their fists in a "black power salute" while the U.S. national anthem played. On a more frivolous but very human level, social reputations of teenagers may depend on a type of dress or a brand of shoes.

Thus, understanding signs and systems of signs is a key ingredient to understanding, and possibly changing, certain aspects of your life and your society. It is preliminary to understanding the most important system of signs—human language.

## Endnotes

1.  Plato, *Phaedrus*, trans. R. Hackforth, *The Collected Dialogues of Plato*, ed. Edith Hamilton and Huntington Cairns (1961; rpt. Princeton: Princeton UP, 1973) 230a.

2.  Aristotle, *Metaphysics*, trans. W. D. Ross, *The Basic Works of Aristotle*, ed. Richard McKeon (New York: Random House, 1941) I 980a.
3.  Aristotle 980b 25.
4.  Ernst Cassirer, *An Essay on Man: An Introduction to a Philosophy of Human Culture* (1944; rpt. New Haven: Yale UP, 1968) 26.
5.  Susanne K. Langer, *Philosophy in a New Key: A Study in the Symbolism of Reason, Rite, and Art* (1942; rpt. New York: New American Library, 1951) 58–61.
6.  A body of literature suggests that animal communication also is symbolic. See, for example, Thomas A. Sebeok, ed., *Animal Communication: Techniques of Study and Results of Research* (Bloomington, IN: Indiana UP, 1968).
7.  Cassirer 25.
8.  Alfred Korzybski, *Manhood of Humanity*, 2nd ed. (Lakeville, CT: International Non-Aristotelian Library, 1950) 58–67.
9.  Kenneth Burke, *Language as Symbolic Action: Essays on Life, Literature, and Method* (Berkeley: U of California P, 1966) 16.
10. Anatol Rapoport, *Semantics* (New York: Thomas Y. Crowell, 1975) 15–16.
11. Burke 9.
12. Kenneth Burke, *The Rhetoric of Religion: Studies in Logology* (Berkeley: U of California P, 1970) 222.
13. Thomas A. Goudge, *The Thought of C. S. Peirce* (New York: Dover, 1950) 140.
14. *Peirce on Signs: Writings on Semiotics by Charles Sanders Peirce*, ed. James Hoopes (Chapel Hill: U of North Carolina P, 1991) 141.
15. Charles S. Peirce, *Collected Papers of Charles Sanders Peirce*, ed. Charles Hartshorne and Paul Weiss, vol. 1 (Cambridge: Harvard UP, 1960) 1.339.
16. *Peirce on Signs* 142–43.
17. *Peirce on Signs* 30.
18. *Peirce on Signs* 28.
19. *Peirce on Signs* 239–40.
20. However, elsewhere in his writings, he suggests that "[a]ny material image . . . is largely conventional in its mode of representation." Peirce, *Collected Papers* 2.276.
21. Ferdinand de Saussure, *Course in General Linguistics*, eds. Charles Bally and Albert Sechehaye, trans. Wade Baskin (New York: Philosophical Library, 1959) 66.
22. Saussure 118–19.
23. Roman Jakobson claims that modern linguistic scholars are coming to realize "the analysis of any linguistic sign whatsoever can be carried out only under the condition that its sensible aspect undergo an investigation in the light of its intelligible aspect (the signifier in light of the signified) and vice versa." *On Language*, ed. Linda R. Waugh and Monique Monville-Burston (Cambridge, MA: Harvard UP, 1990) 50.
24. Saussure 68. He uses the term *symbol* to refer to such things as the scales of justice which have a "rudiment of a natural bond" between signifier and signified.

# Chapter Two

# Language

The study of language extends at least back to 1600 B.C. in Mesopotamia. However, only in the twentieth century has language eclipsed other items as the central object of humanistic study. Linguistics and speech communication departments are of relatively recent vintage in U.S. higher education; also recently, scholars have suggested that language may shape humans rather than the more traditional version of that relationship. These changes have accompanied an explosion in research and writing concerning language. The focus of this chapter is on some of the various perspectives from which scholars approach the study of language, that very sophisticated system of signs.

## A System of Signs

Although the focus of chapter two is on language, the discussion takes place within a broader context of the theory of signs—*semiotics*. A prominent modern semiotician, Thomas Sebeok, suggests that semiotics includes a philosophy of mind, cognition, and language.[1] Thus, it includes study of the immense variety of human signs, the effects of such signs on thought and communication, and nonhuman sign systems. Semiotics begins with C. S. Peirce and Ferdinand de Saussure; their combined influences caused a significant change in the way scholars study language and other signs.[2]

**19**

## Saussure

In addition to the discussion in chapter one, several other of Saussure's ideas are important to a consideration of language. His discussion of signs generally is limited to linguistic signs. The sign, that two-part entity composed of signifier and signified, is the basis for his two basic linguistic principles. Saussure also posits both the mutability and immutability of language, distinguishes between *langue* and *parole*, and sets the stage for modern linguistics.

## Principles I and II

Saussure's Principle I is the arbitrary nature of the sign; Principle II is the linear nature of the signifier. The latter principle is the simpler of the two. Saussure focuses on spoken language as the fundamental form of language. The linear nature of the signifier refers to the fact that the signifier, that is, the sound-image aspect of a sign, occurs in time, in a measurable single dimension. The signifier is the sensation of sound; a listener apprehends sounds one at a time, in a linear fashion. If you read this sentence aloud, your ear will hear the word *sentence* before it hears the word *aloud*. This principle also applies to written signs, over which the eye travels in a similar linear fashion. Visual signs such as nautical flags, according to Saussure, do not demonstrate the same linearity that linguistic signs display.

Principle I—the arbitrary nature of the sign—is a complex notion that both the signified and signifier are arbitrary, not merely that the relationship between them is conventional. First, as other scholars have suggested, the signifier is arbitrary. In the English language, the signifier *lake* represents the mental construct of certain inland bodies of water. Nothing is imperative about this particular signifier. One can imagine that the language might have evolved differently so that the signifier *lago* might refer to inland bodies of water, as is the case in Spanish. Or, for that matter, *washall* or *placide* or any sound-image imaginable could be the conventional signifier for that particular concept.

This arbitrary nature of the signifier is only half the point of Principle I, as Jonathan Culler points out. The signified also is arbitrary:

> A language does not simply assign arbitrary names to a set of independently existing concepts. It sets up an arbitrary relation between signifiers of its own choosing on the one hand, and signifieds of its own choosing on the other. Not only does each language produce a different set of signifiers, articulating and dividing the continuum of sound in a distinctive way, but each

language produces a different set of signifieds; it has a distinctive and thus "arbitrary" way of organizing the world into concepts or categories.[3]

Thus, speakers of any particular language have concepts given by their language as signifieds that do not exist for speakers of another language. That is the reason translation can be so difficult. If concepts had some extra-linguistic existence, translation merely would be a matter of applying the matching signifier from the second language to the signified concept that was common to both. However, concepts are created linguistically.[4] A given language, for example, might have no word for *art*.[5]

The term *arbitrary* may be misleading, which led Saussure to refer to "motivated" and "unmotivated" signs. Although both signifiers and signifieds fundamentally are arbitrary, once one considers a fully developed and operational system of language, neither are arbitrary to language speakers; they have some fixity that comes from relationships among signs. Thus, to refer to a bicycle as a "ten-speed" in a language in which the meaning of *ten* and the meaning of *speed* are somewhat fixed, is "motivated" by preexisting meanings. Similar motivation leads to notions such as *computer terminal* or *easy chair*.[6] Such fixity does not deny, however, the fundamental arbitrariness of signifiers and signifieds. An unmotivated sign is one in which the signifier was chosen with no reference to existing signs, such as naming a model of car a "Miata."

Often, those fluent in more than one language will revert to another language when there is no signifier adequate to express a certain concept in the language presently being spoken. As language is not merely a set of names for preexisting reality but instead gives shape to reality for a language speaker, the set of concepts given to you by the language or languages you speak is arbitrary. Consider the nearly limitless number of possible concepts, just beyond your reach, because you have no word for them; that is, because you have no signifier, you also have no signified. For example, one can imagine a concept roughly involving all humans between the ages of fourteen and seventeen who are missing teeth. The signifier for this signified could be *dewonks*. If this arbitrary signified, and its accompanying signifier, became a part of the English language, we would begin "seeing" dewonks everywhere, perhaps believing that the concept had some necessary existence, as we think of the signifieds presently in our system of linguistic signs. As another example, the signifier *blancas* could refer to the signified concept of all slightly-tilted-from-upright, nearly flat surfaces. If so, you would "see" the similarity in an automobile windshield; the rock faces of the Flatirons in the foothills near

Boulder, Colorado; a newspaper being read by a commuter on the subway; and the screen on a computer monitor. All would be, for speakers of English, blancas.

Linguistic signs operate within a system. We understand signifieds not only as signifiers present them to us, but in relationship to other signifieds. *Hot* has meaning as it is compared to *cold*, and *red* has meaning as compared to that which we do not call red, including *orange*, *pink*, and *purple*. The signifier and signified, individually arbitrary, become interwoven into a complex system of language. Once set, language conventions become, in some sense, immutable.

## Mutability and Immutability

Linguistic signs have the dual nature of *immutability* and *mutability*, according to Saussure. The system of language is immutable in that a human is born into a linguistic community whose conventions are unchangeable. Although signs are conventional, once those conventions are set, speakers have little influence over them. One is unable, at will, to transform the conventions of a particular language, at least so far as those transformations affect the whole linguistic community. To attempt to change the conventions of English, or Spanish, or Swahili is a nearly impossible task. The arbitrary basis for the system, the large number of signs in any language, the tremendous complexity of the system of signs, and the inertia resulting from the enormous number of speakers of any language operate to inhibit intentional change.

On the other hand, ironically, while language is immutable to intentional change, time invariably operates to change language. Over time, shifts occur in the relationship between signifier and signified. Such shifts can occur within the lifetime of an individual. For example, during the lifetime of my grandmother, the term *gay* underwent change. During her early life, *gay* was used most frequently to mean happy and cheerful. More recently, the most frequent use of the word is to refer to a member of the homosexual community. A similar change has occurred in the meaning of *red*; the communist connotations of that word, so prevalent in the United States during the 1950s, largely are gone. This illustrates the mutability of signs. According to Saussure, language "is radically powerless to defend itself against the forces which from one moment to the next are shifting the relationship between the signified and the signifier."[7] That which humans cannot accomplish intentionally—change in the relationship of signifier to signified—operates naturally.

## *Langue* and *Parole*

Saussure also distinguishes between *langue* and *parole*. *Parole* is the particular sounds of linguistic signs, the sounds of your speech as you use the language; *la langue* is the system of language. Consider your native language and all that you know of it, consciously and unconsciously, which allows you to communicate using the language. Subtract from that the actual exercise of speaking—*parole*; what remains is *langue*. *La langue* is the "sum of word-images stored in the minds of all individuals," a "storehouse filled by the members of a given community through their active use of speaking," "a product that is passively assimilated by the individual" that "never requires premeditation."[8] *La langue* can be studied separately, without speaking; thus, scholars can study so-called "dead" languages, although they are unable to reproduce the sounds made by the original speakers of that language. *Parole*, on the other hand, is an individual and intentional action. To respond to a question from a person you meet on the street is to react to *parole*, although a knowledge of *langue* is necessary both to understand and to speak a language. *La langue*, the system, is what Saussure cites as the appropriate object of study for linguistics, rather than individual speech acts, which are studied by rhetorical and literary critics as well as by communication scholars.

Because linguistic signs are arbitrary, they have meaning only in relation to other aspects of the system of signs. To understand those relations, linguists study the system of *la langue*. Only by understanding *la langue* can one understand language, according to Saussure.

## Synchronic and Diachronic Linguistics

Saussure distinguishes between two types of language study— *synchronic* and *diachronic*. The synchronic study of language focuses on language as a system, outside of time; a diachronic study follows the evolution of language through time. Although Saussure understood the mutability of language, that is, its historicity, he proposes a synchronic study. Linguistics, before Saussure, was the study of the evolution of language. However, the evolution of either signifier or signified is irrelevant, Saussure claims, to the study of the nature of *la langue*. He argues that linguists must study language states, much as grammarians did prior to evolutionary linguistics.[9] Further, historical changes largely originate not in *la langue* but in *parole*, as individuals modify their speech acts.

Saussure cites one basic problem of linguistics—language does not have "entities";[10] it is not substance, but form. The form of language derives from its two potential variables; language works by *combination* and *contrast* of its various elements. This means that linguists are not looking for *things* but for relationships, for differences and identities.[11] Thus, the sound or phonological elements of language create identities and differences, such as the aspirated and unaspirated difference in sound between *b*in and *p*in, which creates a difference in meaning. Linguists, then, study the forms of language that cause these differences and identities. In English, for example, word order is important, as it is a very different thing to say, "Pam ate the pig" than to say "the pig ate Pam." The rules and conventions which account for this difference become the substance of linguistic analysis.

Saussure saw his reconceptualized study of linguistics located within a larger science of signs. This science, which he called *semiology*, would be tied closely to linguistics, as the unique characteristics of semiological systems are demonstrated most clearly in language.[12]

## Modern Linguistics

Linguistics has made much progress on the basis of Saussure's insights, with many adding to the discussion of structural linguistics, which is a study of the structure that allows language users to recognize well-formed instances of language. A significant role in that progression was played by Noam Chomsky's theory of transformational or generative grammar.

Fundamental to Chomsky's theory are notions of *competence* and *performance*. Competence refers to the fluent language user's unconscious knowledge of language, that is, his or her linguistic ability. Performance is the actual production and comprehension of language in a specific instance, which may or may not reflect the linguistic competence of the individual. Competence involves the understanding of singular or plural correspondence between nouns and verb forms; one who is competent may, for whatever reason, make a performance mistake by saying "I knows you is hiding in that closet."

Competence is defined by means of a *generative grammar*, which is the set of rules whereby all grammatical sentences in a language can be generated. The components for such a grammar are the *base*, which generates or emerges as the *deep structure* of a sentence. This structure is the simplest possible form the statement can take, which frequently is a simple declarative sentence. For example, a deep structure of a statement might be *Alden ate the potato*. This deep structure is modified by *transformational rules*, indicating which changes in word order and other aspects of a statement are allowable. Such transformations result in the *surface structure*, which is the statement as uttered. Thus, the surface structure of the statement might be: *The potato was eaten by Alden*; or, *Alden ate the delicious red potato*. In the latter case, the deep structure also includes the following statement: *The potato is red and delicious*. Transformational rules identify what transformations are allowable in a given language. Any utterance can be analyzed in terms of the deep structure that linguists infer to be embedded within the statement and the transformational rules that allow the statement as uttered. Consequently, a generative grammar is somewhat akin to a mathematical formula; it authorizes the generation of a number of values (statements), depending upon which values are used in place of variables in the formula.

Competence is something developed naturally by speakers of a language. The job of a linguist, in creating a grammar, is to identify the operation of the language, thus explaining linguistic competence in the language. Chomsky's generative grammar is an admirable effort to define the allowable operations of language. Although his theory is not without its critics, it has had enormous influence on the field of modern linguistics as well as on studies of language and cognition in other fields. It also is used by scholars working on artificial languages and intelligence. These researchers seek an understanding of how humans process language in order to construct computer systems that can approximate human intelligence and creativity.[13]

## Other Studies of Language

Although Saussure deserves homage for his pioneering work in modern linguistics, the work of other scholars also offers insights into language. Some scholars have speculated about the development of human spoken language, while others have traced the development of writing. In addition, researchers have identified defining characteristics of language.

### Development of Language and Writing

Some scholars have delved into the origins of language. Although such speculative reading is fascinating, we likely are no closer to understanding how language originated. Some of the theories suggest that language came from a divine source. Both the Hindu and Christian traditions suggest that a divine being gave language to humans. This theory reportedly has resulted in bizarre experiments. According to a long-standing story, both an Egyptian pharaoh, Psamtik I, and James IV of Scotland took human infants and raised them in isolation, in order to determine the original god-given language of humans. The children in Egypt, as all documented cases of children raised in isolation, did not speak at all. James IV reported that the children in his study started speaking Hebrew, but no evidence supporting the claim of this miracle was forthcoming. In a related theory, Ernst Cassirer suggests that language and myth have the same roots, originating in the religious impulse:

> The formulation of language, too, should not be traced back to any sort of reflective contemplation, to the calm and clearheaded comparison of given sense impressions and the abstraction of definite attributes. . . . The word, like a god or a daemon, confronts man not as a creation of his own, but as something existent and significant in its own right, as an objective reality. As soon as the spark has jumped across, as soon as the tension and emotion of the moment has found its discharge in the word or the mythical image, a sort of turning point has occurred in human mentality; the inner excitement which was a mere subjective state has vanished, and has been resolved into the objective form of myth or of speech.[14]

Of the various other theories, none makes any more sense than Cassirer's. One theory is that language developed onomatopoeically, that is, through making sounds that were similar to natural sounds. Onomatopoeic words sound like their meaning, such as *buzz*, *hiss*, *rattle*, *splash*, and sounds animals make, like *meow*. This theory, sometimes known as the "bow-wow" theory of the origin of language, is that humans began imitating natural sounds which then developed into signs. A related theory, called "yo-heave-ho," is that humans developed a set of natural grunts and groans when working that, over time, became communicative. Yet another, the oral-gesture theory, suggests humans vocalized things that had the effect of creating oral gestures to each other. Others have suggested that, as early humans babbled or vocalized, a sound came to be associated with an object, which another human noticed and imitated.[15]

Other speculation concerning the origin of language involves the search for the original human language—that common root for all current languages. Derek Bickerton claims to find the root in *pidgins* and *creoles*, which are the languages that developed in polyglot communities of laborers, generally working for European colonial powers.[16] The first rudimentary system of communication among such people, pidgin, has a very simple syntax and limited vocabulary. Languages which develop from these rudimentary pidgins are called creoles. Bickerton argues that similarities among all creole languages is evidence for the basis of language acquisition by children, if not of the nature of original language(s). Others argue that although humans share language facility, there was no uniform, original language.[17]

Just as we do not know how spoken language developed, we also cannot identify exactly when writing systems began. The alphabetic script used to inscribe most Western languages is only about three thousand years old; however, pictograms and other forms of writing on stone can be dated much farther back. *Pictograms* are images of objects. Modern pictograms include the images of female and male dancers sometimes painted on bathroom doors in Mexican restaurants. More abstracted representations are known as *ideograms*. They may bear some resemblance to a concept but are more abstract, displaying fewer characteristics of a concept than do pictograms. For example, the international symbols for women and men on airport bathroom doors are ideograms, as are the outline of a telephone that serves as the international sign for a phone booth. Pictograms and ideograms, then, represent concepts, and they are not completely arbitrary; rather they are *iconic*. In other words, some characteristic of the concept is illustrated by the written sign.

If a single sign is used to represent a word, but has a wholly conventional, rather than iconic, relationship to the concept, such a written symbol is known as a *logogram*. Sumerian cuneiform writing was logographic, as is much of modern Chinese writing—individual symbols represent entire words. Even though words are pronounced alike, they likely will not have similar written form in a logographic system of writing. *Syllabic* writing uses symbols for syllables or portions of a word. If the writing system for English were syllabic, the same symbol would be used as a part of the writing for each of the following words, which contain the same syllable: *knee*; *ne*ophyte; *nee*d; and pen*ny*. Sequoyah, a Native American, invented a syllabic writing system that was used by Cherokees to inscribe their spoken language. An *alphabetic* writing system involves symbols for each sound. Arabic and Hebrew writing systems have signs only for consonants. Early Greek writing systems added to this by representing vowel sounds independently. Modern spoken English is inscribed with this latter type of alphabet; however, the alphabet and sounds of the English language do not have an invariable, one-to-one correspondence. As an example, *a* represents a different sound in *a*nt, *a*ward, and l*a*ke; further, the same sounds can be represented by different letters, as in *s*hore and *ch*inook or *s*ip or *ts*unami. The discrepancies in the relationship between sounds and letters of the alphabet have several causes. The pronunciation of English has undergone change over time. Also, many words in English originated in other languages, and their spelling is influenced by spelling in the writing of the original language. In addition, English spelling was fixed when printing was introduced in the fifteenth century. Many early printers were native Dutch speakers, so their pronunciations of spoken English were not "standard," making their decisions about standard spelling not always consistent with sound.[18]

## Characteristics of Human Language

A number of scholars, among them Charles Osgood[19] and Charles Hockett,[20] have attempted to identify the criteria for a language, specifically a human language, at least 4500 of which currently are spoken.[21] Any language involves production of certain physical stimuli in some channel of communication; humans create sounds or marks receivable by auditory or visual channels. To truly be a language, these stimuli must be both producible and receivable by the same group of organisms. Although humans may gain meaning from watching a sunset, no language is involved in the "transmission" of meaning from sunset to human. However, those who speak any given language can both send and receive messages. Another characteristic of language is that the stimuli affect the behavior of organisms that receive them. When one human asks a question, the listener responds; when someone criticizes, it affects the listener, even if a third party is the object of criticism. All languages also have nonrandom rules governing their operation. Such rules include grammar, syntax, and so on. For example, in English, adjectives usually precede nouns, and complete sentences must have both a subject and a predicate. Such rules provide the consistency necessary to allow communication of meaning between language users. Languages also allow production of messages concerning things and events not present. Humans can tell stories about the ancient Anasazi peoples of the Southwest, relive battles of the Civil War, discuss the political situation in Kenya, develop stories about Heidi and her grandfather, and tell tales about the tooth fairy.

Controversy exists about the existence of nonhuman languages. No one disputes that animals have sophisticated communication systems; what is at issue is whether certain animal communication systems are best described as language or by some other term. Some researchers suggest that animals do not meet all the criteria set out for a language; for example, few animals seem able to communicate about things and events not present,[22] and no parallel seems to exist to the human ability for linguistic abstractions.[23] Thomas Sebeok argues that much human communication is similar to animal communication, which he terms *zoosemiotic*. For example, human nonverbal communication, involving visual, olfactory, auditory, and tactile clues, can be classified as zoosemiotic. The means of reference for some zoosemiotic signs seem to be iconic; such signs are not arbitrary or, therefore, mutable. According to Sebeok, humans also use species-specific methods of communication, including language, which he calls *anthroposemiotic*.[24] These methods of communication tend to be arbitrary or conventional. Not all scholars concur with Sebeok, however; those who challenge Sebeok argue that some animal communication, including that of bees and apes, displays all the essential characteristics of language.[25]

Whatever the resolution of this issue, agreement exists that human language has some species-specific characteristics. First, human language displays the characteristic of *arbitrariness*. This means that the relationship between language and its meaning is conventional, which is the same point Saussure made when he discussed the arbitrary nature of the linguistic sign. Second, human languages are *productive*; the potential statements one can make using the language theoretically are unlimited. To catalog all possible expressions in any human language would be impossible, as one always can substitute a different verb, or noun, or adjective into an existing sentence and, thereby, create a new statement. Likely, you have not heard the following sentence before, yet it is a possible statement, given the grammar and syntax of the English language: *Tall and intelligent mice compared vices while primping in front of a full-length mirror*. A more famous example is that of Chomsky: "Colorless green ideas sleep furiously."[26] A third characteristic of human language is *discreetness*. This refers to the sounds of language. The distinctions among sounds become distinctions in meaning, such as the difference between *pin* and *bin*. Fourth, human language exhibits *duality*, which means it has a double level of organization. Not only are sounds distinct, but so are meanings. The words spelled *sun* and *son* have the same sound but different meanings.

Although other writers have increased the list of species-specific characteristics of human language to as many as sixteen, these four—arbitrariness, productivity, discreetness, and duality—seem to be most important. Other characteristics, however, affect human communication in important ways. For example, human languages use the vocal-auditory channels as the primary communication system. Signals in these channels fade rapidly, which led to the creation of writing systems to preserve messages. Also as a result of the evanescence of spoken language, humans must process and store information. In order to understand a sentence spoken aloud, a listener first must recall all the sounds, as one sound "disappears" before the next sound is processed. In addition, the speaker must process all clues, including vocal intonation, which may affect the meaning of a message. If you turn to a friend and say, "Do you suppose that chocolate ice cream, which I love, would be as appealing to my canary?," your friend will not understand unless she can remember all the sounds, process them, and understand (by intonation and visual clues such as gestures and facial expressions) the nuances of your message.

Another apparently species-specific characteristic of human language is that it is transmitted culturally. We learn language from the society into which we are born—thus a child raised in a home where Spanish is spoken will learn Spanish. All humans are born with the innate ability to learn a language, but individuals learn the specific language or languages they hear. As adults, learning new languages can be an arduous task; for young children, it comes naturally.

## Linguistic Units

Linguists study important aspects of language, including *phonetics*, *phonology*, *morphology*, and *syntax*. Phonetics is the study of speech sounds and involves classification of sounds as well as their production by the body. Phonetic categories include *bilabials*, which are sounds formed by the lips (*p*in and *b*in); *alveolars*, which are produced by the front part of the tongue on the alveolar ridge in the top of the mouth (*t*ime and *d*ime); and *labiodentals*, produced by the upper teeth and lower lip (*f*airy and *v*ery). Other categories describe the manner of articulation, that is, obstruction of the airstream as consonants are pronounced. For example, *glides* involve transition from other sounds (*m*y or co*w*), and *fricatives* involve forcing the airstream through a narrow opening to create a noisy sound (*s*ip and *z*ip). This list is only partial, as the science of phonetics is quite detailed.

Phonology is a study of the pattern or system of sounds in a language. Languages do not share the same sounds or even the same potential sounds. For example, the trilled double *r* (pe*rr*o) in Spanish does not occur in American English. Phonology also concerns the variation of sound with particular functions. For example, the sound of the plural form in English (written as *s* or *es*) changes depending upon the sound of the word being pluralized. Thus, rings /z/, books /s/, and witches /iz/ involve different phonemes creating the plural form of the noun. These words are consistent with phonological rules for the English language.

Morphology is the study of the basic elements that form a linguistic message. The word *recalled* has three morphemes—*re*, which means again; *call*, which has several potential meanings; and *ed*, which is an indicator of past tense. Some languages put together, as words, morphemes which, in English, would constitute an entire sentence. Anatol Rapoport describes passing through Germany in 1938. His passport was stamped "*Einundwiederausdurchreisesichtvermerk*"; if broken into morphemes, the rough translation is: *Ein* (in) *und* (and) *wieder* (again) *aus* (out) *durch* (through) *reise* (travel) *sicht* (sight) *vermerk* (notation)—the document was a transit visa.[27] Morphology deals not with sound but with the most basic units of meaning in a language. It concerns ways in which basic language structures can be combined.

Syntax is the study of the structure of phrases and sentences in a language. English syntax allows the following sentence—*The green book is lying on the table in the hall*. It does not allow this sentence—*Green the book the on table lying is hall the in*. Syntax involves more than word order, however; it describes the complex internal structure of languages. For example, the sentence—*I saw the woman from the fort*—can have two different meanings, depending on whether the woman resided at the fort or whether the speaker was standing in the fort, looking at her.

While syntax concerns the structural rules of a language, grammar involves the permitted patterns of words in a language. Included in the study of grammar are traditional categories of number, person, tense, voice, and gender. The rule against splitting infinitives (*to go boldly* rather than *to boldly go*) is a rule of grammar.

## Linguistic Diversity

Although the categories of linguistic study identify commonalities among human languages, the more significant lesson of the study of languages is their enormous diversity and complexity. The variety among languages occurs in both signifiers and signifieds. Variety also exists within languages. For example, regional, ethnic, or other dialects of a language create different standard usages and meanings. In different parts of the United States, people may drink a *soda* or a *coke*, put their groceries in a *bag* or a *sack*, *raise* or *fetch up* children, and drink water from a *bubbler* or a *water fountain*. Some dialects, such as Black English, abbreviate expression (*They not home* versus *They're not home*). Diversity within a language comes not only from dialects but also from formal and informal usage. Each of the following statements conveys the same message to a different audience:

> (to business associate you just met) "I will meet you in the restaurant after I park the car."

(to a parent) "I'll be in after I park."

(to a long-time friend) "Catch up with ya in a sec—lemme park
this."

These and other types of variation in language have convinced linguists
that human language is a rule-governed system with enormous
diversity, allowing creativity and change.

## Summary

One fundamental characteristic of human beings is that, whenever
and wherever we find groups of them, we find language. Although no
one knows for certain how human language developed, we have
attempted to account for language in a variety of ways. In the legends
of the Swampy Cree (Omuskakoo), a metamorphosing trickster,
Wesucechak, gives language to the tribe—"it is said that he 'brought
words over' from animals to people."[28] Whether human language came
from Wesucechak or some other source or whether it is the product
of evolution, some modern scholars would limit the use of the term to
humans, arguing that animal communication systems are not
languages.

Every human language is a complex system of signs. Linguistic signs,
which are arbitrary, become immutable to intentional change when
they are part of the system of language; only time can operate to change
the relationship between signifiers and signifieds. The system of
language, *langue*, is internalized by young children, who are born with
a species-specific potential for language. As they hear other humans
speak a language, young children develop competence in the grammar
and syntax of what becomes their primary language. They do so
without being able to articulate the "rules" they intuitively understand
as competent language speakers. Linguists attempt to identify these
rules and structures that children learn intuitively, in order to make
explicit the operation of language.

Our fascination with language is due in part to the central role
language plays in human experience. The story of Helen Keller's
discovery of language dramatically illustrates that role. Born blind and
deaf, she was unable to develop language, as hearing children are able
to do. Instead, she lived in a dark, quiet, and unthinking world for the
first several years of her life. Eventually, a dedicated teacher began to
work with her. One day, while she and Helen were taking a walk
outside, the teacher placed the child's hand in the stream of cold water
coming from a pump, then spelled *water* on her palm. Recounting this
story as an adult, Helen credits that moment as the beginning of a fully

human life. She suddenly realized the connection between the cold, wet feeling on her hand and the "letters" being traced on her palm. In a surge of excitement and dawning awareness, she tugged the teacher forward, touching things, then holding out her hand while the teacher spelled the names for them on her palm. From this beginning, Helen developed an understanding of the system of language and, with it, human intelligence and understanding. Without language, Helen Keller's life and experiences would have been severely limited.

The study of language is not complete with the consideration of *langue*, however. Rhetorical scholars, although cognizant of linguistic findings, focus more on *parole*, that is, the actual spoken interchanges between people.

## Endnotes

1. Thomas A. Sebeok, *Semiotics in the United States* (Bloomington, IN: Indiana UP, 1991) 3.
2. Jonathan Culler notes that semiotics probably would have developed without them, for it is the logical outcome of an intellectual reorientation of human scholarship forecast by Ernst Cassirer, Susanne K. Langer, and Alfred North Whitehead. *The Pursuit of Signs: Semiotics, Literature, and Deconstruction* (Ithaca, NY: Cornell UP, 1981) 24. Thomas Sebeok suggests that Alexander Bryan Johnson and Jakob von Uexküll also were "neglected figures in the history of semiotic inquiry," and he cites C. K. Ogden and I. A. Richards as early contributors to semiotic discourse. Sebeok 11, 121.
3. Jonathan Culler, *Ferdinand de Saussure*, rvd. ed. (Ithaca, NY: Cornell UP, 1986) 33.
4. Saussure is accused of inconsistency on this point. When discussing various names for oxen (*soeur* and *boeuf*), he implies these are arbitrary signifiers for a fixed signified. See the discussion in Françoise Gadet, *Saussure and Contemporary Culture*, trans. Gregory Elliott (Essex, Great Britain: Hutchinson Radius, 1989) 34.
5. Jamake Highwater makes this claim about American Indian languages. *The Primal Mind: Vision and Reality in Indian America* (1981; rpt. New York: Meridian, 1982) 13. See also, Sam Gill, "It's Where You Put Your Eyes," *I Become Part of It: Sacred Dimensions in Native American Life*, ed. D. M. Dooling and Paul Jordan-Smith (1989; rpt. San Francisco: HarperCollins 1992) 83–87.
6. Saussure 131–34.
7. Saussure 75.
8. Saussure 13–14.
9. He cites the *Port Royal Grammar* as an example. Saussure 82.
10. Saussure 107.
11. Culler, *Ferdinand de Saussure* 57.
12. Saussure 16–17.
13. See, for example, John A. Moyne, *Understanding Language: Man or Machine* (New York: Plenum, 1985) and Jim Jubak, *In the Image of the Brain: Breaking the Barrier between the Human Mind and Intelligent Machines* (Boston: Little, Brown, 1992).

14. Ernst Cassirer, *Language and Myth* (1946; rpt. New York: Dover, n.d.) 34, 36.
15. E. L. Thorndike, "The Origin of Language," 98 *Science* (2 July 1943): 1–6.
16. Derek Bickerton, *Roots of Language* (Ann Arbor: Karoma, 1981).
17. Claude Hagège, *The Dialogic Species: A Linguistic Contribution to the Social Sciences*, trans. Sharon L. Shelly (New York: Columbia UP, 1990) 16–26.
18. George Yule, *The Study of Language* (Cambridge: Cambridge UP, 1985) 14.
19. Charles E. Osgood, "What is Language," *The Signifying Animal: The Grammar of Language and Experience*, ed. Irmengard Rauch and Gerald F. Carr (Bloomington: Indiana UP, 1980) 9–50.
20. Charles F. Hockett, "The Origin of Speech," *Scientific American* 203 (Sept. 1960): 89–96.
21. Hagège 28.
22. Most animals' sounds are tied to their emotional state. However, ground squirrels, velvet monkeys, and robins, for example, respond to different predators with different sounds. Michael Bright, *Animal Language* (Ithaca, NY: Cornell UP, 1984) 231–32.
23. William Kemp and Roy Smith, "Animals, Communication, and Language," *Language: Introductory Readings*, ed. Virginia P. Clark, Paul A. Eschholz and Alfred F. Rosa, 4th ed. (New York: St. Martin's, 1985) 672.
24. Thomas A. Sebeok, "Goals and Limitations of the Study of Animal Communication," *Animal Communication: Techniques of Study and Results of Research*, ed. Thomas A. Sebeok (Bloomington: Indiana UP, 1968) 3–12; See, also, Eric H. Lenneberg, "Language in the Light of Evolution," *Animal Communication: Techniques of Study and Results of Research*, ed. Thomas A. Sebeok (Bloomington: Indiana UP, 1968) 592–613, and Thomas A. Sebeok, *Perspectives in Zoosemiotics* (The Hague: Mouton, 1972) 34–62.
25. See, for example, Osgood 15–20.
26. Noam Chomsky, *Syntactic Structures* (1957; rpt. The Hague: Mouton, 1965) 15.
27. Anatol Rapoport, *Semantics* (New York: Thomas Y. Crowell, 1975) 87.
28. Howard Norman, "Wesucechak Becomes a Deer and Steals Language: An Anecdotal Linguistics Concerning the Swampy Cree Trickster," *Recovering the Word: Essays on Native American Literature*, ed. Brian Swann and Arnold Krupat (Berkeley: U of California P, 1987) 403.

# Chapter Three

# Rhetoric

Communication and rhetorical scholars offer two perspectives on the use of human language. Although methodological questions frequently divide these two camps (with communication researchers using the quantitative research procedures of the social sciences and rhetorical scholars using the humanistic research methods of the liberal arts), the object of their study has become remarkably similar in the last decade of the twentieth century.[1] The perspective adopted by this text is a rhetorical perspective; however, to acknowledge that the studies of rhetoric and communication are related and converging, an overview of basic principles of communication serves as prelude to a discussion of rhetoric.

## Communication

Various scholars have attempted to describe and model the communication process. The main divisions historically used to describe communication and to define areas of research tend to be various communication situations and particular communication activities and skills.

### Definition

Perhaps no question regarding human communication involves less agreement than the definition of communication. In 1976, Frank Dance and Carl Larson identified 126 different definitions, titling their list "*Some* Definitions of Communication" (emphasis mine).[2] The number of available definitions has grown dramatically since then. Despite this maze of competing definitions, some agreement emerges among communication scholars. First, such scholars limit their concern to human communication, leaving to psychologists and those in the natural sciences the study of animal communication. Second, human communication is a process of some sort. That process has been described as a "transmission,"[3] a "transaction,"[4] and an "exchange."[5] Third, the process is an interaction involving one or more individuals acting as stimuli for one or more others. As a result of the interaction, some sort of exchange, variously described as transfer of "information," "meaning," or a "message" usually is attempted or results despite intention. Other scholars note that communication is symbolic and that it requires a response from a receiver.[6]

## Types of Communication

Communication scholars generally identify types of communication based on the number and nature of participants in a communication enterprise. Thus, intrapersonal communication is that communication an individual has with herself or himself. Relatively little communication research is focused in this area, leaving such research by and large to cognitive scholars. Interpersonal communication involves a dyad—two individuals communicating with each other. Small-group communication involves three or more individuals communicating together. Public communication includes public speaking and panel discussions before larger audiences. In such public settings, the communication of the audience is more limited than in other types of communication.

   A second distinction made among types of communication concerns the channel of communication. Thus, researchers distinguish between verbal communication, which relies on language, and nonverbal communication, which uses gestures, space, time, and other resources for communication. Most human communication is complex, involving both the verbal and nonverbal. Thus, in order to understand this message accurately—*Sure, I just love your new haircut*—one needs to hear the tone of voice in which the message is delivered, to observe any facial or body gestures that might indicate sincerity, lying, teasing, or sarcasm, and to comprehend other aspects of the communication situation.

## Communication Situations

Descriptions of communication situations most frequently are done by means of communication models, which are simplified representations of some aspects of the communication process. Most communication models involve some visual representation of a sender, who encodes a message and sends it through a channel of communication to a receiver, who then decodes the message. Receivers also act as senders, encoding feedback and messages of their own. This process takes place in a particular environment, which also affects the communication. This environment not only includes the physical setting, which may be a hot room late on Friday afternoon or the family dinner table, but the situation of the individuals involved in the communication transaction. Thus the mental and physical state of communicators affects communication, as does the occasion for which they are gathered. Prior communicative interactions between the parties, which will affect their feelings toward one another and their understanding of verbal and nonverbal messages, are also components of a communication situation. A communication situation between two individuals running for President from different political parties is different early in a campaign than it is just before the election. Further, if they meet in a televised debate, their communication is affected in different ways than if they meet accidentally in a restaurant, far from cameras and microphones.

## Functions of Human Communication

Various authors have attempted to catalog the functions of human communication. Dance and Larson suggest that human communication has three functions: 1) a linking function, allowing an individual to relate self to the environment and to other human beings; 2) a mentation function, whereby an individual's own higher mental processes are developed; and 3) a regulatory function, in which an individual attempts to regulate the behavior of self and other human beings.[7]

Thus, the study of communication can encompass symbolic interactions between and among individuals in nearly every conceivable circumstance. Communication scholars, using descriptive and experimental methods, attempt to determine effects of particular variables in communication situations in order to explain the communication process and to enable individuals to improve their own communication.

## Rhetoric

Communication can have several ends; one is persuasion. The art of using language to such an end historically was known as rhetoric. Although currently one meaning of the word "rhetoric" is pejorative (referring to "mere rhetoric"—language that sounds good but signifies little), rhetoric also is an art with a long, venerable, and varied history.

In Western civilization, tradition has it that rhetoric began on the island of Sicily during the fifth century, B.C. When a democracy was established following a revolution against dictatorial government, the courts attempted to sort out land claims. As claimants were required to represent themselves in court, those who were skilled in public speaking increased their chances of prevailing before the law. In responding to the need for speaking skills, Corax wrote the "Art of Rhetoric," an instructional treatise on oral communication. Tisias, a pupil of Corax, is credited with introducing his instructor's system to the Greek mainland.[8]

Rhetoric, since its beginning in Greece, has played a central role in the liberal arts. During those two thousand years, however, understandings about the nature of rhetoric have varied significantly.

## Definitions of Rhetoric

Even those who have written about rhetoric are not in complete agreement concerning the definition of the term. A review of noteworthy definitions indicates not only something about the nature of rhetoric but its scope as well:

- Aristotle, as translated by George Kennedy, notes: "Let rhetoric be [defined as] an ability, in each [particular] case, to see the available means of persuasion."[9]
- Francis Bacon argues that "the duty and office of Rhetoric . . . is . . . to apply and recommend the dictates of reason to imagination, in order to excite the appetite and will."[10]
- George Campbell suggests that rhetoric ("eloquence") is "[t]hat art or talent by which the discourse is adapted to its end." The possible ends are "to enlighten the understanding, to please the imagination, to move the passions, or to influence the will."[11]
- Richard Whately states, "The *finding* of suitable arguments to prove a given point, and the skilful *arrangement* of them, may be considered as the immediate and proper province of Rhetoric, and of that alone."[12]

- Douglas Ehninger defines rhetoric as "an organized, consistent, coherent way of talking about practical discourse."[13]
- Donald Bryant calls rhetoric the "*rationale of informative and suasory discourse*," and cites as its function "*adjusting ideas to people and people to ideas.*"[14]
- I. A. Richards argues rhetoric should be "a study of misunderstanding and its remedies."[15]
- Kenneth Burke says rhetoric is "*rooted in an essential function of language itself, a function that is wholly realistic, and is continually born anew; the use of language as a symbolic means of inducing cooperation in beings that by nature respond to symbols.*"[16]
- For Richard Weaver, rhetoric is "truth plus its artful presentation."[17]
- Sonja Foss, Karen Foss, and Robert Trapp suggest that rhetoric is a purposive, symbolic human action as well as a perspective that involves focus on the process of symbolism.[18]

These varied definitions, while not setting the exact parameters of rhetoric, give a general sense about its nature and scope. That general sense can be made more specific by a review of the major rhetorical theorists who view rhetoric, variously, as the art of persuasion, as ornamentation added to language, or as the means by which truth is created.

## The Art of Persuasion

The view that has been most influential is that rhetoric is the art of persuasion. This view, detailed by Aristotle, is reflected in the Roman view of rhetoric, adopted by St. Augustine and reclaimed by several scholars during the Enlightenment. It continues to attract adherents in contemporary times.

**Aristotle.**   The first detailed, systematic rhetoric to which we have access is that of Aristotle. This most important work, the *Rhetoric*, details human emotions, inventional topics, lines of argument, modes of proof, stylistic devices, and patterns of arrangement; in keeping with Aristotle's scientific attitude, the *Rhetoric* categorizes the "available means of persuasion."

Aristotle's rhetoric is based on his conception of knowledge. An important aspect of knowledge—knowledge of particulars—comes from experience. Aristotle also cites knowledge of the probable, that is, *belief*. Because the world of human affairs is in the realm of the contingent, rhetoric, as the art of persuasion, is a necessary art for arriving at decisions in human affairs. Legislators do not come to universal truths when debating whether to raise the sales tax or limit welfare benefits. They make decisions based, at least in part, on belief. Rhetoric, although it cannot yield absolute truth, is the means to probable truth and is, therefore, crucial in politics and everyday life.

To aid in establishing what is probable, Aristotle cites three modes of proof: *ethos*, *pathos*, and *logos*. *Ethos* is the character or credibility of the speaker. Audiences can be persuaded either to believe or disbelieve someone on the basis of the person's character. Mother Theresa is highly credible; a person who has a reputation for dishonesty is not. *Pathos* concerns emotional appeals. The audience can be put into a certain frame of mind to accept a speaker's conclusions, and a speaker will be more persuasive if he or she understands the range of human emotion and how to appeal to particular emotions. Humans are moved to pity by stories or pictures of human suffering, for example. Finally, *logos* is the proof, or apparent proof, provided by the words of the speech, which persuades by appealing to human reason. Citing a statistic, drawing a historical analogy, or using a supporting opinion acts as proof for a claim.

In the *Rhetoric*, Aristotle discusses three situations in which rhetoric occurs. *Deliberative* or political rhetoric is concerned with the future and its ends are expediency or inexpediency. Legislators deliberate about the expediency of raising taxes, allowing gambling within the state, or paying for particular social services. *Forensic* or legal rhetoric is concerned with the past, and its ends are justice or injustice. Attorneys attempt to convince juries that justice will be served by finding a defendant not guilty. *Epideictic* or ceremonial rhetoric is concerned with the present, and its ends are honor or dishonor. An orator at a memorial service praises the life and honors the memory of the recently deceased person.

Aristotle emphasizes the invention of rational arguments in his rhetoric, distinguishing between the types of proof available for such arguments. *Artistic proofs* are those created by the orator, whereas *inartistic proofs* merely are interpreted and used by the speaker. Statistics are inartistic proofs; a hypothetical example is an artistic proof. The method Aristotle gives for generating arguments are the *topoi* or topics, which are stock formulas for arguments. He lays out an entire topical system, not only indicating topics and lines of argument generally available but also identifying those specific to each of the three rhetorical situations as well as those useful in appeals to *ethos*, *pathos*, and *logos*.

The last section of the *Rhetoric* concerns organization. The basic parts of a speech, according to Aristotle, are the *introduction*, the *body* or "proof," and the "epilogue" or *conclusion*. He gives specifics for the creation of each part.

These and other details of Aristotle's system were adopted by the Roman rhetoricians and are used today in modern public speaking courses. However, for many centuries, the *Rhetoric* had little direct influence, for Aristotle's writings were lost and not rediscovered for several centuries.

**Post-classical Hellenistic Period**.   Alexander the Great and his successors spread the Greek model of education and society over a vast geographical territory during the period following classical Athens. The program of education, *paedeia*, was to educate in the Greek model, and it consisted of instruction in grammar, rhetoric, logic, arithmetic, geometry, music, and astronomy. Of all these topics, instruction in rhetoric carried the greatest importance.

Around 150 B.C., Hermagoras wrote a since-lost text concerning *stases*. According to later accounts of this text, which are extant, the issues of a legal dispute will center around one of several questions. The first, the conjectural *stasis*, concerns matters of fact—did certain events happen? The second, the definitive *stasis*, concerns the appropriate definition for an act—can it be categorized as murder or not? The third, the qualitative *stasis*, concerns the justification for the act—was the person to blame? Was the act in self-defense? Finally, the translative *stasis* concerns the competence or jurisdiction of the court to try the case. To defend yourself against a charge, legal or otherwise, you may determine which *stasis* offers the most effective defense. If a friend berates you for late arrival for an engagement, and you point out that you had a flat tire while driving to meet her, the dispute centers around the qualitative *stasis*.

**Romans**.   As they did in many other aspects of their culture, the Romans borrowed or adapted Greek rhetorical theory. Although Aristotle did not use the same terminology, he discussed most of the so-called "canons" of rhetoric, which the Romans set forth as the basic units of rhetorical activity: 1) *invention*; 2) *disposition*; 3) *elocution*; 4) *delivery*; and 5) *memory*. Invention involves the development of the ideas of the orator, the appeals to reason and to the emotions, and the highlighting of the speaker's *ethos*. Disposition is the arrangement of arguments that have been invented by the orator. Elocution is the stylistic devices, the choice of words, that dress up the speaker's ideas. Delivery is the vocal and nonverbal elements of presenting an oration. Finally, memory is the ability to remember what the speaker planned to say. The Romans named the canons and used them to organize rhetorical instruction.

An extant early Roman rhetorical treatise is the *Rhetorica ad Herennium*, a work from approximately 100 B.C. The *Rhetorica ad Herennium*, a manual for schoolboys, includes discussion of the five canons of rhetoric and *stases* in addition to other borrowed Greek concepts. Some speculate that Cicero may have authored this work.

Several works, however, are known to be Cicero's, who not only wrote treatises on rhetoric but was a renowned orator himself. His early work on rhetoric was *De Inventione*, which portrays the ideal orator and is, essentially, a prescriptive model of rhetoric. It largely is restricted to invention and details Hermagoras's system of *stases*. In his major work, *De Oratore*, Cicero posits rhetoric as the practical art for dealing with human affairs. He details what an orator must know and suggests principles of invention, arrangement, and memory. Known for his own ornate style, he devotes a section of the text to the three categories of style—plain, middle, and grand.

Marcus Fabius Quintilian describes the proper education of the citizen/orator throughout his life in *De Institutione Oratoria*, in which he defines an orator as a "good man speaking well." Quintilian was a teacher and a lawyer, who emphasized forensic oratory in this work. His ideas are adaptations of Cicero, the sophists, and the Greeks.

**Middle Ages**.    The decline of the Roman Empire left much of Europe mired in feudalism. During the Middle Ages (400 to 1400 A.D.), rhetoric thus was concerned with preaching, education, and letter writing, as individuals had little chance for political oratory. The key rhetorical theorist during this period was St. Augustine. Early Christians condemned rhetoric as a pagan art, for Christian truth needed no embellishment. However, prior to Augustine's conversion to Christianity, he had taught rhetoric; indeed, his oratorical skill as a preacher was notable. In *De Doctrina Christiana*, he argues that preachers could learn from the art of rhetoric; they need to be able to teach, delight, and move audiences, thereby better carrying the Christian gospel to the people. In the treatise, he argues that preachers have two tasks—to determine the meaning of Scripture and to give eloquence to its teaching.

In education, rhetoric played a significant role as one of the seven liberal arts. The *quadrivium* was concerned with numbers and was comprised of arithmetic, geometry, astronomy, and music. The *trivium* was concerned with language and was comprised of rhetoric, logic, and grammar. In this tradition, scholars concerned with rhetoric include Boethius and Alcuin. Boethius translated some of Aristotle into Latin and drew on both Aristotle and Cicero for a complicated system of topics. Alcuin, on the other hand, wrote a treatise that relies heavily on Cicero.

**Enlightenment**. George Campbell and Richard Whately authored the key epistemological rhetorics of this period. Campbell, a Scottish minister, based *The Philosophy of Rhetoric* on the works of Aristotle and Cicero plus the faculty psychology in vogue during the eighteenth century. Faculty psychology concerned the various faculties of the mind, which were used to explain behavior. Persuasive discourse was directed to the five powers of the mind—understanding, memory, imagination, passion, and will.

Whately, also a preacher, wrote *Elements of Rhetoric*, which focuses on argumentation. Rhetoric, according to Whately, involves finding arguments and arranging them skillfully. He also discusses the corresponding notions of presumption and burden of proof.

**Kenneth Burke**. Burke adopts the view that rhetoric is the art of persuasion. A literary critic, Burke views literature as rhetoric, thereby erasing the distinction between rhetoric and poetic. Instead, he sees rhetoric as symbolic action in a world built by symbols. Thus all discourse is persuasive; both poetry and oratory become forms of propaganda. Burke discusses the persuasive action of rhetoric as *identification*.

Central to his notion of identification is Burke's belief that the world is made of substance. That this substance is found in separate things—people and objects—is due to division. The nature of human life is division; individuals are separate or divided from other things and other people. This division is both the ambiguity of substance and a resource for rhetoric. If rhetoric works as identification, then rhetoric works to bring together what was divided substance; to identify items is to make them *consubstantial*. What Burke means by this term is that rhetoric operates to remind individuals of their shared substance, which allows them to overlook division and to identify. Identification is compensatory to division: "But put identification and division ambiguously together, so that you cannot know for certain just where one ends and the other begins, and you have the characteristic invitation to rhetoric."[19] Persuasion, then, is based on identification: "You persuade a man only insofar as you can talk his language by speech, gesture, tonality, order, image, attitude, idea, *identifying* your ways with his."[20]

Identification may function in many ways. Politicians attempt to identify with middle-class citizens, despite their own personal wealth, in order to gain votes. Advertising is designed to get viewers and listeners to identify with individuals portrayed in the ads, thereby increasing the likelihood they will purchase the product or service advertised. Thus, consumers are shown models and actors who are beautiful, talented, and satisfied—characteristics many individuals wish to have. A student may identify with a teacher of the same gender or race, causing her to respond more favorably to the class material or to learn more than she otherwise would. We also identify with those who share our enemies, no matter how unlike us they are. During the Gulf War, the United States and Syria, formerly bitter enemies, became allies; they identified as a result of their common hatred of Saddam Hussein.

Rhetoric, as the art of persuasion, is a practical art, detailing how discourse can be adapted to the rhetor's desired ends. It draws on the other liberal arts, particularly logic, and frequently it is prescriptive in nature. Not all rhetorical theorists define rhetoric as the art of persuasion, however. Some view rhetoric as the art of ornamentation.

## Ornamentation

Rhetoric also has been viewed as the art of style and delivery, with other canons of rhetoric becoming a part of logic. In this view, rhetoric becomes little more than ornamentation to ideas and arguments created by other means. A chief architect of this perspective on rhetoric was Peter Ramus. Similar views of rhetoric are found in *belles lettres* and elocutionary rhetorics.

**Ramistic**.   In seventeenth-century France, Peter Ramus set out to make his academic career by attacking Aristotle, Cicero, and Quintilian. Pointing out the overlap between the arts, he redefined them, limiting grammar to syntax, rhetoric to style and delivery, and leaving to logic the study of invention and disposition. This departmentalization of the arts had a profound impact on rhetorical education. As Ramistic rhetorics no longer concerned the invention of arguments, students of such rhetorics learned only to make their speech appealing through tropes and figures of speech as well as good delivery.

**Enlightenment**.   During the eighteenth century, French and other rhetorics followed the Ramistic model and focused on style. These *belles lettres* rhetorics concern aesthetic qualities and elevate form over content. They also broaden the scope of rhetoric beyond oratory to literature and criticism. One exemplar of this movement is Hugh Blair. In his *Lectures on Rhetoric and Belles Lettres*, drawn from lectures he gave at the University of Edinburgh, the relationship of literature, criticism, and rhetoric is explored. This work contains a detailed discussion of taste.

A final movement during this period, the elocutionary movement, limited rhetoric further, to the canon of delivery. Elocutionists used faculty psychology to link particular vocal and nonverbal elements to aspects of the mind. Gilbert Austin and Thomas Sheridan were well known as elocutionists who developed elaborate systems of gesture and vocal variations to communicate certain meanings.

The effect of Ramistic, belletristic, and elocutionary rhetorics was to marginalize rhetoric, that is, to make it a fanciful but unimportant art. This is in stark contrast to the view that rhetoric creates truth, which makes of it an "architectonic" art.[21]

## Creation of Truth

An ancient view of rhetoric that has been resurrected in the twentieth century is that rhetoric creates rather than discovers truth. Early proponents of this view were the sophists; in the Renaissance, Italian Humanists espoused similar notions. However, only in the twentieth century has this view had such a profound impact not only on rhetoric but other disciplines as well.

**Sophists**.   Between 450 and 400 B.C. in Athens, a group of itinerant teachers of rhetoric, known as sophists, taught the art of rhetoric for a fee. The political system was ripe for such teachers, as Athens was a democracy whose male citizens could vote in the assembly, hold administrative offices, and bring suit against other citizens in the courts. Therefore, the ability to speak eloquently was prized and in demand; the sophists, from the Greek *sophos*, meaning "wise" or "excellent," found receptive audiences for their rhetorical teachings. Most notable of the sophistic views about rhetoric was the relationship of rhetoric to truth.

One early sophist, Protagoras, believed that absolute truth was inaccessible to humans and, therefore, had to be established by human standards, as "man is the measure of all things." According to Protagoras, the sole basis of human knowledge is human perceptions and sensations. Thus, as all sensations and perceptions are "real," no experience can be wrong, and no individual can move from his or her own experience to universalized, abstract knowledge. To examine the arguments for and against a position was, he felt, the best method for judging probability.

Another sophist, Gorgias, not only started a school in Athens but was himself famous as an orator. He excelled at, and required students to practice, impromptu speaking. Gorgias argued that speech is extremely powerful, creating emotions and evoking perceptions of reality. He, like Protagoras, believed that truth was unavailable to humans, who rely on opinion, *doxa*, as a criterion for action. This *doxa* is, by definition, untrue. But, as humans cannot know truth, the deception presented by rhetoric is the extent of reality accessible to humans.

Like *rhetoric*, the term *sophist* today has a pejorative meaning. One reason is that few sophistic texts are extant. However, the works of Plato, in which he vilifies and mocks the Sophists, have survived. Thus, history views the Sophists through Plato's unflattering and hostile depictions. The sophistic view of truth as unknowable, however, gives to rhetoric a major role—for language creates *doxa*, which becomes the only truth we can know. Not until the Italian Renaissance was rhetoric again viewed as a creator of truth.

**Humanists**.    The end of the Middle Ages came with the Renaissance and the rise of Humanism, which involved the study of ideas and languages from antiquity, particularly classical Rome. Rhetoric was of particular interest to the Humanists, who saw eloquence as a combination of knowledge and style. The Humanists were scholars from a variety of professions, including history and the law. They rediscovered the complete text of *De Oratore* in a cathedral cellar and became particularly enthused by Cicero. In a reversal of the Greeks, the Humanists privileged rhetoric over philosophy, as humans gain access to the natural world through language. Therefore, the Humanists emphasized poetry rather than rational proofs.

The height of Humanism occurred in Italy. Among the Humanists concerned with rhetoric were Francesco Petrarca (Petrarch), a poet of the fourteenth century who discovered a large number of Cicero's personal letters. Petrarch advocated Cicero's ideal of rhetoric and cultivated learning, which became a foundation of Humanism. As many Italian intellectuals of the time were involved in public life, they were drawn to the ideal of wisdom combined with eloquence. Lino Coluccio di Piero Salutati, a political leader and Petrarch's student, and a group of his colleagues studied, practiced, and occasionally taught rhetoric. In a notable break with historical practice, Italian women of this period were educated alongside men. However, few women were allowed to enter public life or pursue scholarly careers.

Although the Italian Renaissance ended when the Spanish Army plundered Rome in 1537, Italian Humanism came to full flower in the eighteenth century in the works of Giambattista Vico. Vico, a professor of rhetoric, suggested that human knowledge comes through language rather than science, as understanding and imagination, the essentials of human experience, are metaphoric. Ernesto Grassi describes Vico's idea:

> [R]ational thought, in the traditional sense, consists of connecting (*legein*) and abstracting in order to define sensory manifestations with a view to attaining universal and necessary principles . . . . Vico confronts this process with metaphorical

> thinking. This is also a process of combining, connecting (*legein*) and abstracting, but not of a rational nature. The ingenious vision of relationships between sensory manifestations, a vision inherent in metaphor, represents the primary aspect of combining, the aspect characteristic of sharp-wittedness. . . .
>
> The connecting, abstracting function contained in the act of the *ingenium* [the capacity to see similarities in dissimilar things] forms the essence of "real" or original thought and speech.[22]

Vico thus sees rhetoric not as persuasion but as expression of the real. The metaphorical capacity of *ingenium* creates that which humans come to know.

A humanistic tone is evident in modern rhetorical theories. For example, I. A. Richards supports the view that language affects the reality humans "see," pointing out that the world "so far from being a solid matter of fact—is rather a fabric of conventions, which for obscure reasons it has suited us in the past to manufacture and support."[23] Humanism also underpins the claim that rhetoric generates knowledge.

**Rhetoric Is Epistemic.** A number of scholars in the field of speech communication have identified the truth-creating role of rhetoric, arguing that it operates epistemically. Because human truths are contingent, they are seen to arise from rhetoric. This social knowledge, argues Thomas Farrell, is derived rhetorically, as consensus is a necessary, although not sufficient, condition for such knowledge.[24] He notes: "The ability of rhetorical transactions gradually to generate what they can initially only assume appears to possess a rather magical ambiance."[25] Walter Carleton suggests that all knowledge is social knowledge, which involves rhetorical processes of creating new ideas (*invention*), naming or classifying ideas (*interpretation*), sequencing ideas within hierarchies (*connection*), and determining first principles or fundamental assumptions, establishing models, and making metaphors (*explanation*).[26]

Richard Cherwitz and James Hikins suggest that rhetoric affects our knowledge of reality by positing relationships among categories for particulars, thus giving meaning to such particulars. They describe the rhetorical processes which allow this creation of meaning as: 1) *differentiative*, whereby discourse distinguishes or differentiates among particulars; 2) *associative*, whereby connections are drawn, inferences suggested, and warrants supplied; 3) *preservative*, whereby ideas are kept alive for discussion and for the testing that occurs in the process of public discussion and debate; 4) *evaluative*, whereby ideas are discussed and tested; and 5) *perspectival*, whereby individual knowers become aware of various perspectives on the world and on particulars.[27] By allowing for, and even embracing, the perspectives of others, true knowledge, which Cherwitz and Hikins define as "justified true belief," is possible.[28] Although "overarching" certainty is only an idea, we can proclaim truths when, tested by debate in the marketplace of ideas, claims to know obtain consensus.[29]

Rhetoric is seen not only in terms of its end—variously, persuasion, ornamentation, or truth—but also in terms of the value of its end. Throughout the history of rhetoric, various scholars have warned of its potential for evil or proclaimed its potential for good.

## Potential for Evil

Rhetoric's potential for evil is the potential that auditors will be led astray or persuaded to bad acts or dysfunctional beliefs. Although many have cautioned against the power of a base rhetoric, none has done so more forcefully than Plato.

**Plato.** Plato, a student of the great philosopher Socrates, writes his philosophical treatises largely in the form of dialogue, with Socrates engaging first one and then another lesser mind in the discussion of philosophical issues. In the works on rhetoric, among his foils are Gorgias and Phaedrus, after whom the dialogues are named. Socrates denounces sophistic notions of a relative truth, arguing that genuine knowledge comes from dialectic, with truth lying in the realm of the ideal, in the unchangeable essence of things. Such essences can be known not by experience but by the minds of true lovers of wisdom, through divine inspiration and dialectic. Reliance on *doxa* leads to deception, which accounts for Plato's scorn of sophists and their "art" of rhetoric.

In the *Gorgias*, Socrates argues that rhetoric is dangerous and corrupt and that it has nothing to do with justice or virtue. Instead, he claims it is merely a form of flattery. Rhetoric is not an art but a mere knack:

> Well then, Gorgias, the activity as a whole, it seems to me, is not an art, but the occupation of a shrewd and enterprising spirit, and of one naturally skilled in its dealings with men, and in sum and substance I call it "flattery." Now it seems to me that there are many other parts of this activity, one of which is cookery. This is considered an art, but in my judgment is no art, only a routine and a knack. And rhetoric I call another part of this general activity, and beautification, and sophistic—four parts with four distinct objects.[30]

In the course of the dialogue, Plato has Socrates condemn not only rhetoric and those who teach it but democracy as well.

In the *Phaedrus*, Socrates analogizes various types of love to rhetoric. He compares sophistic rhetoric to love that is false or has base motives. An ideal rhetoric, which is an art (*techne*), is compared to a true love. This rhetoric is based upon knowledge of the truth, of the forms of discourse, and of the types of souls. Such a rhetoric does not corrupt but instead communicates truth discovered by other means. Only this latter rhetoric is a true rhetoric:

> But can anyone possibly master the art of using similarities for the purpose of bringing people round, and leading them away from the truth about this or that to the opposite of the truth, or again can anyone possibly avoid this happening to himself, unless he has knowledge of what the thing in question really is? . . .
>
> It would seem to follow, my friend, that the art of speech displayed by one who has gone chasing after beliefs, instead of knowing the truth, will be a comical sort of art, in fact no art at all.[31]

Often cited as a neo-Platonist, Richard Weaver also cautions against the dangers of a base rhetoric. Such a rhetoric involves skill in use of signs but lacks a vision of the truth as the central content of the message. Weaver acknowledges "speech which influences us in the direction of what is evil," arguing that such rhetoric is exploitative. He notes that base rhetoric, in modern times, with the "vastly augmented power of propagation" has a "means of deluding which no ancient rhetor in forum or market place could have imagined."[32] However he, like Plato, also acknowledges the potential for good by a noble rhetor.

## Potential for Good

Noble rhetoric is acknowledged by many. Some argue that rhetoric is good when it is in service of the truth. Others argue that rhetoric is essential to the search for truth, or the probable, in the political arena.

**Isocrates**.    Although his thought is closely aligned with the Sophists, Isocrates' career was contemporaneous to Plato and Aristotle. He and his school were famous in his day, as was his system of education in which eloquence was stressed above all other learning. Isocrates believed that humans could attain neither truth nor exact knowledge (*episteme*) so must rely on *doxa*. However, he attempted to distance himself from the Sophists, arguing that rhetoric is more than the skill to prevail in a court, no matter the strength of one's case. He relied on an elaborate style, arguing that by using such style, orators could elevate the character and political consciousness of fellow Athenians. In a well-known passage from *Antidosis*, Isocrates states:

> For in the other powers which we possess, as I have already said on a former occasion, we are in no respect superior to other living creatures; nay, we are inferior to many in swiftness and in strength and in other resources; but, because there has been implanted in us the power to persuade each other and to make clear to each other whatever we desire, not only have we escaped the life of wild beasts, but we have come together and founded cities and made laws and invented arts; and, generally speaking, there is no institution devised by man which the power of speech has not helped us to establish. For this it is which has laid down laws concerning things just and unjust, and things honourable and base; and if it were not for these ordinances we should not be able to live with one another. It is by this also that we confute the bad and extol the good. Through this we educate the ignorant and appraise the wise; for the power to speak well is taken as the surest index of a sound understanding, and discourse which is true and lawful and just is the outward image of a good and faithful soul. With this faculty we both contend against others on matters which are open to dispute and seek light for ourselves on things which are unknown; for the same arguments which we use in persuading others when we speak in public, we employ also when we deliberate in our own thoughts; and, while we call eloquent those who are able to speak before a crowd, we regard as sage those who most skillfully debate their problems in their own minds.[33]

Isocrates' reference to debating ideas relates to another reason for the potential good of rhetoric. Challenging ideas, as Cherwitz and Hikins note, leads to a more justified consensus.

**Marketplace of Ideas.**   The art of rhetoric as practiced in Greece and Rome went into decline following the demise of Roman representative government. This is the beginning of the wax and wane of rhetoric in concert with the political freedom of individuals. If individuals can be punished for expressing opinions contrary to the government in power, the art of rhetoric has little place in that society, at least a rhetoric that involves inventional strategies useful to political oratory. In a society in which citizens have political freedoms, rhetoric holds enormous potential for good in the marketplace of ideas.

The concept of the *marketplace of ideas* was created by John Milton and John Stuart Mill and was introduced into U.S. law by Oliver Wendell Holmes. Milton's discussion in the *Areopagitica* contains this classic, often-quoted statement: "And though all the winds of doctrine were let loose to play upon the earth, so Truth be in the field, we do injuriously, by licensing and prohibiting, to misdoubt her strength. Let her and Falsehood grapple; who ever knew Truth put to the worse, in a free and open encounter?"[34] Although Mill does not use the term, he describes the importance of the marketplace of ideas in *On Liberty*:

> If all mankind minus one were of one opinion, and only one person were of the contrary opinion, mankind would be no more justified in silencing that one person, than he, if he had the power, would be justified in silencing mankind. . . . But the peculiar evil of silencing the expression of an opinion is, that it is robbing the human race; posterity as well as the existing generation; those who dissent from the opinion, still more than those who hold it. If the opinion is right, they are deprived of the opportunity of exchanging error for truth: if wrong, they lose what is almost as great a benefit, the clearer perception and livelier impression of truth, produced by its collision with error.[35]

In his dissenting opinion in the 1919 U.S. Supreme Court case *Abrams v. United States*, Holmes penned what has become the *raison d'être* for free speech: "But when men have realized that time has upset many fighting faiths, they may come to believe even more than they believe the very foundations of their own conduct that the ultimate good desired is better reached by free trade in ideas—that the best test of truth is the power of the thought to get itself accepted in the competition of the market."[36] Thus, the role of rhetoric in the marketplace of ideas is to state, forcefully and effectively, individual ideas, that they might be tested by clash with opposing ideas. This is the preservative and evaluative functions of an epistemic rhetoric to which Cherwitz and Hikins refer.

**Truth in Its Artful Presentation**.   For Richard Weaver, like Plato, rhetoric is useful as a means of conveying dialectically secured truths. The process of dialectic is concerned with abstract concepts, what he calls "dialectical terms." Not all categories are dialectical terms. For example, Weaver is not concerned with specific names for objects or categories, which he calls "positive terms." Instead the categories with which his dialectic is concerned are abstractions, verities, essences, and principles—the good, the true, the just. The dialectical process requires piety, sentimentality, and appropriate vision of the ideal, for the function of dialectic is to define and order and appraise dialectical terms.[37]

Once the nature of these dialectical terms is established, rhetoric communicates this truth to others. The proper role of rhetoric is "truth plus its artful presentation." Therefore, the noble rhetor has a vision of ideal truth and a consideration of the situation of the audience, showing them the ideal and "better versions of themselves."[38] This is why Weaver claims that *language is sermonic,* and, when we use language either in our private or public capacities, we are acting as preachers, urging a particular view of things. As rhetors, we must realize that our statements are not neutral and may persuade others to share our point of view. Therefore, we must not lose sight of the proper order of values so that our discourse, our "sermonizing," will be noble rather than base.[39]

## Summary

Rhetoric, whether seen as the art of persuasion or the means whereby knowledge is created, implies an ethics, for rhetorical choices have results that can affect other human beings in profound ways. Nikos Kazantzakis' fictional character, Zorba, demonstrates the power of rhetoric. Zorba is an older yet vital, energetic, sensuous, story-telling, laboring-class Greek "everyman" who encounters a bookish younger man (the first-person narrator of the story) who inherited a mine on Crete. The two men live and work together, lodging on Crete with an old and broken French woman—Dame Hortense. Zorba's vision of the world is simple, alive, and unencumbered by academic philosophies or political doctrines, and he communicates that vision through his stories and by dancing. The narrator, as a result of Zorba's rhetoric, develops a voracious appetite for life and a passion for living it. Zorba so charms Dame Hortense that she sees herself, once again, as young and desirable, and acts like a foolish coquette. Even the reader is swept up in Zorba's enthusiastic recipe for living life to its fullest. Zorba is able to create the world anew, demonstrating the potential of rhetoric— which can be exercised for evil or for good.

The power of rhetoric—displayed so dramatically by Zorba—arises because humans, through language and other systems of signs, create understandings for themselves and other humans. This is the process of creating meaning.

## Endnotes

1. Perhaps nothing illustrates this point so well as the differences between the second and third edition of Stephen Littlejohn's widely adopted communication theory text. The third edition concerns both structural and poststructural theories of signs, discussion of meaning, review of critical and interpretive theories, dramatistic theories, and other topics also within the purview of contemporary rhetorical theory. Stephen W. Littlejohn, *Theories of Human Communication,* 3rd ed. (Belmont, CA: Wadsworth, 1989).
2. Frank E. X. Dance and Carl E. Larson, *The Functions of Human Communication: A Theoretical Approach* (New York: Holt, Rinehart and Winston, 1976) 171–92.

3. See, for example, Bernard Berelson and Gary A. Steiner, *Human Behavior: An Inventory of Scientific Findings* (New York: Harcourt, Brace & World, 1964) 527.
4. See, for example, Rudolph F. Verderber, *Communicate!* 6th ed. (Belmont, CA: Wadsworth, 1990) 4.
5. Theodore M. Newcomb, Ralph H. Turner, and Philip E. Converse, *Social Psychology: The Study of Human Interaction* (New York: Holt, Rinehart and Winston, 1965) 219.
6. Ronald B. Adler and George Rodman, *Understanding Human Communication*, 4th ed. (Fort Worth: Holt, Rinehart and Winston, 1991) 5–8.
7. Dance and Larson 48.
8. Conley argues that this version of the "birth" of rhetoric may be apocryphal. Thomas M. Conley, *Rhetoric in the European Tradition* (New York: Longman, 1990) 4. Richard Enos suggests that rhetoric evolved through a process starting with Homer. Richard Leo Enos, *Greek Rhetoric Before Aristotle* (Prospect Heights, IL: Waveland, 1993).
9. Aristotle, *On Rhetoric: A Theory of Civic Discourse*, trans. George A. Kennedy (New York: Oxford UP, 1991) I 1355 36–37.
10. Francis Bacon, "Of the Dignity and Advancement of Learning," *The Works of Francis Bacon*, ed. James Spedding, Robert Leslie Ellis, and Douglas Denon Heath, vol. 4 (1870; rpt. New York: Garrett, 1968) VI 3 455.
11. George Campbell, *The Philosophy of Rhetoric*, ed. Lloyd F. Bitzer (Carbondale: Southern Illinois UP, 1963) 1.
12. Richard Whately, *Elements of Rhetoric*, ed. Douglas Ehninger (1828; rpt. Carbondale: Southern Illinois UP, 1963) 39 (capital letters omitted).
13. Douglas Ehninger, "On Systems of Rhetoric," *Contemporary Rhetoric: A Reader's Coursebook*, ed. Douglas Ehninger (Glenview, IL: Scott, Foresman, 1972) 18, 26.
14. Donald C. Bryant, "Rhetoric: Its Function and Its Scope," *Contemporary Rhetoric: A Reader's Coursebook*, ed. Douglas Ehninger (Glenview, IL: Scott, Foresman, 1972) 18, 26.
15. I. A. Richards, *The Philosophy of Rhetoric* (1936; rpt. Oxford: Oxford UP, 1981) 3.
16. Kenneth Burke, *A Rhetoric of Motives* (1950; rpt. Berkeley: University of California P, 1969) 43.
17. Richard M. Weaver, *The Ethics of Rhetoric* (South Bend, IN: Regnery, 1953) 15.
18. Sonja K. Foss, Karen A. Foss and Robert Trapp, *Contemporary Perspectives on Rhetoric*, 2nd ed. (Prospect Heights, IL: Waveland, 1991) 14–18.
19. Burke, *A Rhetoric of Motives* 25.
20. Burke, *A Rhetoric of Motives* 55.
21. Richard McKeon, "The Uses of Rhetoric in a Technological Age: Architectonic Productive Arts," *The Prospect of Rhetoric*, ed. Lloyd F. Bitzer and Edwin Black (Englewood Cliffs, NJ: Prentice-Hall, 1971) 46.
22. Ernesto Grassi, "The Priority of Common Sense and Imagination: Vico's Philosophical Relevance Today," trans. Azizeh Azodi, *Vico and Humanism: Essays on Vico, Heidegger, and Rhetoric* (New York: Peter Lang, 1990) 37–38.
23. Richards 41–42.
24. Thomas B. Farrell, "Knowledge, Consensus, and Rhetorical Theory," *Quarterly Journal of Speech* 62 (1976): 7.
25. Farrell 11. See also, Barry Brummett, "Some Implications of 'Process' or 'Intersubjectivity': Postmodern Rhetoric," *Philosophy and Rhetoric* 9 (1976): 21–51.

26. Walter M. Carleton, "What is Rhetorical Knowledge? A Response to Farrell—and More," *Quarterly Journal of Speech* 64 (1978): 319–21.

27. Richard A. Cherwitz and James W. Hikins, *Communication and Knowledge: An Investigation in Rhetorical Epistemology* (Columbia, SC: U of South Carolina P, 1986) 92–110.

28. Cherwitz and Hikins 21.

29. Cherwitz and Hikins 155–56.

30. Plato, *Gorgias*, trans. W.D. Woodhead, *The Collected Dialogues of Plato*, ed. Edith Hamilton and Huntington Cairns (1961; rpt. Princeton: Princeton UP, 1973) 463a–b.

31. Plato, *Phaedrus*, trans. R. Hackforth, *The Collected Dialogues of Plato*, ed. Edith Hamilton and Huntington Cairns (1961; rpt. Princeton: Princeton UP, 1973) 262b–c.

32. Weaver 11–12.

33. Isocrates, *Antidosis*, trans. George Norlin, Loeb Classical Library (Cambridge: Harvard UP, 1954) 253–57.

34. John Milton, *Areopagitica, Great Books of the Western World*, ed. Robert Maynard Hutchins, vol. 32 (Chicago: Encyclopedia Britannica, 1952) 409.

35. John Stuart Mill, *On Liberty, Great Books of the Western World*, ed. Robert Maynard Hutchins, vol. 43 (Chicago: Encyclopedia Britannica, 1952) 274–75.

36. *Abrams v. United States*, 250 U.S. 616, 630 (1919).

37. Richard M. Weaver, "Ultimate Terms in Contemporary Rhetoric," *Language is Sermonic: Richard M. Weaver on the Nature of Rhetoric*, ed. Richard L. Johannesen, Rennard Strickland, and Ralph T. Eubanks (Baton Rouge: Louisiana State UP, 1970) 87–112.

38. Weaver, *The Ethics of Rhetoric* 25.

39. Weaver, "Language is Sermonic," *Language is Sermonic: Richard M. Weaver on the Nature of Rhetoric*, ed. Richard L. Johannesen, Rennard Strickland, and Ralph T. Eubanks (Baton Rouge: Louisiana State UP, 1970) 224–25.

# Chapter Four

# Meaning

The product of language use, of rhetoric, frequently is referred to as meaning. People communicate with each other to transfer meaning; a failure of communication is declared if the receiver does not understand the meaning intended by the sender. Although the term *meaning* is understood by most who speak the English language, scholarly dispute over the term has occupied a great deal of the latter twentieth century. Indeed, Gilbert Ryle refers to this issue as the "occupational disease" of contemporary philosophers.[1] How do words mean? Should the focus of meaning be on single words? What is meaning? Is meaning created or discovered? This chapter concerns various aspects of meaning, ranging from common-sense notions to philosophical and psychological theories about meaning. Included is a discussion of the role of metaphor in creating meaning.

## Aspects of Meaning

When individuals refer to the "meaning" of a statement or word, they may be referring to a number of things. One concept frequently labeled *meaning* is the denotation of words. Denotations are understood to be those "things" to which words refer. Dictionary definitions are attempts to explain denotative aspects of meanings. When you point to an example of a horse or a hibiscus, you are attempting to identify the denotative meaning of those words.

A second concept that may be an aspect of meaning is the connotation of words or statements. Connotations are the emotional contexts that words or groups of words have for communicators. For anyone who experienced the 1960s in the United States, the term *peace* can have a variety of connotations, including memories of peace marches, sit-ins, love-ins, drugs, wildly painted Volkswagen buses, riots, communes, long hair, and so on. These connotations may be negative, positive, or a mixture of both, depending on the individual's political persuasion and experiences during the 1960s. The connotation of the word *communism* is much different today than it was during the 1950s, when many U.S. citizens in the entertainment business were blacklisted on the basis of Joseph McCarthy's allegations of communist sympathies.

Because certain words have negative connotations, euphemisms have developed. Euphemisms are substitute words or expressions to avoid an offensive term. For example, our society has numerous euphemisms for *toilet*, including *powder room*, *little boys'* (or *girls'*) *room*, *bathroom*, and so on. Various excretory and other bodily functions have numerous euphemisms, and a large number of euphemisms are used to describe sexual intercourse.

Although denotation and connotation have something to do with word meaning, certainly they do not describe adequately the operation of meaning. How do words come to have meaning for human beings? What is the meaning of meaning?

## Philosophical Theories of Meaning

This question has occupied many philosophers during the twentieth century. One category of theory that attempts to answer the question of the meaning of meaning is known as *referential meaning theory*. This type of theory suggests that the meaning of a word is that to which the word refers. John Stuart Mill adopts a referential view of meaning by suggesting that nearly all words and phrases in a language are names.[2] This and other referential theories, however, are too simplistic. Although reference may bear some relationship to meaning, it certainly does not exhaust the notion of meaning. One frequently cited explanation of the limitations of referential theories is that of Bertrand Russell. He points out that although two statements—"Sir Walter Scott" and "The author of *Waverly*"—have the same referent, the two phrases cannot be said to be identical in meaning.[3]

Referential theories also have several other weaknesses. First, some words have no identifiable referents, such as *of*, *and*, *for*, and *nor*. Also, the referent for other types of words is unclear, including, for example, *holy, unicorn,* and *democracy.* Even words that, at first blush, seem to support referential theory are, upon closer examination, problematic. What is *the* referent for *tree* or *automobile* or *cousin*? Thus, some understanding other than reference is needed to get at the meaning of meaning.

A second type of meaning theory involves description of the mind and is referred to by William Alston as *ideational meaning theory.*[4] John Locke, a British philosopher, offers such a theory, suggesting that meanings are the ideas in the mind of the person who uses a word—"The use, then, of words, is to be sensible marks of ideas; and the ideas they stand for are their proper and immediate signification."[5] This may seem to solve the problem of the referent for *tree,* as the meaning is the tree in my mind as I type this sentence. However, as I examine that notion, I find I do not have a mental construct of a particular tree in mind at the moment. If you ask about the tree in front of my parents' home, to which is tied a rope for swinging across the irrigation ditch that runs next to it, then I picture a giant cottonwood tree. However, as most speakers of English have not seen that tree, or choose to picture another tree, the stability of meaning for a word or concept is put into question by this theory. Further, Locke cannot demonstrate that humans actually have separate ideas for each word they use.

The problem with both referential and ideational types of meaning theory is that they force analysis of meaning at the level of words, which is precisely the problem Mill encounters with his conception of words as names. A list of names (the Pope, Whoopi Goldberg, my favorite grocery clerk, Fido, and Superman) neither is representative of all meaningful statements nor does such a list have much meaning for individuals. Thus, as Ryle notes, the notion of "having meaning" is at least partially different from the notion of "standing for," which is what referential and ideational meaning theories seem to describe.[6]

Another type of meaning theory is based on the writings of behaviorists. Such *behavioral meaning theories* suggest that meaning arises from the situation in which the speaker utters a statement and the response of the listener. This moves meaning out of the mind of the language user and accounts for both speaker and listener. In addition, it makes of meaning more than names. However, the same problem of stable meaning occurs with behavioral meaning theory. Surely, meaning has some consistency that is not accounted for by the variety of responses and situations in which one statement might be uttered. On the other hand, situation and response are likely to affect meaning. Thus, these aspects give additional insight into the operation of meaning.

The difficulties with early meaning theories become evident, and are overcome, in later scholarship. Most contemporary scholars of meaning are indebted to the work of German philosopher, Ludwig Wittgenstein.

## Ludwig Wittgenstein

Wittgenstein developed two important conceptions of meaning during his career. His first is found in the *Tractatus Logico-Philosophicus*, often referred to as the "red book." In that tract, he argues that language is a picture of reality:

> The total reality is the world.
> We make to ourselves pictures of facts.
> The picture presents the facts in logical space, the existence and
>     non-existence of atomic facts.
> The picture is a model of reality.
> To the objects correspond in the picture the elements of the
>     picture.
> The elements of the picture stand, in the picture, for the objects.
> The picture consists in the fact that its elements are combined
>     with one another in a definite way.
> The picture is a fact.
> That the elements of the picture are combined with one another
>     in a definite way, represents that the things are so combined
>     with one another.
> This connexion of the elements of the picture is called its
>     structure, and the possibility of this structure is called the form
>     of representation of the picture.[7]

Symbols, as pictures, must portray reality accurately: "What every picture, of whatever form, must have in common with reality in order to be able to represent it at all—rightly or falsely—is the logical form, that is, the form of reality."[8] To determine whether a statement, or picture, is true, one compares it with the reality it purports to represent, according to this theory. Therefore, meaning, in the *Tractatus*, becomes something akin to that posited by the referential meaning theorists.

   Later in his career, Wittgenstein changed his views, although hints of the later position exist in the *Tractatus*.[9] However, certain philosophers maintained their interest in his first position. Most notable of those philosophers adhering to the *Tractatus* are the logical positivists, particularly the so-called Vienna Circle. These philosophers developed the *verifiability criterion* as a test of meaning. According to their view, a concept has meaning only if it is either analytic, that is, a statement true by definition, or if the concept is capable of being verified. An example of an analytic statement is "Bachelors are unmarried males." In such statements, the subject logically contains the predicate. The second half of the criterion concerns statements that are capable of verification by the senses, such as "it is raining outside." The verifiability criterion, then, identifies as meaningless statements such as "God exists." Logical positivists do not mean that this sentence is merely a jumble of words unidentifiable by speakers of English. Instead, as students of symbolic logic, they suggest that it makes no sense to argue over such statements, as verification is impossible. While the logical positivists held to Wittgenstein's early views, he moved forward in his explication of meaning.

In the preface to the *Philosophical Investigations*, the "blue book," Wittgenstein cites "grave mistakes" in his first work and refers to his "old way of thinking."[10] He acknowledges that thinking of language as a picture of reality does not get at the fulsomeness of language use. He gives several exclamations, including "Water!," "Help!," and "No!," then asks, "Are you inclined still to call these words 'names of objects'?"[11]

In this later text, Wittgenstein argues that language is a game. Meaning is how a concept is used in that game: "For a *large* class of cases—though not for all—in which we employ the word 'meaning' it can be defined thus: the meaning of a word is its use in the language."[12] Inquiry into language, then, is an inquiry into how language is used in various situations, which allows for more complete analysis of meaning than does reference of individual words:

> Doesn't the analogy between language and games throw light here? We can easily imagine people amusing themselves in a field by playing with a ball so as to start various existing games, but playing many without finishing them and in between throwing the ball aimlessly into the air, chasing one another with the ball and bombarding one another for a joke and so on. And now someone says: The whole time they are playing a ball-game and following definite rules at every throw.
>
> And is there not also the case where we play and—make up the rules as we go along? And there is even one where we alter them—as we go along.[13]

A group called ordinary language philosophers has adopted this later view of Wittgenstein. Among them is John L. Austin, who studied language behaviors, later termed *speech acts*. He identifies three types of acts in the language game. *Locutionary acts* involve saying something with referential meaning, as in "This pen on the table is red." *Illocutionary acts* involve saying something with the force of communicating an intention. Such acts are to be taken as warnings, compliments, or so on. Examples of illocutionary acts are: "I am hurt by what you said"; "You are handsome"; "I'll have lunch with you on

Wednesday." Finally, *perlocutionary acts* are designed to affect feelings, attitudes, beliefs, or behaviors of witnesses, such as the following: "Come here"; "Vote for Roosevelt"; "Turn the television down"; "Don't cry."

A student of Austin's, John Searle, is a major figure in speech-act theory. In this theory, speech is an action or a form of intentional behavior. Acts are individual utterances, which may be in the form of sentences or phrases. Searle reclassifies speech acts into four types, depending upon the speaker's intention. An *utterance act* involves the intention to utter, but no more. Making random sounds for no other reason than to vocalize is to perform an utterance act. A *propositional act* is similar to Austin's locutionary act; its intention is referential. Searle also adopts Austin's categories of *illocutionary* and *perlocutionary acts*. Utterance propositional acts are part of an illocutionary act; indeed, the same illocutionary act can be performed by a variety of utterance and propositional acts—*I'm tired*; *I'm bushed*; *I'm beat*; *I'm exhausted*.

Searle defines the act of speaking a language as "engaging in a rule-governed form of behavior."[14] These rules are of two major sorts. Rules that create the nature of speech acts are known as *constitutive rules*. They define and set boundaries for the language game. Searle and others detail the types of rules sufficient to constitute particular speech acts, such as promises or threats. Among the several rules for promises, for example, is the *sincerity rule*, which requires that a speaker must intend a speech act for it to be classified as a promise. Rules that guide particular behaviors in an established language game are *regulative rules*. These rules, as the name implies, regulate the game.

These and other aspects of speech-act theory as well as numerous so-called "rules" theories[15] are attempts to describe how meaning is created by language use and to identify regularities of such use. Thus, for these scholars, meaning is neither something to which language refers nor something for which language stands, but it is created by language use. The process by which language creates meaning has fascinated a number of philosophical and rhetorical scholars, including I. A. Richards, C. S. Peirce, Ernst Cassirer, Kenneth Burke, and Richard Weaver.

# I. A. Richards

Richards, although beginning from the level of a word, lays the foundation for a more comprehensive understanding of meaning. Richards begins by attempting to describe the process whereby words develop connotative meanings for individuals. First, he says, humans receive sense data from a variety of sources external to the individual. These perceptions leave what Richards terms an *engram* on the mind, a memory of sorts. This memory of prior sensation is stored for later retrieval. However, sensations are not individual; each human experience occurs in a context, a "cluster of events that recur together."[16] When a part of a context appears, the mind may recall, based on the engram, the context. This one part of the context can affect an individual as much as the whole context. Sorting through items saved from the past demonstrates this principle. Consciously forgotten memories flood back as you read an old letter, touch a present someone gave you, locate a ribbon from an athletic triumph, or examine a feather you found on an excursion through the woods. Each of these items functions as a sign of the entire context, representing the whole.

This notion of *context* is to become central to twentieth-century rhetoric and argumentation. Richards discusses context in several ways. First, he adds to models of communication the idea of *comparison fields*, which are the understandings, based upon experience, of the various participants in a communication event. Each person understands a particular communication transaction from his or her own unique perspective. Therefore, words are not accepted in some objective sense but are understood in terms of the hearer's (or speaker's) frame of reference. Richards speaks of *utterances-within-situations*, because the comprehension of an utterance "is guided by any number of partially similar situations in which partially similar utterances have occurred."[17] In addition to personal comparison fields, the notion of context includes the situation in which discourse occurs as well as the associations of meaning built up around words through use.

Richards and C. K. Ogden describe the meaning of words as a three-part relationship, using as a model the *semantic triangle*, which represents Richard's theory of meaning. Each point of the triangle is a component of the process of meaning—*symbol*, *reference*, and *referent*. References are the memories of past experiences and understandings of concepts that exist in individuals' minds. Referents are those perceived objects and events which relate to references in the mind. Symbol is the word or other sign which calls up the referent through the reference; in other words, Richards uses the term *symbol* to refer to that which Saussure calls the *signifier*.

The relationship between the symbol and the referent is not direct. Symbols directly relate to references by *symbolizing* them, and references *refer* to referents. This latter relationship can be either direct or indirect, depending upon whether the referent is physically present. However, no necessary relationship exists between symbol and referent.[18] Richards refers to the belief in this relationship as the "proper meaning superstition."[19] Because individual references for symbols differ, the "meaning" individuals have for various symbols can be dramatically different. For example, although most speakers of English understand some essential meaning of the term *grandmother*, one person whose contextual experience involved an abusive grandmother, another person who has two living grandmothers with whom he is close, another whose grandmother is terminally ill, and one whose grandmothers died before she was born each would have different references, therefore somewhat different meanings, for *grandmother*.

If meaning is created rather than discovered, how does the process occur? Several scholars suggest that meaning is created by a three-part process.

## C. S. Peirce

In Peirce's writings on semiotics, he discusses the basic components of human consciousness, which are essential to the process whereby meaning is created. He labels these components *firstness*, *secondness*, and *thirdness*. Several descriptions of firstness, secondness, and thirdness are located in Peirce's writings. One such description is: "1st, Feeling, the consciousness which can be included with an instant of time, passive consciousness of quality, without recognition or analysis; 2nd, Consciousness of an interruption into the field of consciousness, sense of resistance, of an external fact, of another something; 3rd, synthetic consciousness binding time together, sense of learning, thought."[20] This three-part distinction of firstness, secondness, and thirdness describes aspects of meaningful human experience. Firstness is a sensation in itself, "not referring to anything or lying behind anything." It is immediate, present, spontaneous, free, vivid, and prior to synthesis. He gives as an example the experience of the color purple, without any thought, linguistic expression, or other representation or synthesis. Firstness is what "the world was to Adam on the day he opened his eyes to it, before he had drawn any distinctions." Perhaps easier to understand is the firstness experience we have, in that first moment of awareness, when awakened at night by some stimulus. In that first moment of semi-consciousness, before the world is set right by the categories of language, is the pure experience of firstness. Firstness is nearly impossible to talk about, because whatever you are talking about no longer is firstness, as description turns it into secondness.

Secondness is our humanly lived reality, Adam's conscious experience, the categorization of purple as a color by comparison to pink. Secondness becomes a thing, an existent, because it is "other" to something or by force of something to which it is a second. An occurrence is secondness because it is something "whose existence consists in our knocking up against it." Secondness, says Peirce, is much easier to comprehend than firstness. If you touch firstness, you spoil it. However, secondness is tangible and firm to the touch. The moment our awakened sleeper comprehends that the firstness experience is a ringing telephone, she has entered the realm of secondness.

Thirdness is the aspect of relationship, the world of theories and abstractions. Concepts of force, of gravity, or the laws of nature, are thirdness. The study of anything, from mathematics to human communication, involves drawing comparisons, relationships, and principles. Such is the awareness of thirdness. Thirdness involves the intelligent comprehension of the consciousness of existence.[21]

The combination of firstness, secondness, and thirdness is the layers of human experience by which human meaning is created. Using the thirdness understandings we have, humans make secondness statements, giving form to firstness experience. These same aspects are described, using different terminology, by Ernst Cassirer.

## Ernst Cassirer

Cassirer, who acknowledges that the "meaning of meaning" is the most bewildering of problems,[22] does not explicitly give a theory of meaning. However, his explanation of human consciousness, tripartite and very nearly identical with Peirce's, explains the process by which the world becomes meaningful to humans. His terms for the three processes are *sensuous*, *intuitive*, and *conceptual*. Says Cassirer, "Sensibility, intuition, understanding are not mere successive phases of knowledge to be apprehended in their simple succession, but are necessarily intertwined as its constitutive factors."[23] Cassirer uses this three-part distinction in several ways. First, he describes human experience as involving three parts—sensuous matter, the intellectual symbol (that is, signifier), and the law or relationship that unites the two. Further, each symbol involves these parts. Finally, human awareness of the symbolic relationship can exist in one of three stages. At the expressive or sensuous level, signifier and meaning are fused. Such state of awareness is exemplified in some primal cultures, where individuals do not distinguish between word and meaning. The discussion of word magic in chapter six describes the expressive level of awareness. At the intuitive level, the conventional nature of the symbol is realized; that is, signifier and meaning are separate. This is the awareness of common-sense reality in which we live our daily lives. At the conceptual stage, an individual is conscious of the nature of signs, understanding the arbitrary nature of the relationship. Much discussion in this text is conceptual in nature, as are discussions about quantum physics, music theory, and epistemology.

Perhaps an example will illustrate these distinctions. If two people walking in opposite directions round a corner on a busy city street and run into each other, that moment of sensation of physical contact with another body is at the sensuous level; it correlates to Peirce's firstness. After that first moment, as they step back, they begin to make sense of the sensuous experience: "Hey, that hurt." "Yeah. Wow. Sorry." "Oh, yeah. Me, too." This is experience at the intuitive level of secondness. If, however, one of them says, "Gosh. I wonder if the utterances we both made were illocutionary acts, that is, speech acts that communicate intention," the experience, at least for the speaker, is raised to the level of the conceptual, of thirdness.

A related three-part distinction in the writings of Richard Weaver lends insight into a larger category of the creation of meaning. His description attempts to describe how categories of understanding affect rationality.

## Richard Weaver

Human knowledge, at least our conscious reflection, is of three types, according to Weaver. We have specific *ideas*, generalized *beliefs*, and a *metaphysical dream*. Ideas are particular notions and understandings about life. Facts, such as historical, geographical, or scientific facts, can be categorized as ideas. Bits of information you have about your friends, the political system, particular musical groups, automobiles, and so on, are ideas. When we go about our day-to-day existence, we are conscious of ideas or details; this is the level of practical knowledge, similar to Peirce's level of secondness.

The second level of conscious reflection involves beliefs. This level is more abstract than ideas; it involves more generalized knowledge. Theories, generalizations, and laws all are at this level. Your prejudices, your understanding of scientific or physical laws, your knowledge of legal principles, your personal code of conduct, and general understandings about human nature and yourself—all of these are beliefs. Weaver suggests that some of your beliefs are inherited—you are socialized into particular beliefs about the world by family, school, and society. This level most closely approximates Peirce's thirdness.

The third, and most important, level for Weaver is the metaphysical dream. The metaphysical dream is "an intuitive feeling about the immanent nature of reality." The metaphysical dream sanctions and tempers both ideas and beliefs; it is the core of an individual's reflection, the standard by which things are judged. If individuals possess similar metaphysical dreams, they are bonded into a "spiritual community."[24] The metaphysical dream is not rational knowledge, like a theory, but an intuitive sense about the nature of things and of the good. Thus, the metaphysical dream operates as a template, structuring and driving ideas and beliefs. Kenneth Burke specifically focuses on the template aspect of the rhetorical creation of meaning.

## Kenneth Burke

Language is, for Burke, a terministic screen whereby humans filter sensation through an intellectual, linguistic screen, coming to individual, human understandings of the world. The words we use focus our attention on particular aspects of reality and present to us a world organized into the categories of our language. Different words, different terminologies, lead to different observations and different understandings. Burke, like Cassirer and Peirce, argues that the "objects" of human experience are humanly defined (if not created) as *"many of the 'observations' are but implications of the particular terminology in terms of which the observations are made."* Terministic screens filter sensation, making our experience of the world both human and individual: "Even if any given terminology is a *reflection* of reality, by its very nature as a terminology it must be a *selection* of reality; and to this extent it must function also as a *deflection* of reality."[25] This notion of meaning is much broader than that with which we began the chapter. This, however, is the meaning that is most important to our examination of sign systems and the world that signs present to us.

Contemporary discussions of metaphor are another way to discuss this view of meaning. However, metaphor has not always been viewed so broadly.

## Metaphor

Recognized since antiquity, metaphor has been chastised as well as championed as a linguistic device. Some scholars banish metaphor to a role as mere embellishment and argue that it obfuscates the search for truth. Others elevate metaphor as the foundational principle of language, analogizing and, in some cases, defining the operation of metaphor as the process of human intelligence. This latter view of metaphor offers insight into the creation of meaning. This section investigates the two views of metaphor—as trope and as the basic form of conception—in order to further our understanding of meaning.

## Metaphor as a Trope

Aristotle finds for metaphor a role in both rhetoric and poetry. In his work, the *Poetics*, Aristotle defines this figure: "Metaphor consists in giving the thing a name that belongs to something else; the transference being either from genus to species, or from species to genus, or from species to species, or on grounds of analogy."[26] Metaphor, for Aristotle, is a borrowing of proper meaning from another name, another word.

The metaphor with which Aristotle is concerned is, by nature, a trope, a figure of speech; that is, if one can distinguish between the proper names for certain objects, on the one hand, and tropes, on the other, then the latter are words which are decorative and which serve to add color to discourse. Metaphors add to the connotative meaning of a statement, beyond the meaning a "proper" name would create. To use a metaphorical signifier, to call, for example, the world a stage, is to add to the meaning of the signified. As a trope, the term *metaphor* often is reserved for direct attribution while *simile* is an indirect attribution. However, metaphor also is used to refer to a broad category of figure, with simile a subset of that category.

Nearly all scholars acknowledge the role metaphor plays in poetry. According to Aristotle, however, metaphor plays an even more significant role in prose, for all figures are fitting in prose. The resources available to orators are less abundant than those available to poets, making metaphor of great value.[27] Aristotle does acknowledge the importance of metaphor: "But the greatest thing by far is to be a master of metaphor. It is the one thing that cannot be learnt from others; and it is also a sign of genius, since a good metaphor implies an intuitive perception of the similarity in dissimilars."[28]

To regard metaphor only as a trope is to deny it any philosophical or epistemic importance. Such was the position of British empiricists as well as logical positivists from the Vienna Circle. Thomas Hobbes distinguished between general and special uses of speech. Generally, speech is used to transfer mental ideas into verbal discourse. Special uses include:

> first, to register, what by cogitation, we find to be the cause of any thing, present or past; and what we find things present or past may produce, or effect; which in sum, is acquiring of arts. Secondly, to show to others that knowledge which we have

> attained, which is, to counsel and teach one another. Thirdly,
> to make known to others our wills and purposes, that we may
> have the mutual help of one another. Fourthly, to please and
> delight ourselves and others, by playing with our words, for
> pleasure or ornament, innocently.

However, he also cites abuses. That most relevant here is, "when they
use words metaphorically; that is, in other sense than that they are
ordained for; and thereby deceive others." Metaphors and other tropes
cannot be "true grounds of any ratiocination."[29]

John Locke's judgment is even more strident. Because he castigates
not only metaphor but rhetoric for the damage it can do, his discussion,
although lengthy, is reproduced in whole:

> Since wit and fancy find easier entertainment in the world than
> dry truth and real knowledge, figurative speeches and allusion
> in language will hardly be admitted as an imperfection or abuse
> of it. I confess, in discourses where we seek rather pleasure and
> delight than information and improvement, such ornaments as
> are borrowed from them can scarce pass for faults. But yet if
> we would speak of things as they are, we must allow that all
> the art of rhetoric, besides order and clearness; all the artificial
> and figurative application of words eloquence hath invented, are
> for nothing else but to insinuate wrong ideas, move the passions,
> and thereby mislead the judgment; and so indeed are perfect
> cheats: and therefore, however laudable or allowable oratory
> may render them in harangues and popular addresses, they are
> certainly, in all discourses that pretend to inform or instruct,
> wholly to be avoided; and where truth and knowledge are
> concerned, cannot but be thought a great fault, either of the
> language or person that makes use of them. What and how
> various they are, will be superfluous here to take notice; the
> books of rhetoric which abound in the world, will instruct those
> who want to be informed: only I cannot but observe how little
> the preservation and improvement of truth and knowledge is
> the care and concern of mankind; since the arts of fallacy are
> endowed and preferred. It is evident how much men love to
> deceive and be deceived, since rhetoric, that powerful
> instrument of error and deceit, has its established professors,
> is publicly taught, and has always been had in great reputation:
> and I doubt not but it will be thought great boldness, if not
> brutality, in me to have said thus much against it. Eloquence,
> like the fair sex, has too prevailing beauties in it to suffer itself
> ever to be spoken against. And it is in vain to find fault with those
> arts of deceiving, wherein men find pleasure to be deceived.[30]

Throughout much of the history of rhetoric, metaphor played a role
as ornamentation and, lurking constantly, was the danger that artifice

would be used to deceive. Such a view of metaphor no longer predominates. The changing fate of metaphor's reputation is largely a twentieth-century phenomenon.

In addition, two other long-held assumptions about metaphor are challenged by twentieth-century scholars. The first is that one must have an eye for resemblances to make good metaphors, that to apprehend or to see similarity is the master stroke of the metaphor, and not everyone has that ability. Aristotle, in the *Rhetoric*, says "it is characteristic of a well-directed mind to observe the likeness even in things very different."[31] The second assumption about metaphor that Aristotle has willed to Western thought is that metaphor is a thing, a name. Paul Ricoeur explains, "Thus the destiny of metaphor is sealed for centuries to come; henceforth it is connected to poetry and rhetoric, not at the level of discourse, but at the level of a segment of discourse, the name or noun."[32] All three assumptions, then, with roots in Aristotle—that metaphor is merely trope, that skill in using metaphor is an unusual talent, and that metaphors are things or names—are discarded in the twentieth century as metaphor is credited with a new, far more significant role than ornamentation.

## Metaphor as the Fundamental Form of Conception

Cassirer argues that "[l]anguage is, by its very nature and essence, metaphorical."[33] This view has predominated during the twentieth century. Burke defines metaphor as "a device for seeing something *in terms of* something else. It brings out the thisness of a that, or the thatness of a this." It is used, he says, to gain perspective.[34] George Lakoff and Mark Johnson suggest "[t]*he essence of metaphor is understanding and experiencing one kind of thing in terms of another*."[35] Although these definitions are not unlike Aristotle's, the role these and other contemporary scholars posit for metaphor is much broader.

Richards was one of the first modern students of metaphor. Contrary to Aristotle, Richards argues that everyone has an eye for resemblances. Rather than a gift or an unusual facility with language, the ability to use metaphor is innate in all language speakers. This view belies a much different view of metaphor than its role as trope. For Richards, metaphor is not ornamentation added to language; it is the constitutive form of language.[36] Thought is metaphoric and "proceeds by comparison, and the metaphors of language derive therefrom."[37]

To better analyze the operation of metaphors, Richards identifies the two ideas that exist in the simplest of metaphors—*tenor* and *vehicle*. The underlying idea is the tenor; the vehicle is the particular means of expression. Therefore, to say "love is a red rose" is to make of love the tenor and a red rose the vehicle in what, taken as a whole, is a metaphor. The presence of a tenor and a vehicle results in *meaning*, which Richards urges not be confused with the tenor. The vehicle and tenor cooperate to create a meaning that cannot be ascribed to either.[38] Neither meaning nor metaphor has anything to do with images, copies, or duplications of reality. Indeed, metaphor operates, according to Richards, much the same as his semantic triangle. Tenor and vehicle create a transaction between contexts that results in a redescribed reality.

Ricoeur agrees that metaphor involves a reference that redescribes reality, making metaphor a rhetorical process. Ricoeur argues that the bearer of metaphorical meaning is not the word but the whole sentence. Therefore, metaphor does not operate by substitution but, rather, by interaction of logical subject and predicate, which he calls "deviant predication rather than a deviant denomination."[39] This deviance is what he calls a "semantic impertinence," which violates a code of ordinary usage, creating a new semantic pertinence. A new predicative meaning arises from the ashes of the "literal" meaning.

So-called literal meanings, however, merely are products of earlier, unwitting metaphors. The process of using metaphor is frequently unconscious, for all language has a basis in metaphor, which works whether or not we are able to articulate why. Over time, the vehicle comes to be seen not as part of a metaphor but a literal description of or name for the meaning created by the metaphor. Thus, meanings grow much as an organism grows.[40] For example, most English-speaking individuals do not recognize the metaphor involved in the *leg of a chair* or in talking about arguments as if they were wars: *defending one's own position*; *shooting down the arguments of another*; and ultimately *winning the dispute*.

The "reality" in which humans live literally is built up by metaphors. We do not live by our sensations but rather by what our sign systems tell us, or what we tell each other through our sign systems, about our sensations. "Our world is a projected world, shot through with characters lent to it from our own life." Richards goes on to explain: "The processes of metaphor in language, the exchanges between the meanings of words which we study in explicit verbal metaphors, are super-imposed upon a perceived world which is itself a product of earlier or unwitting metaphor."[41] This unwitting metaphor is the very operation of the human mind. The mind brings together disparate ideas that come before it. Richards explains:

> Words are the meeting points at which regions of experience
> which can never combine in sensation or intuition, come
> together. They are the occasion and the means of that growth
> which is the mind's endless endeavor to order itself. That is why
> we have language. It is no mere signalling system. It is the
> instrument of all our distinctively human development.[42]

Drawing on Vico, Ernesto Grassi argues that metaphor is the original form of mental interpretation, which becomes generalized by representation in language.[43] The original metaphoric activity of the human mind, "seeing" similarities, he calls *ingenium*. By *ingenium*, humans decipher sensations, creating "an order in the midst of the chaos of sensory impressions."[44] Humans must make sense of this chaos, and they do so metaphorically. That sense is *meaning*—a humanly constructed web of understanding. Original metaphors, the generalized product of *ingenium*, now are imbedded in our language and are treated as literal usage. Thus, Grassi calls for a study of dialogue, or metaphorical speech, as the "source of the human world," a world which is ordered and framed by metaphor to give meaning to sensory appearances.[45]

Lakoff, Johnson, and Turner are engaged in research very much like that for which Grassi calls; they study metaphors embedded in ordinary language and resulting human understanding. Metaphor, they argue, is not an extraordinary but the most ordinary of uses of language; it is conventional, automatic, and an integral part of our language and thought. Aspects of sensate reality are either highlighted or hidden, depending upon the metaphors embedded in the language used to talk about things. For example, our understanding of human communication, as discussed in chapter three, is structured by the metaphor of "sending," which is embedded in our language about communication, thereby structuring our concept of communication. Thus, we understand communication as something that can be "sent," as it has "senders," "receivers," "channels," and so on. After discussing a large number of similar instances of metaphorical structuring of concepts in the English language, Lakoff and Turner note:

> To study metaphor is to be confronted with hidden aspects of
> one's own mind and one's own culture. To understand poetic
> metaphor, one must understand conventional metaphor. To do
> so is to discover that one has a worldview, that one's imagination
> is constrained, and that metaphor plays an enormous role in
> shaping one's everyday understanding of everyday events. . . .
> Recent discoveries about the nature of metaphor suggest that
> metaphor is anything but peripheral to the life of the mind. It

> is central to our understanding of our selves, our culture, and
> the world at large.[46]

Metaphors operate to structure our conceptual system and, thereby, to build our cultural coherence. Metaphors are not a matter of words but of thought—indispensable not only to imagination but to reason as they create the structure whereby reason operates.[47]

In addition to embedded metaphors, which structure our understandings and appear as literal meaning, new metaphors can operate to *re*describe reality. This is the "semantic impertinence" of which Ricoeur speaks. Creation of new metaphors challenges existing categories and structured views of reality. José Ortega y Gasset describes this emergence of new meanings as a result of metaphors: "their hard carapaces crack and the internal matter, in a molten state, acquires the softness of plasm, ready to receive a new form and structure."[48] Poetic metaphor redescribes a reality created by earlier metaphor. The poetic metaphor creates a new semantic pertinence that, at some future date, may operate as literal usage, becoming embedded in ordinary language and a part of the structure of human meaning.

Metaphor constitutes a primordial activity that reveals or unconceals the deep structures of reality as experienced by humans. These deep structures do not exist in nature but in humans. Each of us, as makers of metaphor, whether intentional or unwitting, thereby participate in the societal creation of meaning. We are, according to Grassi, "actors and spectators in an uninterrupted game which bears witness to the metaphorical value of reality."[49]

## Summary

This view of metaphor, and of meaning, corresponds with the view that rhetoric shapes our social reality. As Grassi notes, "[t]he task of rhetoric is therefore no longer one of 'persuasion,' intended to convince us of an ahistorical truth, but to disclose the reality signified in terms of constantly new 'situations,' and in this way to reveal the 'succession' of the different worlds as they follow one another" as humans create and recreate meaning and describe and redescribe reality metaphorically.[50] Grassi calls for a "principle rejection of formal semiotics, strict linguistics, and rhetoric understood only as an art of persuasion."[51] To do so is to opt for a humanistic perspective on the study of signs, language, rhetoric, and meaning—a rhetorical point of view.

This rhetorical point of view is delightfully illustrated in Jane Wagner's play, *The Search for Signs of Intelligent Life in the Universe*. Trudy, the bag lady, explains how going mad was the best thing that ever happened to her:

I don't say it's for everybody;
some people couldn't cope.
But for me it came at a time when nothing else seemed to be
working. I got the kind of madness Socrates talked about,
"A divine release of the soul from the yoke of
custom and convention." I refuse to be intimidated by
reality anymore.
After all, what is reality anyway? Nothin' but a
collective hunch. . . . a
primitive method of crowd control that got out of hand. . . .

See, the human mind is kind of like . . .

a piñata. When it breaks open,
there's a lot of surprises inside. Once you get the piñata
perspective, you see that losing your mind
can be a peak experience.[52]

To understand, as Trudy does, that a particular worldview is not
necessary is to adopt a rhetorical point of view.


## Endnotes

1. Gilbert Ryle, "The Theory of Meaning," *The Importance of Language*, ed. Max Black (Englewood Cliffs, NJ: Prentice-Hall, 1962) 147.
2. John Stuart Mill, "A System of Logic Ratiocinative and Inductive," *Collected Works of John Stuart Mill*, vol. 7 (1974; rpt. Toronto: U of Toronto P, 1981) I 1–3. Ryle acknowledges that Mill's discussion is more complex than claiming language is only names, a notion he calls a "monstrous howler." Ryle 150.
3. Bertrand Russell, *An Inquiry into Meaning and Truth* (1940; rpt. London: George Allen and Unwin, 1961) 47. He notes: "When we ask what constitutes meaning . . . we are asking, not who is the individual meant, but what is the relation of the word to the individual which makes the one mean the other." *Analysis of Mind* (London: George Allen & Unwin, 1921) 191.
4. William P. Alston, *Philosophy of Language*, Foundations of Philosophy Ser. (Englewood Cliffs, NJ: Prentice-Hall, 1964) 22.
5. John Locke, *An Essay Concerning Human Understanding, Great Books of the Western World*, ed. Robert Maynard Hutchins, vol. 35 (1937; rpt. Chicago: Encyclopedia Britannica, 1952) III II 1.
6. Ryle 151 (emphasis omitted).
7. Ludwig Wittgenstein, *Tractatus Logico-Philosophicus*, trans. C. K. Ogden (1922; rpt. Boston: Routledge & Kegan Paul, 1985) 2.063–2.151.
8. Wittgenstein 2.18.
9. For example, he says: "In order to recognize the symbol in the sign we must consider the significant use." 3.326.
10. Ludwig Wittgenstein, *Philosophical Investigations*, trans. G.E.M. Anscombe, 3rd ed. (1958; rpt. New York: MacMillan, n.d.) vi.
11. Wittgenstein, *Philosophical Investigations* I 27.
12. Wittgenstein, *Philosophical Investigations* I 43.

13. Wittgenstein, *Philosophical Investigations* I 83.
14. John R. Searle, *Speech Acts: An Essay in the Philosophy of Language* (London: Cambridge UP, 1969) 22.
15. See, for example, Vernon E. Cronen, W. Barnett Pearce, and Linda M. Harris, "The Coordinated Management of Meaning: A Theory of Communication," *Human Communication Theory: Comparative Essays*, ed. Frank E. X. Dance (New York: Harper & Row, 1982) 61–89 and Susan B. Shimanoff, *Communication Rules: Theory and Research* (Beverly Hills: Sage, 1980).
16. I. A. Richards, *The Philosophy of Rhetoric* (1936; rpt. New York: Oxford UP, 1981) 34.
17. I. A. Richards, *Speculative Instruments* (New York: Harcourt, Brace & World, 1955) 23.
18. C. K. Ogden and I. A. Richards, *The Meaning of Meaning: A Study of the Influence of Language upon Thought and of the Science of Symbolism* (New York: Harcourt, Brace & World, 1956) 10–13.
19. Richards, *The Philosophy of Rhetoric* 11.
20. *Peirce on Signs: Writings on Semiotic by Charles Sanders Peirce*, ed. James Hoopes (Chapel Hill: U of North Carolina P, 1991) 185.
21. *Peirce on Signs* 188–91.
22. Ernst Cassirer, *An Essay on Man: An Introduction to a Philosophy of Human Culture* (1944; rpt. New Haven: Yale UP, 1968) 112.
23. Ernst Cassirer, *Philosophy of Symbolic Forms*, trans. Ralph Manheim, vol. 3 (1955; rpt. New Haven: Yale UP, 1972) 9.
24. Richard A. Weaver, *Ideas Have Consequences* (1948; rpt. Chicago: U of Chicago P, 1976) 18.
25. Kenneth Burke, *Language as Symbolic Action: Essays on Life, Literature, and Method* (Berkeley: U of California P, 1966) 45, 46.
26. Aristotle, *Poetics*, trans. Ingram Bywater, *The Basic Works of Aristotle*, ed. Richard McKeon (New York: Random House, 1941) 1457b 7.
27. Aristotle, *On Rhetoric: A Theory of Civic Discourse*, trans. George A. Kennedy (New York: Oxford UP) 3 2 1405a.
28. Aristotle, *Poetics* 1459a 5–8.
29. Thomas Hobbes, *Leviathan: Or the Matter, Forme and Power of a Commonwealth Ecclesiastical and Civil*, ed. Michael Oakeshott (New York: Collier, 1962) 34, 40.
30. Locke III X 34.
31. Aristotle, *On Rhetoric*, 3 11 1412a.
32. Paul Ricoeur, *The Rule of Metaphor: Multi-disciplinary Studies of the Creation of Meaning in Language*, trans. Robert Czerny (1977; rpt. Toronto: U of Toronto P, 1981) 14.
33. Cassirer, *An Essay On Man* 109.
34. Kenneth Burke, *A Grammar of Motives* (1945; rpt. Berkeley: U of California P, 1969) 503–04.
35. George Lakoff and Mark Johnson, *Metaphors We Live By* (Chicago: U of Chicago P, 1980) 5.
36. A similar notion arises in Ernst Cassirer's discussion of metaphor as the basis both of language and myth. *Language and Myth*, trans. Susanne K. Langer (1946; rpt. New York: Dover, n.d.) 83–99.
37. Richards, *The Philosophy of Rhetoric* 94.
38. Richards, *The Philosophy of Rhetoric* 100.
39. Paul Ricoeur, "The Metaphorical Process as Cognition, Imagination, and

Feeling," *On Metaphor*, ed. Sheldon Sacks (1979; rpt. Chicago: U of Chicago P, 1981) 143.

40. Richards, *The Philosophy of Rhetoric* 30.
41. Richards, *The Philosophy of Retoric* 108–09.
42. Richards, *The Philosophy of Retoric* 131.
43. Ernesto Grassi, "Introduction: The Roots of Italian Humanistic Tradition," trans. John Michael Krois, *Rhetoric as Philosophy: The Humanist Tradition* (University Park: Pennsylvania State UP, 1980) 7.
44. Ernesto Grassi, "Language as the Presupposition of Religion: A Problem of Rhetoric as Philosophy?," trans. John Michael Krois, *Rhetoric as Philosophy: The Humanist Tradition* (University Park: Pennsylvania State UP, 1980) 112.
45. Grassi, "Language" 112.
46. George Lakoff and Mark Turner, *More Than Cool Reason: A Field Guide to Poetic Metaphor* (Chicago: U of Chicago P, 1989) 214.
47. This discussion is found in Lakoff and Johnson and in Lakoff and Turner. See, also, George Lakoff, *Women, Fire, and Dangerous Things: What Categories Reveal about the Mind* (Chicago: U of Chicago P, 1987).
48. José Ortega y Gasset, *Phenomenology and Art*, trans. Philip W. Silver (New York: Norton, 1975) 143.
49. Ernesto Grassi, "Why Rhetoric is Philosophy," trans. Kiaran O'Malley, *Vico and Humanism: Essays on Vico, Heidegger, and Rhetoric* (New York: Peter Lang, 1990) 209.
50. Grassi, "Why Rhetoric is Philosophy" 209.
51. Grassi, "Language" 114.
52. Jane Wagner, *The Search for Signs of Intelligent Life in the Universe* (New York: Harper & Row, 1986) 17–19.

# Part Two

## The Mythological Mind

As rhetoric creates meaning, it creates societal and individual understandings—particular ways of looking at the world. This understanding is known as a *Weltanschauung*, a "worldview," which serves as the terministic screen for interpreting and enabling our interactions with each other and with our environment. To "see" the world through our own *Weltanschauung*, our own particular terministic screen, is so natural that acknowledging, much less understanding, other worldviews is extremely difficult. However, only by attempting to understand other ways of viewing the world can we identify ways in which our own understanding may be constrained.

Part Two describes societies whose worldview was unlike that of modern Western society. These societies were marked by their communication technology; they were oral societies whose only means of transmitting and storing information was through the spoken word. Oral societies exist currently, and some are referenced in this section. However, the focus is on oral societies of the past—societies which existed in a world that, by and large, was non-literate. Scholars suggest that individuals in these societies used language differently than we do, thought in ways markedly different than modern Western humans think, and as a result, understood the world in very different ways. An understanding of the particulars of their language and communication—the oral tradition—and of the power and magic of the spoken word may bring a clearer understanding of the operation of rhetoric in our own lives.

# Chapter Five

# Oral Traditions

Those of us who live in contemporary Western society frequently take many things for granted, including the marvels of modern medicine and travel, the hectic pace of modern life, and the amazing developments in communication. Although not a recent development, we also take for granted the writing system that allows us to make a permanent record of our thoughts, ideas, discoveries, and histories, preserving them for another day or another audience. Literacy and all its trappings so permeate our lives that we seldom consider what a different world it would be if we did not have a written language. This chapter delves into that world, into non-literate societies and their magnificent means of transmitting culture—the oral tradition. It also considers the worldview of individuals in oral societies.

## The Challenges of an Oral Society

The dependence which a literate society places upon the written word and other semipermanent means of encoding messages is enormous. Nearly all things that humans know currently are stored in books or on videotape, microfilm, or computer disks. We use these resources whenever we want information that is not readily available, either in our own memories or in the memories of those available for questioning. We also make notes to ourselves about things we want to remember. Imagine your life and the lives of those around you if such

**77**

semipermanent means of encoding messages were taken away and if our writing systems somehow were eliminated. We would have no means of "looking something up," no means of creating written reminders to ourselves. Having no way to make records, our vast knowledge would become very precarious; if forgotten, it would be lost. People without a remembered history, with no traditions, laws, learning, or knowledge, are no longer a society.

However, many oral societies of the past were highly developed and quite cohesive. How can the knowledge of a group be preserved, from one generation to the next, without the technologies of writing upon which we depend so heavily? The only way to preserve information in an oral society is to preserve it in human memory. At least one living person must remember each part of the information of the society and be able to transmit that information orally to other members of society. The total societal encyclopedia—all the law, history, medicine, genealogy, religion, and other important societal information—must exist in the collective living human memory of the group.

For highly developed oral societies to survive, individuals' memories had to be developed far beyond the capacity of our memories. As we depend very little on memory, our potential to remember has atrophied. Individuals in oral societies, however, had prodigious memories, developed in proportion to their dependence upon it. But memory alone does not explain the ability of preliterate humans to maintain a society without semipermanent means of encoding information. The form of their oral communication also was central to preserving cultural information in memory.

The language we use for everyday speech is poorly designed for the mnemonic task required of oral societies, as the childhood rumor game illustrates. Someone makes up a story, whispers it to the person next to him, who in turn whispers it to the person next to her, and so on until the story is told to the last person—who is asked to say, aloud, what she heard. The final version of the story never duplicates the original and often, in that short span of time, has been altered remarkably. The knowledge of an oral society needs a more efficient packaging than the language of our everyday speech to ensure that it remains in the memory of the members of society; it must be in a verbal form that is conducive to recall. Knowledge in oral societies is packaged in what has come to be known as the "oral tradition"—oral narratives that involve a particular format and certain stylistic devices that appeal to memory.

# Characteristics of Oral Traditions

A group of twentieth-century scholars has produced a fascinating discussion about the nature of oral societies and their communication technology. These scholars identify characteristics of oral traditions that make them successful as a means of storing and transmitting information. Eric Havelock, a classics scholar at Yale, examined the Greek oral society in Athens prior to 5th century, B.C. He identified three characteristics of the oral communication of that society which enabled the Greeks to pass down a tradition and a culture through several hundred years of the Dark Ages, during which the society had no writing technology. These characteristics, which literally make information memorable, are common in the communication of many oral societies. First, the form of the oral tradition is narrative. Second, the style of the oral tradition involves rhyme and rhythm. Third, in order to keep the tradition alive in the society, it is repeated, again and again.[1]

## Narrative

The knowledge carried by the oral tradition is contained in narrative, in a story. Havelock studied the works attributed to Homer, which are the written form of the oral tradition of the Greek people during the Dark Ages. The narratives in the *Odyssey* and the *Iliad* include descriptions of proper procedure and conduct, such as how to trim sails and how to treat parents or elders; details of military strategy; and other information critical to Greek society. The details of the Greek store of knowledge, including codes of public law and private behavior, are not set out in the same manner as contemporary laws and rules (that is, as abstract principles which cover a variety of specific instances). Instead, they are part of the formula of the story. The actions of characters in the narrative illustrate various principles and rules, thereby serving as examples which members of the oral society can remember and imitate. A military leader would behave as Odysseus behaves; a child would be expected to display the same respect to elders that the children of Odysseus display.

Nearly all oral traditions are narrative in form. For example, the oral tradition of the Apache includes stories about White Painted Woman, who "existed 'from the beginning,'" and the Mountain People (*Gan*) and the Water People, groups of supernatural beings.[2] In Apache oral tradition, as well as that of other tribes, Coyote is a trickster who makes trouble for other characters. Navaho or the *Dineh* ("the people") stories include First Man and First Woman. In these stories, the people lived among the spirits in the Black World. They climbed out through an opening into a second world, and eventually they moved through two or three more worlds. During their journey, they encountered many adventures. Versions of the story include Woman Who Changes (or Changing Woman), Sun Bearer, Spider Woman, and Mirage People.[3] The Cherokee tell of the coming of the sun. Grandmother Spider, who made a clay bowl, went to "the place of the sun people," spinning a thread behind her. When she reached the place of the sun people, Grandmother Spider put a tiny piece of the sun in her clay bowl and followed the thread she had left. As she moved back from east to west, the light from the clay bowl glowed and spread before her.[4]

These and other oral-tradition narratives include the cultural encyclopedia of the oral society. In Celtic oral tradition, the storyteller in that society, the *fili*, learned and performed narratives which contained "paradigms of societal behavior and an ideological world-view" which were "interlaced with the legendary, genealogical, toponymical, and even legal lore that it was the *fili*'s responsibility to transmit."[5] The Welsh oral tradition, or body of "native learning," was the *cyfarwyddyd*, remembered and told by a *cyfarwyddiaid*, one of the "knowledgeable" within society. The narratives they told concerned "history, genealogies and origin narratives, topography, boundaries and geography, religious myths, tribal and family lore, antiquities and legends, social and legal procedures, and medicine."[6]

The story is a form of communication that involves the audience and appeals to the psychology of memory. Little human memory is verbatim. Humans remember the "gist" of things, having episodic as well as general memory. A story allows audience members to remember by association; they remember details of the plot and the manner of expression. Other detail can be "filled in" around the data stored in and retrievable from memory. Thus, remembering oral traditions "is not a reduplicative process . . . but a procedure of creative reconstruction."[7]

Various other aspects of oral-tradition narratives also aid in the recall of the critical elements of the story. Walter Ong, a Jesuit scholar, details particular narrative characteristics found in most oral traditions, characteristics which assist in this mnemonic process. Most significant among these characteristics are their additive and aggregate nature, their redundancy, and their tendency to be concrete.[8]

**Additive**. Oral narratives tend to use an additive instead of a subordinate logical form. That is, rather than having subordinate clauses and using short, declarative sentence structure, the narratives are characterized by what we would call "run-on sentences"— numerous clauses connected by *and* or other connecting words. Ong points to the first chapter of Genesis as an example. The first five verses have nine introductory *and*s in places where we might use *therefore*, *because*, or other structuring or subordinating words. Even in literate societies, oral speech is less elaborate and has a simpler grammatical structure than writing does. As Ong suggests, writing lacks the context of oral situations, so it is more dependent upon linguistic structure to transfer meaning. Purely oral societies, he argues, have even more additive, less complex grammatical forms than oral speech in literate societies. This additive structure is demonstrated in South Slavic oral tradition. A significant number of statements begin with *i*, *a*, or *pa*, which translate "and" or "and then." When "translated" into written form, the selection below appears to be short, declarative sentences. However, when read aloud, its additive nature is apparent:

| | |
|---|---|
| *Ta' put tatar ferman dofatijo,* | Then the messenger took the firman, |
| *Pa istera carskogo mezila,* | Then he rode out the imperial post-horse, |
| *Pa on krenu zemlji carevini.* | Then he set out through the empire. |
| *Lak' polako Bosnu pogazijo.* | Easily he crossed Bosnia. |
| *Bosnu prodje, do Kajnidja dodje.* | He passed Bosnia, he came to Kajnidja. |
| *Pa ga vide kajnidjki muftija,* | Then the mufti of Kajnidja saw him, |
| *Pa on zovnu bajraktara svoga:* | Then he called his standard-bearer.[9] |

**Aggregative**. Ong points out that oral-tradition narratives are aggregative, by which he means they are dependent upon verbal formulas. The narratives do not use words or names alone but depend on phrases or clusters of phrases that predictably appear together—similar to clichés in contemporary speech. For example, narratives might speak not of an "oak tree," but of a "strong and spreading oak," of "the beautiful princess" rather than "the princess." Each time the tree or the princess is mentioned, the same phrase is used. This aggregate language operates as a slogan of sorts, a phrase which is remembered more easily than unique and unpredictable verbal phrasing.

The language of oral traditions also serves as amplification. Describing Odysseus consistently as "wily Odysseus" serves not a referring function, for the reference is superfluous, but a mnemonic and an aesthetic function. Stereotyped phrases and themes serve to create caricatures rather than individualized characters, as names become ceremonial and, as Ong describes it, "heavy" due to the formula of adjective(s) consistently used with the name ("wise Nestor" or "faithful Penelope").[10]

**Redundant**. Oral-tradition narratives also are characterized by redundancy. The plot of the story itself moves along very slowly, and items are repeated, again and again. Written narratives can be reread; oral narratives move forward with no chance for review. Redundancy assists oral-tradition narratives in the same fashion that the potential for rereading affects writing; the audience is sure to "get" the oral message if it is repeated over and over. In the *Odyssey* and the *Iliad*, approximately one-third of the lines are repeated, often more than once.[11] The repetition can come not only in repeated words, lines, phrases, or verses, but in parallel structure or recurrent formulaic expression. Ong says: "Oral cultures encourage fluency, fulsomeness, volubility. Rhetoricians were to call this *copia*."[12] The repetitive aspects allow the audience to participate not only in the details of the story but in the phrasing as well.

**Close to the Human Lifeworld**.   Detail in the narratives is neither abstract nor alien to the society but rather is familiar and immediate to its members. For example, lists do not work well; instead, lists are worked into the narrative, with the items on the list portrayed in active roles. In the last half of the *Iliad* is the famous Catalogue of Ships— over four hundred lines that include the names of Greek leaders and the regions they ruled. However, the information is not merely listed but occurs in the context of human action. Each of the leaders is given a bit of narrative, is portrayed doing something. Thus, names and places become a part of episodes of activity, which are more memorable than lists.[13] Further, procedures for accomplishing tasks are illustrated by the narratives. An example of this is found in Havelock, who cites the *Iliad*:

> As for now a black ship let us draw to the great salt sea
> And therein oarsmen let us advisedly gather and thereupon a
>    hecatomb
> Let us set and upon the deck Chryseis of fair cheeks
> Let us embark. And one man as captain, a man of counsel, there
>    must be.[14]

This sort of detail is not necessary to a modern story; however, it works well to preserve details about sailing and appropriate duties for captains of ships in an oral tradition. Details of a society are preserved in the oral tradition by means of narratives describing those details through the actions of characters.

Some, but not all, of Ong's characteristics of oral-tradition narratives are similar to characteristics of stories you might tell orally. You likely use run-on sentences, connected by "and" or "then," and you likely use concrete details, although you also may include abstract terms and concepts. In addition, you may use aggregate phrases, such as "my best friend Stephen" or "my black-haired roommate Celeste," although you are not likely to use the same phrase every time you mention Stephen or Celeste. Also, a contemporary storyteller is not likely to be as repetitive as a storyteller in an oral society. Another unique aspect of oral-tradition narratives is the rhythmic, rhyming nature of both the tale and the telling.

## Rhyme and Rhythm

The oral-tradition narratives, as well as everyday speech in oral societies, tend to use rhyme and rhythm, which appeal to the psychology of memory. The rhymes and rhythms of poetry are remembered more easily than non-rhythmic prose. Likely, you can remember simple childhood poetry or rhymes, things you neither have heard nor said for years. Just as likely, you have forgotten much of what you read in an earlier chapter of this text, particularly the specific language used to express the ideas. Song lyrics also are remembered and recalled with amazing ease. Since rhythmic, rhyming patterns are recalled more easily, oral-tradition narratives not surprisingly employ both devices.

Oral-tradition narratives are performed. The singer of tales is a person of high esteem in an oral society, frequently chosen for both the ability to remember and to perform. Individuals take this as a sacred duty. Mamadou Kouyaté, a modern West African *griot* or storyteller, expresses his historical duty: "We are vessels of speech, we are the repositories which harbour secrets many centuries old . . . . We are the memory of mankind; by the spoken word we bring to life the deeds and exploits of kings for younger generations."[15] Storytellers, such as a *griot*, serve long apprenticeships, learning the tales and learning techniques of oral performance. *Griots* often inherit their position from an elder family member who serves as mentor during the apprenticeship; Yugoslav storytellers, on the other hand, do not gain their position by inheritance but by ability.[16]

The storyteller chants the narratives before an audience, sometimes with accompaniment of a musical instrument. The strumming of the lyre or other instrument, along with the chanting human voice, adds to the psychological operation of rhyme and rhythm on human memory. Frederick Turner suggests that chanting is a form of rhythm which affects the limbic system of the brain. The stimulation of chanting, rhythmic poetry, and rhythmic music can produce trance-like feelings and mystical elevation. It is, he suggests, a stimulation which unites the functions of the two hemispheres of the brain, involving both left-brain linguistic processing and right-brain musical or pictorial processing; thus the brain operates in a "'stereo' mode." Turner suggests that integration between right and left brain "constitutes what various researchers have called the human 'cognitive imperative,' the 'aha' or 'eureka' moment" that allows humans to make sense out of the world.[17] Thus, the appeal of rhyme and rhythm to memory combine with their effect on understanding to create a particular oral worldview.

## Repetition

Havelock's final characteristic of the rhyming, rhythmic narratives of oral traditions is that they are repeated. Every social event is cause to perform the oral tradition. Such constant repetition keeps it always in the minds of people, where it must be to avoid extinction.

The repetition is made to be ritual. Ritual is a means by which oral humans make sense of their environment. Rituals are a means of transforming certain aspects of experience, creating patterns of meaning for a people. The rituals are magic. Ruth Benedict discusses this aspect of oral society in her study of the Zuñi culture. She suggests that ritual is the foremost activity in life:

> No field of activity competes with ritual for foremost place in their attention. Probably most grown men among the western Pueblos give to it the greater part of their waking life. It requires the memorizing of an amount of word-perfect ritual that our less trained minds find staggering, and the performance of neatly dovetailed ceremonies that are charted by the calendar and complexly interlock all the different cults and the governing body in endless formal procedure. . . . Zuñi religious practices are believed to be supernaturally powerful in their own right. At every step of the way, if the procedure is correct, the costume of the masked god traditional to the last detail, the offerings unimpeachable, the words of the hours-long prayers letter-perfect, the effect will follow according to man's desires. One has only, in the phrase they have always on their tongues, to "know how." . . .
>
> Their prayers also are formulas, the effectiveness of which comes from their faithful rendition. The amount of traditional prayer forms of this sort in Zuñi can hardly be exaggerated. Typically they describe in ritualistic language the whole course of the reciter's ceremonial obligations leading up to the present culmination of the ceremony. They itemize the appointment of the impersonator, the gathering of willow shoots for prayer-sticks, the binding of the bird feathers to them with cotton string,

> the painting of the sticks, the offering to the gods of the finished
> plume wands, the visits to sacred springs, the periods of retreat.
> No less than the original religious act, the recital must be
> meticulously correct.[18]

The emphasis on accuracy is to maintain the efficacy of the ritual
performance. It also serves the needs of oral transmission.

## Accuracy in Transmission

The insistence on accuracy in the many repetitions is another way to
maintain the knowledge of the society. Knowledge is not something
to be squandered, so oral societies place a high value on the accurate
transfer of information. Therefore, the important details of narratives,
those involving the knowledge and traditions of the society, must be
preserved. This does not mean that oral narratives lack creativity;
however, the creativity comes from variety in other aspects than the
important details of the narrative. Certainly minor variations happen
frequently if not every time a tale is retold. However, details about the
history, medicine, or religion of the group must be preserved unaltered.

Ruth Finnegan, who studied contemporary oral societies, notes that
one impulse for change is the effect on a society from present-day
fashions and allocations of power:

> As we all know, we tend to "remember" events and narratives
> in accordance with our own preconceptions and expectations—
> to *interpret* them in fact. Interpretations of the past which,
> perhaps quite innocently, fall in with current power
> relationships are to be found everywhere—it is the pretender
> who wins in the end who is added to the official genealogies as
> the "true" king, while his opponent and the loser is then
> assumed to have been unjustified in his claims.[19]

However, most oral societies Finnegan reviews place a strong emphasis
on a correct rendition of the narrative. Also, in most oral societies,
individuals with good memories, who give correct versions, are praised.
As correct performance is stressed, those who learn a narrative or a
song take upon themselves the corresponding burden of memory and
correct rendition.

Evidence for the accuracy in transmission of oral-tradition narratives
over long periods of time comes from the narratives themselves.
Scholars who have studied various oral-tradition narratives find
detailed and accurate descriptions of objects and places that did not
exist at the point in time at which the oral-tradition narrative was
studied or inscribed. For example, the *Iliad* contains descriptions of

the shield of Achilles and the boar's tusk helmet, both of which were
not in existence in the twelfth century but which archeological evidence
demonstrates to be described accurately.[20] Burton Raffel argues that,
when written material must be recopied by hand, again and again, the
accuracy of transmission actually is less than oral-tradition narratives
handed down over generations.[21] Thus, the efficiency of the oral
tradition in transmitting information of an oral society from one
generation to the next is amazing.

The ritual performance of oral-tradition narratives also is a means
of creating understanding—an oral worldview. According to Turner,
ritual is a means of "setting the stage, creating the frame, arranging
the agenda, and picking the topic in such a way as to give human beings
a home ground advantage in making the ontological contract."[22] Oral-
tradition ritual functions in this way to create meaning for members
of the oral society. The meaning is a function of many factors, including
the dependence of oral societies upon human memory, the psychology
of the performance of oral traditions, and the way in which ritual
presents the world. These factors create a distinct oral worldview, one
very different from the contemporary *Weltanschauung*. This
worldview also is reflected in the nature of early oral societies.

## Worldview of Early Oral Societies

Early oral societies were organized differently and had different
strengths and potentialities than contemporary literate societies have.
They also had different patterns of reasoning and modes of
comprehension, possibly related to their means of storing and
communicating information.

### Nature of Early Oral Societies

Certain aspects of Western, twentieth-century civilization are not
possible in the absence of literacy. Finnegan acknowledges that oral
societies face much different challenges than literate societies face, for
such a society is unable to accumulate the same quantity of information
that a literate society can. As individuals in a literate society are not
responsible for remembering, collectively, all the information of the
society, the increased potential for accumulation is enormous. As a
result, literacy allows industrialization, bureaucracy, economic
development, science, and the development of technology.

Writing supports economic, technological, and scientific development
in another manner. Oral societies do not have the same ability to

communicate with others not immediately present, particularly with those in other societies or from different cultures. As a result, oral societies are not nearly so likely to encourage the spread of ideas throughout a broad area; they tend to remain very insular. With writing comes the opening of society, the discovery and transmission of ideas over great distances, both in space and in time. As discussed in chapter eight, modern communication technologies have increased the interaction among societies exponentially, escalating the rate of discovery, change, and development.

Development of the communication technology of writing does not always lead to industrial and economic development, however. Finnegan illustrates this claim by noting the experience of India. "It is worth remembering too the many developing countries of the present world in which print *exists*; but, without the intervening social factors of, for instance, widespread education, capital investment or political policies, it does not have the same consequences as apparently it did in western Europe."[23] Thus, she argues, writing technology is a *necessary* but not *sufficient* condition for development. Widespread literacy, however, may be a sufficient condition for change. Certainly the combination of the technology of writing and widespread literacy have been significant factors in the development of industry, bureaucracy, science, and other technologies throughout the world. Oral societies simply do not have the means to store the amount of information necessary for such activities.

Thus, early oral societies were not bureaucratized or highly economically developed. Instead, such societies were relatively small, cohesive, and tightly knit groups which "possessed" a common knowledge. This knowledge reinforced group membership and enforced group values. The narratives and their performance operated to include rather than exclude, creating a unity among the group members. Reading is an individual experience, but oral performance of the narratives becomes participatory and unifying. Thus members of early oral societies did not develop the extreme self-consciousness of modern, literate humans in the West. Individuals in oral societies also reasoned differently and viewed their world in distinct ways.

## State of Mind in Early Oral Societies

Havelock, in his study of the Homeric Greek culture, suggests that the enormous amount of concentration and memory required by the oral societies resulted in a particular oral state of mind. He argues that the oral mindset was not rational in the modern Western sense of that term: "You did not learn your ethics and politics, skills and directives, by having them presented to you as a corpus for silent study, reflection and absorption. You were not asked to grasp their principles through rational analysis. You were not invited to so much as think of them. Instead you submitted to the . . . spell [of the oral performance]."[24]

The oral nature of these societies called for memory and passivity rather than independent judgment or critical analysis. Reflection was not important; remembering was. Life in an early oral society was "a life without self-examination," a life "without a chance to ask a question or raise a doubt" about the truth of what the narrative tells us.[25] Individuals in early oral society answered questions by reference to the narrative. Rather than ask "why?," the query was "from whence came?"; that is, where in the tradition does such information come, for that is the source of all knowledge. The oral state of mind described by Havelock was mystical and accepting; it involved a self-surrender to the narrative and to the greater society. As he explains it, the knower did not feel independence from that which was known:

> From the standpoint of a developed self-conscious critical intelligence [a member of an oral society] was a part of all he had seen and heard and remembered. His job was not to form individual and unique convictions but to retain tenaciously a precious hoard of exemplars. These were constantly present with him in his acoustic reflexes and also visually imagined before his mind's eye. In short, he went along with the tradition. His mental condition, though not his character, was one of passivity. . . .[26]

Such an individual did not have a highly developed sense of self—certainly not of an autonomous thinking and reasoning self. This description contrasts with the excessive self-awareness that contemporary Western individuals develop.

Joseph Epes Brown describes this communal state of mind as one of "interconnections." Native American cultures see all life—nature, animals, the heavens, people—as connected, and the thread that connects them is the sacred. Brown illustrates his explanation with a segment of a Navajo chant:

> "The mountains, I become part of it . . .
> The herbs, the fir tree, I become part of it.
> The morning mists, the clouds, the gathering waters,
> I become part of it.
> The wilderness, the dew drops, the pollen . . .
> I become part of it."[27]

All things are related in a system of kinship, which gives a solidarity to life. The oneness of experience in a primal oral worldview also is described by Cassirer:

> What is characteristic of primitive mentality is not its logic but
> its general sentiment of life. Primitive man does not look at
> nature with the eyes of a naturalist who wishes to classify things
> in order to satisfy an intellectual curiosity. . . . His view of nature
> is neither merely theoretical nor merely practical; it is
> *sympathetic*. . . . Primitive man by no means lacks the ability
> to grasp the empirical differences of things. But in his conception
> of nature and life all these differences are obliterated by a
> stronger feeling: the deep conviction of a fundamental and
> indelible *solidarity of life* that bridges over the multiplicity and
> variety of its single forms. He does not ascribe to himself a
> unique and privileged place in the scale of nature. The con-
> sanguinity of all forms of life seems to be a general
> presupposition of mythical thought.

The primal mind sees itself bound inextricably with the animals that
are its totemic ancestors. Humans thus have no particular rank in
nature; both the "highest" and "lowest" forms of life have the same
"religious dignity." Unity of life is so strong, according to Cassirer, that
generations form an unbroken chain, and the soul of a grandparent
reappears in a newborn child.[28]

Marvin Bram illustrates his understanding of the different states of
mind in oral and literate societies by describing a modern university
professor who wakes up from a dream. In the dream, which he
remembers vividly, his grandmother, who is dead, comes to his office,
lays a wooden flute on his desk, talks about the meaning of the carvings
on the flute, and asks him to devote the rest of his life to playing the
flute. When the professor, now awakened, begins his new day, he goes
about his life as he had the day before, thinking about the dream, *his*
dream, but in no way "confusing" his awakened state with the dream.
Nor does he learn to play the flute. He does not "confuse" past and
present or the fact he is alive and his grandmother dead. However, says
Bram, if the dreamer had been a Chinese villager during the Han period,
upon awakening, he

> might have walked slowly to an elder's house, gesturing
> respectfully to empty space . . . [as the] space through which
> he walked was filled with the presences of every kinsperson who
> had ever occupied that space—including, naturally, the
> grandmother whom he had seen in his dream. . . . The dead
> grandmother was alive. She moved among her kin in both past
> and present, daylight and dream. . . . Since the reality of the
> villager's kin-group preceded the reality of his individual person,
> it was the kin-group too that dreamt that dream. And all such
> dreams together were the possession of each kinsperson.[29]

These two men Bram describes represent two poles of consciousness,
two poles of linguistic behavior. The contemporary, literate, Western

human rationalizes, creates hierarchies, and thinks in terms of abstract concepts. "We want to know about 'trees' or 'the tree as such,' a tree that cannot be touched. That knowledge is more satisfactory than knowledge about 'that particular maple.'"[30] The oral Chinese villager's world, however, does not have the same or as many hierarchies and abstractions as the Western professor's world. In our literate world, we have so many modifiers and adjectives and verb tenses that we have fewer specific names. We can put an object in a category, then distinguish it by modifiers—*There is a very young maple in my back yard that turned red and orange last autumn.* In an oral world, without the same linguistic complexity, many more names exist. Individuals in such a society "see" more particulars and fewer general concepts. For example, as discussed in the next chapter, humans in some oral societies are given different names at each stage of their lives, becoming, in a very real sense, a different person than the one who bore the former name.

Early oral and Western literate worldviews also understand metaphors differently, according to Bram. In the oral world, metaphors do not operate as stylistic devices; they are believed. "I am a wind" does not mean "I am like a wind" as it does in the Western world—for someone from an early oral society, an identity exists with the wind. Giving a young woman the name of an animal gives her the power, the magical efficacy, of that animal.

Time also is understood differently in oral societies. In literate societies, we learn from the past and plan for the future. In oral societies, according to Bram, the "past will not be combed for patterns and the present for opportunities; the future will just be awaited."[31] When thinking back, the Western mind uses memory and creates history; the oral mind relies on myth and reverie. Primal people do not treat time as linear and successive, as literate Westerners do. Hopis deal with time as day and night, as seasons and phases of the moon. Time is sacred, such as the Australian aborigine's *dreamtime.* For the oral mind, all the past and present happens in a perpetual present.

The state of mind in early oral societies is sympathetic rather than logical, holistic rather than linear and hierarchical, accepting rather than critical, and communal rather than individualistic. This state of mind contrasts with the modern Western state of mind, described in Part Three of this text. The contrast in no way implies superiority, as each state of mind has its own unique strengths and weaknesses.

The very unself-consciousness and lack of analysis characteristic of oral societies allows a unity with the natural world and with other humans that Western literate societies have difficulty capturing. Oral culture allows a sense of participation because oral utterance is itself participatory.[32] Such a life is emotional and in harmony with the natural world. It is spiritual and open to the sacred. To describe the state of mind in oral societies as "primitive" is to adopt a limited, linear, and very narrow point of view. Instead, it is mythological, primal, and natural.

## Summary

The fundamental form of language is oral; it is spoken.[33] Many languages have no written code, even today. As Ong notes, written words are "residue," a characteristic which oral speech cannot duplicate. In oral societies, when a particular tale is not being told, "all that exists of it is the potential in certain human beings to tell it." Understanding what it is like to be a member of an oral society is extremely difficult for literate people; we also may find it intimidating. Ong claims that to "dissociate words from writing is psychologically threatening" as our sense of control over language is closely tied to the visual transformations of language.[34]

However, an understanding of the primal mind can bring enrichment to literate people. To understand ourselves, we must understand those aspects of our own worldview which are not necessary, and we must open ourselves to various ways of comprehending experience. So much of what we take for granted, what we assume to be reality, is only appearance from our particular point of view. This multiplicity of experience not only allows us to understand those with a different worldview but also to better understand our own.

Robert Pirsig's novel, *Zen and the Art of Motorcycle Maintenance*, is the story of a man's journey to discover a lost worldview. The narrator sets out on a journey from the Midwest to the West coast, traveling through Bozeman, Montana, where he formerly taught English at Montana State University. As he travels, he gathers bits of memory about himself prior to the electro-shock therapy that was used to treat his "insanity"—therapy that left him a different person. As he travels, and as he confronts the ghosts from the past, he comes to realize that the only thing insane about his former self is that he did not share the same worldview as his contemporaries; his problems came from challenging the assumptions of the dominant paradigm. He also comes to realize that, in most societies, a person who does not fit in the dominant paradigm is marginalized, institutionalized, banished, or "treated." By silencing those who see reality from a different vantage point, the truth of the dominant point of view remains unchallenged.

Attempting to understand early oral cultures can expand our own vision as well as explain some aspects of contemporary life. Our link to our oral past lies in the power of the words. Although we do not depend upon words in the same way oral humans did, we still retain a belief in their magic.

## Endnotes

1. Ruth Finnegan, who studies contemporary oral cultures, refers to oral traditions as "oral literature," claiming the narratives serve an aesthetic function that involves a performance aspect more than serving as mnemonic technology. Ruth Finnegan, *Literacy and Orality: Studies in the Technology of Communication* (Oxford: Basil Blackwell, 1988) 50. Walter Ong, a leading scholar on orality, denounces the use of the term "oral literature" as "monstrous" and "preposterous," arguing that the nature of oral narrative is considerably different than written literature. Walter J. Ong, *Orality and Literacy: The Technologizing of the Word* (New York: Methuen, 1982) 11–12.
2. Tom Bahti, *Southwestern Indian Ceremonials* (1970; rpt. Las Vegas, NV: KC, 1987) 46–47.
3. See, for example, D. M. Dooling and Paul Jordan-Smith, ed., *I Become Part of It: Sacred Dimensions in Native American Life* (1989; rpt. San Francisco: HarperCollins, 1992) 233–39 and Richard Erdoes and Alfonso Ortiz, ed., *American Indian Myths and Legends* (New York: Pantheon, 1984) 39–41.
4. Dooling and Jordan-Smith 72–74.
5. Joseph Falaky Nagy, "Orality in Medieval Irish Narrative: An Overview," *Oral Tradition* 1 (1986): 274.
6. Brynley F. Roberts, "Oral Tradition and Welsh Literature: A Description and Survey," *Oral Tradition* 3 (1988): 62.
7. Bruce A. Rosenberg, "The Complexity of Oral Tradition," *Oral Tradition* 2 (1987): 81.
8. Ong 36–43.
9. Albert B. Lord, "Characteristics of Orality," *Oral Tradition* 2 (1987): 54.
10. Walter J. Ong, *Interfaces of the Word: Studies in the Evolution of Consciousness and Culture* (Ithaca: Cornell UP, 1977) 104–08
11. Donna Rosenberg, *World Mythology: An Anthology of the Great Myths and Epics* (Lincolnwood, IL: National Textbook, 1986) 35.
12. Ong, *Orality and Literacy* 40–41. Alfred Lord suggests that redundancy in oral-tradition narratives is related to ritual rather than mnemonic purposes. Lord 58.
13. Eric A. Havelock, *Preface to Plato* (1963; rpt. New York: Grosset & Dunlap, 1971) 176–80.
14. Havelock 81.
15. Cited in Viv Edwards and Thomas J. Sienkewicz, *Oral Cultures Past and Present: Rappin' and Homer* (Cambridge, MA: Basil Blackwell, 1991) 15.
16. Edwards and Sienkewicz 25.
17. Frederick Turner, "Performed Being: Word Art as a Human Inheritance," *Oral Tradition* 1 (1986): 78–79.
18. Ruth Benedict, *Patterns of Culture* (1934; rpt. Boston: Houghton Mifflin, 1959) 60–62.
19. Finnegan 20.
20. Denys L. Page, *History and the Homeric Iliad* (Berkeley: U of California P, 1959) 218.
21. Burton Raffel, "The Manner of Boyen: Translation Oral Literature," *Oral Tradition* 1 (1986): 11–12.
22. Turner 77.
23. Finnegan 40.
24. Havelock 159.
25. Havelock 190.
26. Havelock 199.

27. Joseph Epes Brown, "Becoming Part of It," *I Become Part of It: Sacred Dimensions in Native American Life*, ed. D. M. Dooling and Paul Jordan-Smith (1989; rpt. San Francisco: HarperCollins, 1992) 11, 20.
28. Ernst Cassirer, *An Essay On Man: An Introduction to a Philosophy of Human Culture* (1944; rpt. New Haven: Yale UP, 1968) 82–83.
29. Marvin Bram, "Elements of Symbolic History, Part I," *Semiotica* 36 (1981): 212–13.
30. Bram 215.
31. Bram 228.
32. Ong, *Interfaces of the Word* 21.
33. Ferdinand de Saussure, *Course in General Linguistics*, trans. Wade Baskin, ed. Charles Bally and Albert Sechehaye (New York: Philosophical Library, 1959) 23–24.
34. Ong, *Orality and Literacy* 14.

# Chapter Six

# Word Magic

Words can be powerful in many ways. Historically, rhetoric has been the study of language used to persuade, as discussed in chapter three; such language can have a significant impact on an audience. Great speakers can sway groups of people to do their bidding, whether for good or ill. A list of powerful orators includes the great leaders as well as the biggest scoundrels of our time—the Reverend Martin Luther King, Jr., Winston Churchill, Franklin Roosevelt, Huey Long, and Adolph Hitler, to name but a few.

Humans also attribute other effects to language; words can have a magical efficacy. Such efficacy, called "word magic" by Cassirer, occurs when language seems to display mythical powers, when "the Word, in fact, becomes a sort of primary force, in which all being and doing originate."[1] Word magic has roots in the oral traditions of our past, yet it also is a force in modern Western society. This chapter discusses the magic of words as agents of creation, as names, and as means of affecting audiences, whether that effect is described as persuasion or the creation of knowledge.

## Words as Agents of Creation

Cassirer argues that, in the murky past of human evolution, language and myth had the same roots. Imagine that you are an early human being, before language. As you walk about your world, you are bombarded by a variety of stimuli. However, as you have no words by which to distinguish the various sensations, you have only an animal-like awareness of the world around you. Then, at the dawning moment of human language, out of all the sensations bombarding you, something is "noticed," that is, something becomes figure, standing out against the background of the rest of sensation. Startled by this presence of some overpowering sensation, you utter a sound, a word which becomes inextricably bound to your perception of sensation. The bonding of sound to sensation is reminiscent of the experience of Helen Keller, described in chapter two. Her sensation of the cold water from the pump was related, in her understanding, to the letters spelled out on her palm. For you, the sound is linked to the sensation. This sound, this word, then confronts you not as your own creation but as something separate, as something which has objective, independent existence. As Cassirer describes it: something "is selected from the uniform flux of sense impressions, and is 'noticed' in the midst of them—that is to say, receives a special linguistic accent, a name." The name allows that which was noticed to be noted and remembered. By creating a distinction among sensations, by this linguistic fixing with a name, the sensation—or more accurately, your conception of it— becomes fixed in consciousness and memory. "What the mind has once created, what has been culled from the total sphere of consciousness, does not fade away again when the spoken word has set its seal upon it and given it definite form."[2] This process, argues Cassirer, is the root for both language and myth, which he sees as the original religious impulse. Thus, reverence for "the word" comes out of this primordial experience, in which the word becomes name and thereby differentiates some aspect of experience.

Cassirer argues that this mystical origin of the word explains not only the reverence for language evident in some oral societies but the magical efficacy of words in many oral traditions. This efficacy is particularly displayed in creation myths.

A striking number of creation myths feature the word of a god or gods as the originating source of existence or as a tool employed in the act of creation. In the Judeo-Christian tradition found in the Old Testament of the *Bible*, for example, God says "let there be light" and, based on that command, that *word*, light is created. By similar vocal command, firmament appears in the midst of waters, and night is separated from day. This vocal origin of creation is found in many other oral traditions. In early Egyptian theology, Ptah, the god who creates the world and other gods, has primary force of heart and tongue. All that he desires comes about. He creates by the tongue, which repeats the thoughts of his heart.[3] In another Egyptian myth, Khepri, the morning sun, was the first deity in the pantheon. He creates himself by saying his own name. The Uitoto creation myth, from Colombia, asserts that in the beginning "the word gave origin to the Father."[4] According to the creation myth of Polynesia, in the beginning, neither voice nor sound existed. Then, sound began. In India, the spoken word (*Vāc*) was exalted even above the gods: "On the Spoken Word all the gods depend, all beasts and men; in the Word live all creatures . . . the Word is the Imperishable, the firstborn of the eternal Law, the mother of the Veddas, the navel of the divine world."[5] The creation myths of several tribes of North American Indians begin from a watery world. In the Maidu myth, Coyote *announced* that the water would become sand, and it happened. Nichant, a god in the lore of the Gros Ventre, made a mound of mud large enough to stand on, stood upon it with closed eyes, and announced, "Let there be land as far as my eyes can see." When he opened his eyes, the water had receded and he could see land.[6] The Inca creation myth features Con Ticci Viracocha, the creator god whose first creations angered him, so he turned them into stone and flooded the earth. When the floods receded, he fashioned humans from stone, then *commanded* the stone figures to sink beneath the earth. Later he shouted, "Con Ticci Viracocha, who helped create the universe, commands his beings to emerge from the stone figures he has created."[7] In the Sumerian epic, *Gilgamesh*, the "naming" of things is the creative act.[8] In the Babylonian creation myth, "the heaven had not been named, Firm ground below had not been called by name . . . no gods whatever had been brought into being, Uncalled by name, their destinies undetermined."[9] Later in the story, after much discord between gods, Marduk announces, "Let my word determine the fates! Let whatever I created remain fixed. Let my command be everlasting, and let my word endure!" The other gods bow down to Marduk, announcing, "Your word will be supreme. Your decrees will be everlasting. No one among the gods will disobey your word." Although Marduk creates things by his actions, he announces his intentions first, and the gods acknowledge the power of his words.[10]

The power of the word is demonstrated in the creation myth of the Quiche Indians, who live in scattered communities in Guatemala and speak a language belonging to the Mayan family. Their creation myth is "The *Popul Vuh*: The Book of Counsel."

> It was quiet.
> Truly it was calm.
> Truly it was solitary
> And it was also still empty,
> the womb of heaven.
> These are truly then the first words,
> the first utterances.
> There was not one person yet,

one animal,
deer, bird, fish, crab,
tree, rock, hole,
canyon,
meadow or forest.
All by itself the sky existed.
The face of the earth was not yet visible.
All by itself the sea lay dammed,
. . .
There was nothing whatever
silenced or at rest.
Each thing was made silent,
each thing was made calm,
was made invisible,
. . .
All alone the Former and Shaper,
Majesty, and Quetzal Serpent,
The Mothers and Fathers
were in the water.
Brilliant they were then,
and wrapped in quetzal
and dove feathers.
Thence came the name
of Quetzal Serpent.
Great sages they were
and great thinkers in their essence,
for indeed there is heaven
and there is also the Heart of Heaven.
That is the name
of the deity, it is said.

So then came His word here.
It reached to Majesty
and Quetzal Serpent,
there in the obscurity, in the nighttime.
It spoke to Majesty
and Quetzal Serpent, and they spoke.
Then they thought;
then they pondered.
Then they found themselves.
They assembled their words, their thoughts.
Then they gave birth,
then they heartened themselves.
Then they caused to be created
and they bore men.
. . .

So then this, the earth, was created by them,
only their word was the creation of it.
To create the earth, "Earth," they said.
Immediately it was created.[11]

Creation myths such as these are called "edict-myths" by Philip Freund, who suggests they derive from human's "deep respect for the magic of the spoken word."[12] In some traditions, the efficacy of such words extends beyond the creation of the world. The power of the words used to create the world is invoked by prayer and ritual for energy, fecundity, or other purposes in human lives. For example, the same words used by Io, the Polynesian creator god, to fashion the universe are used in the ritual designed to make a barren woman pregnant. The words whereby Io created light are repeated in rituals to help raise the spirits of someone who is despondent, to aid in understanding secret matters, and to bring inspiration in songwriting; just as these words allowed Io to dispel darkness, they are used to bring cheer and enlightenment to humans.[13] For the Navaho, creation results not from a creator but the power of thought and ritual—both speech and prayer. Speech and thought existed before creation. They arise from the medicine bundle from which the rest of creation comes and embody the power of the bundle. Following this story, the Navaho "continue to perform acts of creation through the power of ritual representation in sand paintings and the ritual language of song and prayer."[14] This magic of knowing the words of creation and repeating them is found also in the culture of the Australian Arunta and the Kai of New Guinea, in Tibetan ritual, and in Hindu theology and ritual.[15]

This belief in word magic extends beyond the word as agent of creation, however. The potency of the word also comes from its power as a name.

## Magic of Names

Words can have magical efficacy in their own right. Words become merged with their referents, gaining not just equal but in some cases more importance than that which they name. It is the fact of naming, of culling certain aspects of sensation for particular notice, that gives root to this magic. Such magic of words is found in the names of gods, the names for individuals, and the names for other things, wherein the signifier reigns supreme.

## Names of Gods

In some oral traditions and mythologies, knowing the name of a god gives the knower certain power—in some cases, power greater than that possessed by the god. The great Egyptian sorceress Isis tricked Ra, the sun god, into revealing his name to her. By possessing his name, she gained power over him and all other gods.[16]

The very name of a god deserves honor. In the Old Testament, a psalm announces, "O Lord, our Lord, how majestic is thy *name* in all the earth" (emphasis added).[17] One of the Judeo-Christian ten commandments exhorts believers not to take the *name* of the Lord in vain. In some traditions, pronouncing the name of god also is required when honoring the deity. The Babylonian gods celebrated the creation feat of Marduk by "proclaiming the 50 names and qualities that Marduk possessed, for they wished to honor their supreme god's glorious ways and deeds."[18] The Mayan creation gods tried several times before succeeding in creating human beings. Their goal was creatures who will "praise us and love us," and they were not satisfied until they created creatures with speech.[19]

Some gods have many names. As noted above, Marduk had "50 names." The Norse god, Odin, who is the oldest and greatest of the gods, is called many names, including "high one" and "father of the slain."[20] If the god has several names, each of the names may be pronounced when addressing the deity, to avoid offense and so as not to risk losing the efficacy granted to those who utter the "true" name. Some Christian prayers and affirmations demonstrate this litany of names for the deity, as in the following excerpt from the Nicene Creed:

> I believe in one God: the Father Almighty, maker of heaven and earth, and of all things visible and invisible;
>
> And in one Lord Jesus Christ, the only begotten Son of God: begotten of the Father before all worlds, God of God, Light of Light, Very God of Very God . . . .[21]

In some religions the real name of god is too holy to be spoken, so other names are used, to avoid offense. In the Hebrew Old Testament, the name of God is *Yahweh*, but some pious Jews pronounce the word "Adonai."[22]

The magic residing in the name of a god indicates that the name either has a status equal to the being or is an inseparable part of the being's power. This oneness of name and being is what gives magical efficacy to the names of individuals.

## Names of Individuals

In many societies, the name of an individual also has magic or special significance. Thus, the name is seen not as a symbol or a sign but as a part of the person or thing. Cassirer describes the relationship of name to person as similar to property, which must be protected if it is to be retained. He recalls an edict of a Chinese emperor in the third century, B.C., reserving a first-person pronoun for himself alone. In ancient Rome, only legal persons had names. As a slave had no legal personhood, he or she had no legal name.[23]

Eskimo tribes believed that an individual is composed of three parts—body, soul, and name—and a person is not complete without all three. The name has a life independent of the individual and brings with it the qualities of all who shared that name.

> [O]ne may imagine it as a procession of ancestors stretching into the dim past and surrounding the present bearer of the name with a sort of magic protective aura. When a person dies and has been buried, the name may not be mentioned again until it has been reborn. Many Eskimos believe[d] that a newborn baby cries because it wants its name, and will not be complete until it gets it.[24]

An angakok or wise old one of the village determined the name to be given the child. It might be the name of an ancestor who recently died. Many times, a child was given several names, so as to have the most possible protection. In some polar Eskimo tribes, an individual would not pronounce his or her own name, for to do so could break its magical protection.

A number of cultures share this practice of giving a child the name of an ancestor; in these groups, the name rather than the individual is significant and unique. Among the Algonquin, if two individuals had the same name, they were the alter ego of the other; thus, children given the name of an ancestor shared the essence of that person. A ceremonial priest determined which ancestor had been reborn in the child in order to determine what name to bestow on the baby.[25] The Osage have a naming ceremony. Each of the tribe's clans or gens has its own version, reflecting the animal which is its "power-being," and its own special tie to the earth, sky, and other creatures; however, all the gens participate in the naming ceremony, to give the child the strength of each gen. In the naming ceremony of the Puma gen, part of the ceremony recounts how the tribe was created—when the beings assembled among the stars and decided to descend to this world but were in need of names so they could become people. They appealed to a god (Wa-kon-da hon-ba) for names. He told the beings to name their children after him so they would have long lives. Then he gave them names for their children—"Child-of-the-Sun, Sacred-arrowshaft, Giver-of-clear-speech, Woman-who-travels-over-the-earth, Arrow-maker, Beloved-child-of-the-sun, and Dark Eyes." After this ritual recitation of the tribal lore, the child is given a name, which is necessary for becoming a person.[26]

Most North American tribes gave names in tribal ceremonies; these names recognized the uniqueness of individuals. In most of the rest of the Western world, the surname given a baby merely recognizes the male genetic line. In the European tradition, names are public; the name of a Native American, however, is private and singular—it is part of that person. In some tribes, one cannot speak the name of a person who has died. The Kiowas would not, until recent times, speak the name of a dead person, who takes his or her name out of the world at death. To speak the name of the dead was disrespectful and dishonest.[27]

In some cultures, when the name changes, the human personality changes. At a new phase of life, or after a significant deed or event, a new name is given, and a new self or persona results. Native American tribes gave names related to the deeds of the individual. In James Welch's highly acclaimed fictional account of a band of Blackfeet Indians around 1870, the main character, White Man's Dog, behaves bravely and wisely during a raid on a Crow camp. After being shot, he falls down and plays dead. When an old Crow chief advances on him, he jumps up and kills him. When White Man's Dog returns to his own camp, he is renamed Fools Crow at a naming ceremony, and he becomes a "man of much medicine."[28] Attempts by biographers of European lineage to write the biography of Sacajawea, the Native American woman who led Lewis and Clark on their search for the Northwest passage, have been frustrated. They are not certain what happened to her after the expedition returned. Although they are able to track her for several years, they are not certain where she spent her final years because her name changed later in life.

Names also create personal power. In some cultures, if an older child has died, the parents give a frightening name to their other children, to scare the angel of death.[29] In other cultures, individuals' "true names" are kept secret, since to know the name is to gain power over the person. Recall the story of Rumpelstiltskin—in order to break a wizard's power over her, the queen had to discover his true name. If a personal name is sacred, using that name will dissipate the power. Thus, to honor one's fellow humans, "one has to refer to a person in a very circuitous manner, or use a term which expresses relationship."[30]

As with the name of gods, the magical power of the name of individuals is both a protection to individuals and a definition of their character. You may know people who have changed their names. Some women choose to retain their maiden name after marriage. Other individuals opt for names that express their individuality; a former student of mine legally changed his name to a single word—"Cosmo." A name, therefore, has real power. It is no mere signifier of some referent or signified. It is immediate and effective; it is magic. The signifier and signified are merged.

## Identification with Referent

The merger of signifier and signified is explained by Cassirer: "Whatever has been fixed by a name, henceforth is not only real, but is Reality."[31] Word magic is, at its foundation, the identification of words with objects, with referents. Some of this tendency is rooted in early childhood experience; when a child calls for Mother, she appears. Wishes are gratified by pronouncing names, such as "cookie," or "drink." The child discovers that saying the "right" names will result in the materialization of the desired item. If a person does not understand the arbitrary nature of the sign, then words have a tremendous significance; their relationship to meaning is of great importance.

## Power of the Spoken Word

The power of the spoken word stretches back into the oral past. Joseph Epes Brown explains the magic of language for Native Americans:

> In Native languages the understanding is that the meaning *is* in the sound, it *is* in the word; the word is not a symbol for meaning which has been abstracted out, word and meaning are together in one experience. . . . Added to this is the fact that when we create words we use our breath, and for these people and these traditions breath is associated with the principle of life; breath is life itself. And so if a word is born from this sacred principle of breath, this lends an added sacred dimension to the spoken word.[32]

In a magnificent book about the experience of a young Native American caught between his own and the white culture, N. Scott Momaday, in *House Made of Dawn*, describes a revival minister's sermon, part of which deals with "the Word." By tying creation by the word to the importance of the word to oral people, he encapsulates the magic of words. The minister begins by exhorting the congregation to think of Genesis, reminding them that the world was created by the word of God, by a sound made in the silence:

> But . . . in the darkness something happened. . . . There was a single sound. Far away in the darkness there was a single sound. . . . It was almost nothing in itself, a single sound, a word—a word broken off at the darkest center of the night and let go in the awful void, forever and forever. . . . [A]nd everything began.

The minister then takes as his text the first verse of the Gospel of John: "In the beginning was the Word, and the Word was with God, and the Word was God." This section of the sermon is reproduced not for what it says about Christianity, but for what it says about the power of words for oral people. The minister suggests that John caught sight of the truth one day, and in his hurry to tell someone, he said too much.

> And he said, "In the beginning was the Word. . . ." And, man, right then and there he should have stopped. There was nothing more to say, but he went on. . . .

> Now, brothers and sisters, old John was a white man, and the white man has his ways. Oh gracious me, he has his ways. He talks about the Word. . . . He builds upon it with syllables, with prefixes and suffixes, and hyphens and accents. He adds and divides and multiplies the Word. And in all of this he subtracts the Truth. And, brothers and sisters, you have come here to live in the white man's world. Now the white man deals with words, and he deals easily, with grace and sleight of hand. And in his presence, here on his ground, you are as children, mere babes in the woods. You must not mind, for in this you have a certain advantage. A child can listen and learn. The Word is sacred to a child. . . .

The preacher then talks about language in the white man's world. Because the white man's culture is so thoroughly literate, the minister argues, he takes words for granted, as they are so abundant and common. "On every side of him there are words by the millions, an unending succession of pamphlets and papers, letters and books, bills and bulletins, commentaries and conversations." As the white culture has multiplied the word, so the word has been diluted. People in white culture have become insensitive to the magic of words. "[H]is regard for language—for the Word itself—as an instrument of creation has diminished nearly to the point of no return." Then the minister begins to talk about his grandmother, an old Kiowa woman. His grandmother was a storyteller who "knew her way around words." Because she did not know how to read and write, because her use of language was oral, words were precious to her; her regard for words was in direct proportion to her dependence upon them. For her, "words were medicine; they were magic and invisible. They came from nothing into sound and meaning." The Kiowa oral tradition, like all oral traditions, was precarious; if not remembered, it was "but one generation from extinction." But, for the same reason, "it was cherished and revered." The minister describes the reverence that his grandmother had for words, a reverence he saw in her eyes and heard in her voice. "It was that [reverence], I think, that old Saint John had in mind when he said, 'In the beginning was the Word. . . .'"[33]

In addition to the power of words in oral societies, literate societies also find a magic of sorts in the spoken word. In many Western societies, a person's word acts as an oath. A person of her word is a person to be trusted; one who gives his word thereby is committed to act. We ask individuals to give their "word of honor" as evidence for the truth of their statement.

In literate societies one also finds a distinction between the oral and the written word. To use the example at the beginning of the chapter, the Reverend Martin Luther King, Jr., was able to electrify an audience by his magnificent and powerful oral discourse. Even today, many years after his death, watching a grainy, poor quality film of his "I Have a Dream" speech, delivered from the steps of the Lincoln Memorial, can create a profound effect on individuals. How much more magnificent and powerful that feeling must have been for those people standing in front of the Memorial, hearing him speak. In such oral situations, audience members develop, in Ong's words, a "unity, with themselves and with the speaker." Imagine what would have happened if, halfway through his speech, King had asked a group of his followers to hand out a written flier to the audience for them to read. As each person began to read silently, the unity and the magic of the oral moment would have been broken. Individuals enter into private interaction with words on a paper. "Writing and print isolate," claims Ong.[34] The spoken word has a magic efficacy; it erases distance between people.

The power of the spoken word occurs partly because it comes from nothing and, as Momaday suggests, "gives origin to all things."[35] Because it is evanescent, and because if you do not listen closely, you will miss it, the spoken word has the power to spellbind an audience in a way that writing cannot accomplish. This power is demonstrated by great orators and demagogues alike.

Richard Weaver, although not always distinguishing between its oral and written forms, understands the potential power of language, of words. As described in chapter three, he argues that "language is sermonic" and that, in our public and private lives, we are all in some sense preachers: "We have no sooner uttered words than we have given impulse to other people to look at the world, or some small part of it, in our way."[36] This, too, is word magic. By portraying experience in a particular way, words work their unconscious magic on humans, making them see, for example, products as necessary for success or creating distinctions between better and worse—be it body shape, hair style, or brand of blue jeans. Words create belief in religions, governments, and art forms; they create allegiances to football teams, politicians, movie stars, and certain brands of beer. Words are the windows to our own souls and to the world beyond our fingertips. Their essential persuasive efficacy works its magic on every person in every society.

## Summary

The epilogue to Kenneth Burke's *The Rhetoric of Religion* is a scene between Satan and "The Lord." The Lord discusses his plans for the creation of humans, and Satan, a young "over-hasty, mercurial" admirer of the older man, responds.

> TL. And thus nature can circle back on itself. Yes, I'll go ahead with it. And in any case, the project as a whole is so much more inclusive, by comparison that stretch of symbol-using will not be as long as one flicker in all eternity. A protracted evolutionary process leads up to the point where the language-using animal emerges. And then there will be an infinitely long time of wordlessness again, as regards their kind of words, after the evolutionary process has moved on, in developments that leave this troubled species far behind.

> S. (*pondering, half to himself*). But that odd kind of word they will use . . . with syllables and sentences and whole speeches stretched out through time . . . that's so different from our single, eternal, Unitive Word that creatively sums up all, in your exceptional Self, combining your Power, your wisdom and your eternal Love in the perfect simplicity of infinitely complex harmony.[37]

Whether it is the Word or the word, both have magical efficacy for human beings, whether they be in oral or literate societies. By creating either the world or the objects of the world, words present to humans a particular reality in which to live and laugh and love.

## Endnotes

1. Ernst Cassirer, *Language and Myth*, trans. Susanne K. Langer (1946; rpt. New York: Dover, n.d.) 45.
2. Cassirer 38.
3. Marie-Louise von Franz, *Patterns of Creativity Mirrored in Creation Myths* (Zurich: Spring, 1972) 87.
4. Philip Freund, *Myths of Creation* (1965; rpt. Levittown, NY: Transatlantic Arts, 1975) 61.
5. Cassirer 47–48.
6. Freund 62.
7. Donna Rosenberg, *World Mythology: An Anthology of the Great Myths and Epics* (Lincolnwood, IL: National Textbook, 1986) 460.
8. Freund 62.
9. James B. Pritchard, ed. *Ancient Near East Texts Relating to the Old Testament*, 2nd ed. (Princeton: Princeton UP, 1955) 60–61.
10. Rosenberg 163.
11. "The *Popul Vuh*: The Book of Counsel," trans. Munro S. Edmonson, *Native Mesoamerican Spirituality: Ancient Myths, Discourses, Stories, Doctrines, Hymns, Poems from the Aztec, Yucatec, Quiche-Maya and other Sacred Traditions*, ed. Miguel Léon-Portilla (New York: Paulist, 1980) 103–06.
12. Freund 61.
13. Mircea Eliade, *Myth and Reality*, trans. Willard R. Trask (1963; rpt. New York: Harper & Row, 1975) 30–31.
14. Sam Gill, "The Trees Stood Deep Rooted," *I Become Part of It: Sacred Dimensions in Native American Life*, ed. D. M. Dooling and Paul Jordan-Smith (1989; rpt. New York: HarperCollins, 1992) 23–26.
15. Eliade 6–7.
16. Cassirer 48.
17. Psalms 8. 1.
18. Rosenberg 166.
19. Rosenberg 472.
20. Rosenberg 224.
21. *The Methodist Hymnal* (Nashville: Methodist Publishing House, 1966) 739.
22. Anatol Rapoport, *Semantics* (New York: Thomas Y. Crowell, 1975) 32.
23. Cassirer 50–51.
24. Peter Freuchen, *Book of the Eskimos*, ed. Dagmar Freuchen (Greenwich, CT: Fawcett, 1961) 154–55.
25. Cassirer 51.
26. Carter Revard, "Traditional Osage Naming Ceremonies: Entering the Circle of Being," *Recovering the Word: Essays on Native American Literature*, ed. Brian Swann and Arnold Krupat (Berkeley: U of California P, 1987) 452–54.
27. N. Scott Momaday, *The Way to Rainy Mountain* (1969; rpt. Albuquerque: U of New Mexico P, 1985) 33.
28. James Welch, *Fools Crow* (1986; rpt. New York: Penguin, 1987) 151.
29. Cassirer 52.
30. Joseph Epes Brown, "Becoming Part of It," *I Become Part of It: Sacred Dimensions in Native American Life*, ed. D. M. Dooling and Paul Jordan-Smith (1989; rpt. New York: HarperCollins, 1992) 13.
31. Cassirer 58.
32. Brown 13.

33. N. Scott Momaday, *House Made of Dawn* (1968; rpt. New York: Harper & Row, 1989) 85–90.

34. Walter J. Ong, *Orality and Literacy: The Technologizing of the Word* (New York: Methuen, 1982) 74.

35. Momaday, *The Way to Rainy Mountain* 33.

36. Richard Weaver, "Language is Sermonic," *Language is Sermonic: Richard M. Weaver on the Nature of Rhetoric*, eds. Richard L. Johannesen, Rennard Strickland, and Ralph Y. Eubanks (Baton Rouge: Louisiana State UP, 1970) 224.

37. Kenneth Burke, *The Rhetoric of Religion: Studies in Logology* (Berkeley: U of California P, 1970) 276–77.

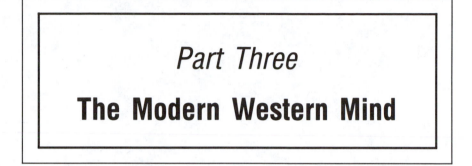

# Part Three
# The Modern Western Mind

Discussion of the ancient Greek worldview is relevant to our attempts to discover the role rhetoric plays in creating human understanding. The modern Western mind is influenced to a significant degree by the ideas and worldview of classical Greece. Part Three examines possible explanations of how this Western mind developed, specifically what may have occurred to move humans from emersion in an oral tradition to a level of cognitive awareness and self-conscious rationality. It includes a very brief overview of the ideas, individuals, and events that influenced developing Western civilization, including communication technologies. Also reviewed are traditional logic, inductive patterns of reasoning, and contemporary theories of argument, to develop awareness of the critical mindset that is valued in the West. The intent of this section is to explain, in broad outline, the modern Western worldview, thus providing a context for understanding the challenges to that so-called "rational paradigm," which are set out in Part Four of this text.

# Chapter Seven

# Beginnings of the Western Mind

A literate human being raised in the West during the twentieth century likely has a different mindset, reasons differently, and, in a very real sense, sees a different world than did a person in an oral society many centuries ago. By fifth century B.C., the Greek mind was beginning to evolve from the oral traditions of the Homeric period to the understandings associated with classical Athens, which are acknowledged as the intellectual foundations of the modern Western mind. This chapter is devoted to theories about this early development of the Western mind. Included in the discussion are several questions. How did the Homeric state of mind differ from its counterpart in Athens in fifth century B.C.? What social forces may have caused these changes? What are the characteristics imputed to the literate state of mind? And, what legacy did the Greeks bequeath to the modern Western mind?

## Changing State of Mind

The state of mind in early oral societies, as described in chapter five, was sympathetic, holistic, accepting, and communal. Such a life was spiritual, emotional, and in harmony with the natural world. Humans were not accorded special status over animals; indeed, animals were the totems or part of the kinship of clans or of individuals. Early oral minds did not reflect, they remembered; they were mystical, reverent,

and respectful. Early oral individuals did not have a highly developed
sense of self—the knower did not feel independence from that which
was known. Humans were very tied to each other, to their collective
past, and to their culture.

The character of thought and mind displayed in extant writings from
the fifth century B.C. in Athens departs sharply from this early oral
model. Key changes come in the development of the individual, the
view of reality, the individual's relationship to knowledge, and the
nature of thought.

## The Individual

In early oral societies, humans did not have such a highly developed
sense of self as do modern Western individuals. Thoughts, volitions,
and impulses were not the result of one's own thought processes but
were given from without, either by some external stimulus or as the
result of a deity giving divine guidance. When a human was faced with
a choice, a god, an oracle, or the fates intervened. As Bruno Snell, who
chronicles the Greek origins of the European mind, notes: "It follows
that Homer's men act with perfect assurance, and that they do not
know what it means to be burdened with scruples or doubts. Nor do
they feel the weight of a personal responsibility for right or wrong."[1]
By the fifth century B.C., the writings of the Greek poets, playwrights,
philosophers, and historians indicate a very specific sense of
individuality, self-consciousness, and individual responsibility. These
changes are evident in the meaning of words, in syntax, and in the
content of discourse.

One indication that the Greek mind was changing was the
development of the concept of *psyche*, which the Greeks of classical
Athens discussed as the soul—a separate personality or an independent
self. This is the meaning of *psyche* we associate with Socrates. Before
this period, *psyche* was the breath or bloodlife of a person. Descriptions
of *psyche* depend, in Homer, on analogies to physical organs of the body
rather than to the intellect or mind. By the fifth century B.C., the
classical meaning had developed, and *psyche* became the essence of
humans whereby moral judgment and cognition are possible—in short,
the "ghost that thinks."[2]

Heraclitus is among the first to refer to the *psyche* as the soul, which
he distinguishes from the body. He refers to the soul with various
metaphors involving depth—a depth which is ephemeral rather than
physical, a "non-spatial substance."[3] He says, "You could not discover
the limits of soul, even if you traveled by every path in order to do so;
such is the depth of its meaning."[4] This description is the foundation

for the classical Greek concept of the soul, which is not physical; it "exists" in some realm other than the realm of the body. This changed meaning of *psyche* is the beginning of the notion of a mental sphere, which is the locus of the thinking self.

Eric Havelock argues that other linguistic clues also indicate the changing mental state of humans in classical Athens. He cites as evidence in support of this claim the new syntactical uses of pronouns, which were attached to verbs indicating thought or cognition.[5]

The development of the self also is seen in the rise of the concept of the individual in Greek lyric poetry, particularly the notion of author. The oral traditions simply are; no one created them.[6] The lyric poets such as Pindar, however, are acknowledged as creators. They identify and speak about themselves, and they are recognized as authors. This is the beginning of individuals in a variety of roles—leaders, writers, philosophers, and so on—who record their names and deeds, and who begin, as Snell notes, to "pierce through the veil of anonymity" which covers the oral period.[7] The transition is from actions caused by deities to actions caused by individuals, who are responsible and held accountable for those actions.

Sometime between the Dark Ages of Greece and the end of the classical period, the Greek mind developed a sense of individuality— of a thinking, autonomous self that was the originator of its own deeds. This may have been the most important aspect in the development of the modern Western mind.[8] As Havelock notes, the notion of an autonomous *psyche* parallels the rejection of the oral culture. This discovery of self is a discovery of a thinking self. It is a self that is distanced from the rest of existence, a self which begins to posit a separate reality—one that can be known and explored.[9]

## Reality

The notion of reality as something distinct from myth also arises in classical Athens. Mythical reality *was* reality; the oral traditions gave to the early oral Greeks a unified and unchallenged reality. A very different understanding of reality arises in classical Greek drama. Drama is not imitation or even a reenactment of reality. The limitations of drama, including the space limitations of the stage itself, time limitations, and various other demands, make drama only a portrayal of reality. A portrayal is not the same as the version of reality given by the epics or oral traditions in which myth and reality are merged. Drama, which has no part in the ritual of myth, is removed from reality; it is instead *art*. Thus is born the so-called "deception of the play." Even the Greek tragedies, which concern the same events as myth, are striking in their differences. The tragedies are not intended to be faithful renditions of the incidents of myth; instead they trace the causes of human action.[10] The dramas give a separate version of events, a version which represents rather than recreates. In Euripides' plays, according to Snell: "Reality is no longer something that is simply given. The meaningful no longer impresses itself as an incontrovertible fact, and appearances have ceased to reveal their significance directly to man. All this really means is that myth has come to an end."[11] Similarly, knowledge is something apart from human beings and distinct from reality.

## Knowledge

In early oral traditions, knowledge was not a concept. The group knew that which was in the oral tradition, not as a knowledge to be learned but as a reality to be lived. It came from the gods, and those who recounted it were inspired by the muses. No distinction existed between the knower and that body of information which was known. In classical Greece, however, knowledge comes as a result of reflection and individual thought and experience. For example, in a fragment from Xenophanes, he notes: "Quite evidently the gods have not revealed everything to mortals at the outset; for mortals are obliged, in the slow course of time, to discover for themselves what is best."[12] Heraclitus argues, "Men who love wisdom should acquaint themselves with a great many particulars."[13] Herodotus also displayed an enthusiasm for investigation. In his history he says, "In the wish to get the best information that I could on these matters, I made a voyage to Tyre. . . . In a conversation which I held with the priests, I inquired how long their temple had been built. . . ."[14] For him, experience is the basis of knowledge.[15]

A key change is that knowledge becomes not concrete but abstract. Rather than knowing by means of the examples of characters in the oral traditions (as myth is connected to particular, concrete situations), concepts are expressed as universal situations. Abstractions allow generalization. Snell notes:

> Before long the problem of human action which is the concern of tragedy was to become a matter for intellectual cognition; Socrates insists on solving the problem through knowledge of the good. That is the ultimate abstraction of the real, its transformation into a teleological concept. Where a divine world had endowed the human world with meaning, we now find the universal determining the particular.[16]

Abstractions are necessary for the reasoning process, as principles or generalities serve as deductive main premises, which will be discussed in detail in chapter nine.

## Thought

In the early oral society, individuals acted in accordance with the oral tradition, neither pausing for reflection nor generalization from instance to broader principle. Further, no distinction was made between parts of objects and the whole. Western logical reasoning developed as an individual activity, a process of conscious thought. Such activity happens only when one is self-conscious and when knowledge becomes something independent of oneself.

The mythic individual likely reasoned by unconscious "comparison," establishing a kinship between self and the mythic personage described by the oral tradition. The kinship was more than comparison; it was actually a relatedness in the sense of ancestry. Comparisons thus did not rest on notions of similarity, as they do in modern Western reasoning, but on an absolute identity—a person *is* the ancestor or the totem animal. As G. S. Kirk notes, oral narratives see the world in "personal and genealogical terms."[17]

By classical Greece, this absolute identity of comparisons is loosened, and comparison proceeds by means of similarity. In addition, Greeks begin to see nature as lawful, that is, following predictable sequences. This leads to the concept of cause and effect, which is central to modern Western thought. The notions of sequence, of causation, and of abstraction allow thinking that leads to new conclusions, that moves beyond the ever-present and ever-existent world of the early oral tradition. Snell argues that logic, as well as the notion of the soul, likely was implicit in Greek life before it became explicit in classical Greece. At the point at which it "intrudes into consciousness," human thinking is changed radically.[18] Mythical thought depends on receptivity; it involves passive acceptance of dream-like images. Logical thought involves an active seeking and a willful progression toward a truth that is separate.

This change of thought has been described as a movement from *mythos* to *logos*, that is, from the word as being to the word as representation or the logical form of expression. In the former, human thought unconsciously synthesizes, seeing the world as a whole. Individuals relate to these synthetic constructions by identifying with them. In the latter, the human quest to know is analytic.[19] Aristotle exemplifies this analytic, scientific view in the ancient Greek world; he is credited as the "father" of modern logic.[20] His writings are systematic descriptions; in the *Rhetoric*, for example, he classifies arguments and rhetorical strategies, making the art of rhetoric a logical system.[21]

Thus, the classical Greek mind, unlike its oral predecessor, has developed a sense of self, of an independent reality, of knowledge as separate from the individual, and of consciousness of thought. Both Heraclitus and the lyric poets who preceded him adopted *depth* as a metaphor, using it to describe thinking and knowledge. This metaphor has special significance to the change in state of mind, as Snell notes: "It is more than an ordinary metaphor; it is almost as if speech were by this means trying to break through its confines, to trespass on a forbidden field of adventure."[22] The metaphor reflected a virtual revolution of intellection which included, not incidentally, the displacement of the oral tradition and the so-called Homeric state of mind with a different system of education and a Platonic mindset. These changes likely were wrought by a combination of forces.

## Possible Agents of Change

Many agents converged to cause the dramatic changes in the Greek mindset in fifth and fourth centuries B.C. Among those changes were literacy, dialectic as an educational tool, and Platonism. The roots of the change, however, extend back into the Greek oral traditions themselves.

### Roots in the Oral Tradition

Although the separation of the oral mindset from that of the classical Greek was great, the myths of Greece contain the foundations of the modern Western mind and themselves were separated from the imitative magic of previous cultures. Merlin Donald traces the evolution of the modern mind from what he terms "episodic understandings," such as exhibited by apes and higher order animals, through a mimetic stage, at which point humans developed language. From this beginning stage, human intellect evolved to the mythic stage, then to the present stage of theoretical understandings. He argues that the mythic or oral-tradition stage was as large a change from the mimetic as the theoretical is from the mythic. The mythic stage featured narration, which allowed, among other things, improvement in the conscious manipulation of the mental modeling process. In addition, mythic narratives "gave events contextual meaning" and gave new structure and shape to experience.[23] The oral traditions, then, were integral to the development of theoretical understanding. As Snell describes it, the Homeric individuals did not feel controlled by irrational forces but by gods who created an ordered and meaningful world. The step to individual ordering and creation is a natural one.[24]

## Literacy

The development of the Western mind would not have been possible without certain changes in Greek society, and surely literacy is among the most significant. With writing comes the potential for release of self from the necessity of identification with the traditional narratives, for now the results of forgetting are not nearly so significant; memory can be refreshed by reference to a written record. All the individual and societal effort that has gone into memorization now is released for other tasks, among which are intellection and independent thought.

Donald describes the impact of literacy in modern, technological terms:

> Individuals in possession of reading, writing, and other visuographic skills thus become somewhat like computers with networking capabilities; they are equipped to interface, to plug into whatever network becomes available. And once plugged in, their skills are determined by both the network and their own biological inheritance. Humans without such skills are isolated from the external memory system. . . .
>
> The memory system, once collectivized into the external symbolic storage system, becomes virtually unlimited in capacity and much more robust and precise. Thought moves from the relatively informal narrative ramblings of the isolated mind to the collective arena, and ideas thus accumulate over the centuries.[25]

Writing serves more than a mnemonic function in the changing intellectual landscape of ancient Greece, however, for writing serves as a constant reminder of abstract and symbolic relationships.[26] The process of rereading and revising texts creates a sense, in ways that retelling a story cannot, of the distinction between the signifier and the signified. It helps to sever the link between the knower and the known, for the known, encoded in writing, now has an existence apart from the knower.

## Dialectic

Havelock suggests that the dialectic method used by Socrates also leads away from identification with the narrative and the merging of self and other. The dialogues of Plato involve Socrates dealing with one or more lesser intellects, leading that individual, by a series of questions, to some truth. Thus, dialectic separates the knower from the known, for it involves "asking a speaker to repeat himself and explain what he had meant."[27] That process breaks the performance; it requires a critical mindset, a self-conscious thought process. Questions break rhythm, involve non-imagistic responses, and require consideration, in a different form, of that which was stated.

## Platonism

Havelock credits Plato with delivering the final blow to the oral mindset of Greece. He does so not only by the dialectic method but by acknowledging the hold of the oral tradition on the minds of Greeks. For evidence of this claim, Havelock cites Plato's animosity toward poetry. In the *Republic*, Plato's description of an ideal society, poets are banned. From the perspective of contemporary Western society, his antipathy to poetry seems out of proportion to its power. However, the poetry to which Plato refers is the Greek oral tradition. Plato calls poetry "a corruption of the mind." To foment change, the hold of the oral tradition on the minds of Greeks must be released; the oral tradition becomes, for Plato, a type of disease—the antidote for which is knowledge of the true nature of things.[28] He feels he must rid the Greek educational apparatus of this effect in order to create his own educational system. This system—Platonism—contains the essential elements of the Western mind.

One tenet of Platonism is the movement from consideration of particulars to the contemplation of ideas. In order for that to happen, there must be an independent self capable of abstract thought. As Plato describes it, this thinking subject or personality involves the individual *psyche* or soul, which is divided into the power of learning, the spirit or will, and the "appetites" or desires. The will allies with reason to control the appetites, creating a harmonious whole.

Plato's point becomes very clear in Book Seven of the *Republic*, in which he discusses appropriate leadership for his ideal society. Rather than putting government in the hands of mere guardians, Plato announces the republic is to be led by intellectuals, by philosopher-kings. Only the latter have the analytic ability to come to a knowledge of the Forms, that is, the intelligence to critically examine the chimera of individual daily experience and to see beyond it, to the categories that lie in the realm of Truth.

Plato's parable of the line is an attempt to explain knowledge and the Forms. The parable compares the visible (things seen) with the intelligible (things thought). In the visible world in which human sight can operate, Plato identifies concrete objects and compares them to mere images, that is, shadows and reflections of objects. By analogy, he identifies the "true" objects in the realm of the intelligible, the world of thought. These true objects are the ideals, the Forms. If individuals have knowledge only of things seen, of individual objects in sensate reality, they have only a shadow or reflection of true knowledge. The Forms are the ideal categories of thought, which are represented only imperfectly in the visible world; individual trees or horses are but reflections of the ideal Form of tree and horse in this abstract world of thought. The "knowledge" obtained from the visible world is flawed; it is merely opinion (*doxa*). Only dialectic and philosophical reasoning can bring knowledge of the Truth, of the Forms.[29]

In another parable, that of the cave, Plato describes his ideas in a different manner. Imagine, if you will, humans who have spent their entire lives chained, unable to move, in a cave into which no light can enter. Behind these humans, unseen by them, is a fire. In front of the fire, but also unseen by the humans, someone parades objects and cutouts of people, trees, animals, and other objects. What these chained humans see is the flickering shadows caused by this parade of objects and pseudo-objects before the fire. As the humans cannot see the things as they truly are, they are convinced that what they do see, the flickering shadows on the wall of the cave, is reality. Eventually, one of the humans breaks his chains and escapes, leaving the cave and entering, for the first time, the world of sunlight and actual objects. After enjoying the variety and fulsomeness of this reality, he returns to the cave to tell his former fellow captives of the "truth." However, as is frequently the case, this prophet who challenges the beliefs of the society inspires only suspicion and fear. As those still chained see only shadows, they do not believe him, and they perceive him as a danger to their society and their way of life. Ultimately, they kill him.[30]

The implicit reference may be to Socrates as the person who brings truth to a society unwilling to hear. However, Plato's parable of the cave also illustrates his belief that truth lies not in what we see but in something beyond physical, observable reality, that is, in the Forms. Truth lies in ideal knowledge, not in empirical, sensate experience, which is merely shadows of the ideal, despite what our senses tell us. Intelligence and reason should inform the senses rather than the other way around.

In order to develop human intellect, Plato's educational program involved neither the process of learning the traditional narratives of the oral tradition nor the adding of new, specific information to the *psyche* but instead the opening of humans to the innate abilities within their intelligence, teaching them to think and to refocus their *psyches* to the service of reason. Havelock argues that the method Plato chooses to develop these abilities in the elite is the study of mathematics, including number and calculation.[31] Study of a system that does not depend on sensation but purely cognition sets into motion the processes of abstract thought. To understand a numerical relationship is to be aware of abstraction, of moving from the particular to the general; to adopt C.S. Peirce's terminology, it requires self-conscious understanding of thirdness. To accomplish thirdness involves apprehension of phenomena and ideas as separate from oneself, as something one can challenge, understand, and change. These ideas express general truths rather than describe specific aspects of immediate sensation. This development of an awareness of thirdness involves a rejection of the poetic identification that was so necessary to oral society.

The process of abstraction is at the heart of Plato's educational system and is essential to the Western mind. Constant reminders of the importance of the abstract and the conceptual come from Plato, who urges that the Forms rather than individual objects be the focus of a person's attention; thus he urges attention not to acts that are just but to justice, to the city rather than to things in the city, to the idea of bed rather than to a particular bed.[32] Such is the process of abstraction, which considers not individual instances but the concepts that capture their essences. Rules, laws, principles, and theories "exist" at this abstract level. They are essential to rational thought, and, according to Havelock, they are antithetical to the oral mindset in the Dark Ages of Greece.

One result of abstracting is the creation of ideas that cannot be visualized. In a detailed narrative, visualization of action is very easy. However, number, concepts, and Forms are not intellectualizable in a visionary mode. Concern with the abstract changes the nature of intellection, removing it to the level of pure thought. These abstracted essences become the objects of rational thought which, with a developing logic, constitute a system within which knowledge can be developed.

Abstraction also tears objects out of individual contexts, separating ideas from actions and actors, allowing concepts to be considered in intellectual isolation or with other concepts with which those individual items do not immediately appear. Indeed, intellection is taken not only out of individual contexts but out of time. Such timelessness is necessary to scientific theorizing, for scientific laws generally are held to be true irrespective of time. Abstraction replaces an imagistic discourse with a conceptual one. This is the basis for Plato's supreme discipline—philosophy. A philosopher is one who has an aptitude for intellection and abstract thought, one who loves knowledge.

Plato's insistence on the conceptual and his accompanying

educational apparatus operated to separate the knower from the known. This is the basis for the rationality that is found in modern Western societies, a rationality not possible in the oral society that existed in Greece during the Dark Ages. A parallel description of the change in mind from oral to literate societies is discussed as the development of consciousness, drawing largely from psychological studies.

## The Development of Consciousness

Another version of the evolution of the Western mind concerns the development of *consciousness*. Although definitions of this term vary, essentially consciousness is awareness, more specifically, individuals' awareness of themselves in their surroundings. Currently, the notion of consciousness is much debated. The discussion centers on whether consciousness is explainable entirely in physical terms, as activities of the brain, or whether some aspects of consciousness are best discussed in so-called mentalist terms.

### Nature of Consciousness

Understanding consciousness as a nonphysical existence finds roots in Descartes' notion of the *cogito*, which is the thinking self that he discovered as a result of his famous thought experiment. If some evil force made everything you think false, could you be sure of anything? Yes, says Descartes, even if everything you believe to be true is false, the one thing about which there is no doubt is the self, which is thinking even if the thoughts are false. Thus, his famous adage—"I think, therefore I am." Descartes sets the *res cogitans*, that is, consciousness and subjective experience, in opposition to the physical world—the *res extensa*.[33] This view of consciousness identifies the *mind* as something not reducible to the brain.

Modern science is most comfortable with the *res extensa*, with physical explanations.[34] In this world, consciousness increasingly is deemed to be nothing more than activities of the brain.[35] Thus biologists and many psychologists claim that the study of neuronal activity in the brain eventually will lead to a complete understanding of consciousness, eliminating the need for the mind/brain dualism involved in descriptions of consciousness as a mental phenomenon, thus exorcising once and for all the Cartesian ghost.

Whichever of these two notions are accepted, consciousness is deemed only one aspect of human mental activity. In a controversial theory, Julian Jaynes, in his book *The Origin of Consciousness in the Breakdown of the Bicameral Mind*,[36] suggests that the characteristic of consciousness has developed in humans over time. Further, he claims that consciousness is not necessary for human existence. Consciousness is not the opposite of the unconscious state of someone who has received a bump on the head. Rather, he argues, it contrasts to that "non-conscious" state of someone who is driving down the road, all the while thinking about something else. The portion of the human that successfully navigates the road (although fifteen minutes later, no memory of that process exists) is operating in a non-conscious state. In that non-conscious state, argues Jaynes, humans can function, do work, learn, and carry on quite adequately. Thus, consciousness is not necessary to most human activity, including thinking. For example, Jaynes argues that one can make judgments, such as determining which of two things held in either hand is heavier, without conscious reflection.

Indeed, some things are accomplished much better without consciousness, according to Jaynes. Accomplished musicians do not consciously think about fingering or other actions of playing an instrument—they act almost instinctively. A basketball player who begins consciously fretting when his shot is "off" is much less likely to get it back than those who merely keep shooting, hoping to regain the rhythm that makes the shot almost "automatic." Becoming "conscious" of physical activities may disrupt their operation.

Consciousness, then, is a specific mental state involving images, ideas, and actions within the brain. Jaynes describes this notion of consciousness as composed of several mental abilities.

**Spatialization**.   Consciousness involves mental space, which is inhabited. Individuals, when conscious of a particular item, have the ability to imagine things spatially. If you think of five different items—a jeep, Pikes Peak, a banana split, Mother Theresa, and a safety pin— they are spatially separated in your mind as you focus on each one. Events, locations, and actions can be "seen" spatially in consciousness, even if they are not perceived spatially by the senses. The example Jaynes gives of this is time—which Westerners tend to see linearly, with the past stretching out to the left and the future, to the right.

**Excerption**.   In consciousness, humans never "see" all of something; instead, we excerpt parts of events, just as we experience only a part of the sense data that bombards us at any given moment. To illustrate: think about an event you attended in the past—a birthday party, a gathering of family or friends, a community event—and remember what you can of it. That which you "see" in your consciousness is an excerpt of the events. If you become conscious of a soccer game you once attended, you will excerpt from all aspects of that event only portions. The way in which you excerpt any given experience affects your attitudes towards things; for example, you may excerpt your mother as insensitive and mean while your brother may excerpt her as good, caring, and kind. As Jaynes notes, "we are never conscious of things in their true nature, only of the excerpts we make of them."[37]

**Analog I**. In our consciousness, we can move about, doing things. While you read this text, probably seated somewhere inside a building, imagine yourself driving along an interstate highway. Look to your right, outside your window, and "see" a range of snow-capped peaks. Now, turn left, and look at a meadow with a white wooden fence around it, thoroughbred horses grazing on freshly mowed green grass. Now look ahead, at the car in front of you, and sense the motion of your car, moving through this imaginary territory. Thus, consciousness contains an analog of your own experience in life.

**Metaphor Me**. Further, you are able to step back, become the third party, and see yourself—taking an omniscient point of view. You can see yourself seated in that car. Now, still "outside" your body, watch yourself pull to the side of the road, exit the car, and walk around, checking each tire to see if you have a flat. You are creating, in your conscious mindspace, a metaphor of yourself.

**Narratization**. You also have the ability, in this conscious mode, to create a story connecting your sensations. When you lie in bed at night, if you hear a noise outside, you can create an entire narrative associated with that noise. You can imagine a terribly dangerous person, lurking in the dark, holding a knife or gun, waiting until you are asleep, when he will pounce! As he lurks in the dark, he stubs his toe on your bicycle, which causes the sound you have heard. Although none of this "actually" happened, you can "see" the entire narrative in your imagination.

**Conciliation**. Not only can the conscious mind create a narrative but it also can bring together items that do not exist together. For example, if you imagine the Rocky Mountains, then the Pacific Ocean, you can bring them together in consciousness, although they do not exist together in fact. You can "people" a room with individuals who have never met each other, then put that room in a house, in a town, where none of those people have ever been.

Jaynes argues that the state of mind in certain very early oral societies is what he calls "bicameral." Among the characteristics of the bicameral mind is the absence of "mindspace" in which narratization, conciliation, and the other characteristics of consciousness can occur. As an example, he points out that characters in the *Iliad* do not sit down and think what to do or feel guilty after doing it, which he argues requires the mindspace which he has described as being central to the modern state of consciousness.

In a sense what Jaynes is describing as consciousness is the *cogito*, Descartes' thinking self. This independent, thinking self is what creates modern Western individualism, and it may be partially a function of writing, for literacy plays a role in encouraging free thought, skepticism, questioning—items which are the bases of Western rationality. Certainly consciousness is a function of language. Jaynes notes that although consciousness "is not all language," it is "generated" and "accessed" by language.[38]

Jaynes argues that the very process of abstraction, which happens on the basis of metaphors, is linked to the development of consciousness. "In early times, language and its referents climbed up from the concrete to the abstract on the steps of metaphors, even, we may say, created the abstract on the bases of metaphors."[39] This happened because words that originally had very limited and specific referents were used metaphorically to describe new and broader concepts. As they used metaphors to describe concepts, humans began to "see" connections in the world, and understanding things as relationships increased human powers of perception. For example, from the *leaf* on a tree, humans moved to turning a new *leaf* in life, which is a much broader concept. Jaynes quaintly describes this process: "Abstract words are ancient coins whose concrete images in the busy give-and-take of talk have worn away with use."[40] Jaynes further illuminates his ideas by calling theory a metaphor; similarly, says Jaynes, the conscious mind is a metaphor of the real world—and the structure of the world is "echoed" in the structure of consciousness.

Walter Ong argues that, as humans can accumulate knowledge, they gain more conscious understanding of the cosmos as well as control over it. Humans in early oral society had myths to integrate the cosmos into their "lifeworld"; they did not need and perhaps did not develop self-consciousness to the degree modern humans have.[41] Jaynes attributes the development of consciousness to literacy, the weakening authority of traditions and gods, natural disasters resulting in migration, and conquest, which brought different cultures into contact with each other. He, like Havelock, finds the real roots of Western consciousness in classical Athens:

> The Greek subjective conscious mind, quite apart from its pseudostructure of soul, has been born out of song and poetry. From here it moves out into its own history, into the narratizing

introspections of a Socrates and the spatialized classifications and analyses of an Aristotle, and from there into Hebrew, Alexandrian, and Roman thought. And then into the history of a world which, because of it, will never be the same again.[42]

# Legacy of the Greeks

The intellectual tradition begun in ancient Greece is the foundation of those developments which formed the modern Western mind. The Greeks set us on a course of critical inquiry, exploring the world of objects and the world of ideas. Among the assumptions that the contemporary West inherited from the Greeks are: 1) reality is ordered, thus empirical understanding is possible; 2) knowledge is a combination of human reason and empirical observation; 3) the search for truth must be ongoing and critical; 4) human opinion (*doxa*) is fallible and must be constantly analyzed, challenged, and updated; 5) causes are natural and observable rather than supernatural; and 6) a deeper reality also exists, apprehension of which satisfies the soul.[43] Plato's search for Forms and ideal truth is balanced and tempered by Aristotle's identification and classification of particulars. Thus, the West is bequeathed a tradition of metaphysical speculation and skeptical observation as modes of intellection.

# Summary

Our quest to understand the modern Western mind begins in Greece, in the ancient struggle to evolve from the oral-tradition mindset to that of classical Athens. Jaynes' description of consciousness is not unlike Havelock's and Snell's descriptions of the self-conscious knower who is able to think abstractly and who conceptualizes. In all three cases, literacy and the use of abstract concepts lead eventually to the state of mind found in those who were born and raised in the modern West. These accounts lay groundwork for understanding this Western mind.

This change in the collective state of mind is analogous to changes Joe Mondragon brings to the mindset of the poor Hispanic people of Milagro, New Mexico, when he irrigates his beanfield in John Nichols' novel, *The Milagro Beanfield War*. In New Mexico, like many arid Western states, water is a scarce and precious commodity. Developers must have water to build subdivisions, which often involves buying the water rights of farmers, causing agriculture literally to "dry up" as cities expand. As Joe, an impoverished, feisty farmer, contemplated his beanfield, shriveling during a drought, and thought about the swimming pools in the nearby wealthy subdivisions, he flouted the 1935 Interstate Water Compact, which had reallocated the water in the creek that flowed next to his beanfield to monied interests in southern New Mexico and Texas, and began irrigating his beanfield. The book concerns the political upheaval and tense standoff which follows this illegal act. The crisis forces all parties to think about their lives, particularly those ideas and the very existence they previously have taken for granted. The ultimate result of his illegal irrigation is to create a sense of pride and power in the minds of the Hispanics of Milagro, a change that made a difference even as their lives continued much as they had for centuries.

The changes in the Greek mind came to the modern West in a less-than-direct manner. The transmission of the mindset of classical Athens was affected by various historical events as well as the development of communication technologies.

## Endnotes

1. Bruno Snell, *The Discovery of the Mind: The Greek Origins of European Thought*, trans. T. G. Rosenmeyer (1953; rpt. New York: Harper & Row, 1960) 123.
2. Eric A. Havelock, *Preface to Plato* (1963; rpt. New York: Grosset & Dunlap, 1971) 197.
3. Snell 17.
4. *The Presocratics*, ed. Philip Wheelwright (New York: Odyssey, 1966) 72, which is a translation of fragment 45 in Hermann Diels and Walther Kranz, eds., *Die Fragmente der Vorsokratiker* (1934; rpt. Berlin: Weidmann, 1960). See also Snell 17.
5. Havelock 198.
6. Even the existence of Homer is in doubt. Some have suggested that several individuals set the Greek oral traditions to writing.
7. Snell 44.
8. Jerome Bruner and Susan Weisser, "The Invention of Self: Autobiography and Its Forms," *Literacy and Orality*, ed. David R. Olson and Nancy Torrance (Cambridge: Cambridge UP, 1991) 146.
9. Havelock 200.
10. Snell 94, 107.
11. Snell 111.
12. *The Presocratics* 33; fragment 18 in Diels and Kranz. See also, Snell 139.
13. *The Presocratics* 69; fragment 35 in Diels and Kranz.
14. Herodotus, *The History of Herodotus*, trans. George Rawlinson, *Great Books of the Western World*, ed. Robert Maynard Hutchins, vol. 6 (Chicago: Encyclopedia Britannica, 1952) II 44.
15. Snell 144.
16. Snell 112.
17. G. S. Kirk, "Orality and Sequence," *Language and Thought in Early Greek Philosophy*, ed. Kevin Robb (La Salle, IL: Monist, 1983) 86.

18. Snell 213.
19. Alexander S. Kohanski, *The Greek Mode of Thought in Western Philosophy* (Cranbury, NJ: Associated UP, 1984) 17–18.
20. Tony M. Lentz, *Orality and Literacy in Hellenic Greece* (Carbondale, IL: Southern Illinois UP, 1989) 168.
21. Lentz 170.
22. Snell 18.
23. Merlin Donald, *Origins of the Modern Mind: Three Stages in the Evolution of Culture and Cognition* (Cambridge, MA: Harvard UP, 1991) 268.
24. Snell 22.
25. Donald 311.
26. Lentz 4.
27. Havelock 208.
28. Plato, *Republic*, trans. Paul Shorey, *The Collected Dialogues of Plato*, ed. Edith Hamilton and Huntington Cairns (1961; rpt. Princeton: Princeton UP, 1973) X 595b.
29. Plato VI 509–11.
30. Plato VII 514–16.
31. Havelock 230.
32. Havelock 217.
33. Rene Descartes, *Meditation on First Philosophy*, trans. Laurence J. Lafleur, 2nd ed. (Indianapolis: Bobbs-Merrill, 1960).
34. Alastair Hannay, *Human Consciousness* (New York: Routledge, 1990) 3.
35. See, for example, Daniel C. Dennett, *Consciousness Explained* (Boston: Little, Brown, 1991) and Ray Jackendoff, *Consciousness and the Computational Mind* (Cambridge, MA: Massachusetts Institute of Technology P, 1987).
36. Julian Jaynes, *The Origin of Consciousness in the Breakdown of the Bicameral Mind* (1976; rpt. Boston: Houghton Mifflin, 1990).
37. Jaynes 61.
38. Jaynes 49.
39. Jaynes 51.
40. Jaynes 51.
41. Walter J. Ong, *Interfaces of the Word: Studies in the Evolution of Consciousness and Culture* (Ithaca, NY: Cornell UP, 1977) 43.
42. Jaynes 292.
43. Richard Tarnas, *The Passion of the Western Mind: Understanding the Ideas That Have Shaped Our World View* (New York: Harmony, 1991) 69–71.

# Chapter Eight

# Evolution of the Western Mind

The evolution described in this chapter was by no means an unbroken continuation of the intellectual changes begun in ancient Greece. Instead, the development of the Western mind was a plodding and precarious process. For great periods of history, a significant number of Western humans were not able to read nor did they have access to the discoveries or thoughts of the Greeks. The story of the tenacity of Greek ideas and their eventual renaissance and revision is a story of Western civilization as well as a story of the development of communication technologies.

## Western Civilization

To reduce to a summary the vast expanse of people, ideas, and events in the period ranging from ancient Greece to the modern West is a gross oversimplification of that history. However, even this cursory tracking of Greek ideas and learning will give some sense of the path by which these items arrived on our modern doorstep. Even better, it may encourage additional study of this history in considerably more depth.

### Hellenic World

Although the political power of Greece waned when Alexander the Great of Macedonia created an empire encompassing most of the

ancient West and Near East, Alexander—himself a student of
Aristotle—promoted Greek language and ideas, and populations of non-
Greeks became Hellenized by Greek culture. This Hellenic period lasted
through Alexander's successors up to the rule of the Roman Emperor
Augustus, and it included three major Hellenistic kingdoms—Egypt,
Macedonia, and the Seleucid empire, including Asia Minor, Iran, Syria,
Mesopotamia, and Afghanistan. During the third century B.C.,
Alexandria became the center of Hellenistic culture. It was the site of
the most famous library of antiquity, one which contained the largest
collection of Greek works anywhere. Ancient sacred books were
translated into Greek in Alexandria, including the Jewish Old
Testament, the translation known as the Septuagint. Throughout
Hellenistic kingdoms, rulers subsidized public education and culture,
with an emphasis on Greek learning, including rhetoric.

## Roman Empire

Following this period, the Romans conquered much of the eastern
Mediterranean, beginning over eight hundred years of Roman rule.
Rome's political might, however, outstripped its intellectual
achievement; much of Roman culture was borrowed from, or imitated,
the Greeks. For example, scholars such as Cicero created Latin texts
that were heavily influenced by Greek writings. During the Augustan
Roman empire in the first century A.D., the four Christian Gospels were
drafted and the new religion, with its blend of Judaic and Platonic ideas,
spread rapidly throughout Asia Minor, Egypt, Greece, and Rome. Also
during the Roman period, the status of women began to change,
although significant change was to take many, many centuries.[1]

During the third century, the Romans made a concerted effort to wipe
out Christianity, which was attracting too many converts. In the fourth
century, however, Constantine let persecution of the Christians lapse;
he also reunited the Roman empire and moved the capital to
Byzantium, which was renamed Constantinople. Constantine seized
vast sums from pagan churches, giving some of the plundered wealth
to Christians. During his reign, many lavish churches were built, from
Rome to Jerusalem, and Christianity prospered. For the first time, two
great powers existed within the Roman empire—church and state. Once
in power, Christians began persecution of "heretics," both pagans and
Jews. The growth of the Church accompanied a growth in church
property and personnel. By Justinian's reign, high church officials lived
in lavish style, and a power struggle broke out between religious leaders
in Rome and those in Constantinople.

## Middle Ages

The Middle Ages lasted from approximately 395 to 1500. Early in this period, Greek ideas were adopted by Christians, notably St. Augustine, whose views on rhetoric were described in chapter three. Thus, Christianity played some role in perpetuating classical culture, bringing it to the "barbarians" at the edges of the empire. The Christian tradition outlasted the Romans; the western Roman empire began to fall to invaders from the North during the fifth century. The eastern empire lasted until 640 A.D., when the Arabs took Egypt.

The Church became the intellectual authority in medieval Western Europe after the decline of the empire. It dominated, by conversion, the Germanic and Scandinavian pagan tribes, leading to the triumph of orthodoxy; nearly all of Western Europe was Catholic, and even the calendar revolved around the birth of Jesus. However, literacy largely was limited to the religious elite, as scholarship lost political patronage in the wave of invasions that changed the political landscape—Vikings from the north, Moslems from the south, and Magyars from the east. In addition, communication was difficult without centralized rule. It was left to the monks and nuns of the Church, specifically in the monasteries and in some cases the cathedral libraries, to preserve writing and a few classical texts. For example, Boethius' translations and digests of Aristotle's logic and other Greek texts were copied in the monasteries. Islamic expansion, particularly the capture of Alexandria, had cut off access to most Greek texts; however, Church teachings, particularly the notions of individual freedom and responsibility, laid the foundation for a later rebirth of Greek ideas in Western culture as a whole. According to Richard Tarnas: "While in classical times the introspective life was characteristic of a few philosophers, the Christian focus on personal responsibility, awareness of sin, and withdrawal from the secular world all encouraged an attentiveness to the inner life among a much wider population."[2]

More significant than the Church in Rome in the continuation of classical learning, however, was the Eastern Roman empire. Constantinople was the greatest of Christian cities, with incomparable wealth and influence. Not until the city was sacked in 1204 by the crusaders sent by Rome did its influence wane. Classical learning also was kept alive, to an even greater degree, by the Arabs. In the early ninth century, the Arabs began a major push to translate ancient Greek (frequently using Syriac translations rather than original Greek) and other texts into Arabic, sometimes searching as far as Constantinople for manuscripts. By the middle of the eleventh century, most of Aristotle's works had been translated into Arabic. Thus, the West owes much to the Arabs for saving Greek learning in mathematics, natural sciences, and metaphysics.

The middle of the medieval period saw a cultural revival. Referred to as the "Carolingian renaissance," it saw the wane of feudalism. The work of Boethius and that of Martianus Capella led to a revival of logic. The educational curriculum of the period was the Seven Liberal Arts— the Trivium included grammar, logic, and rhetoric; the Quadrivium included geometry, arithmetic, astronomy, and music. Scholars in the West translated into Latin a nearly complete corpus of Aristotle, preserved by the Arabs and Byzantines; in addition, the West recovered other Greek works as well as Arabic commentaries on Greek texts. This period also saw the rise of the university and the formation of guilds. After early bans on pagan teachings, the universities were allowed access to the newly translated Greek texts. Scholastic philosophers such as Thomas Aquinas confronted faith with reason, and they and rising secular thinkers paved the way for the Scientific Revolution.

After this relatively prosperous period, the fourteenth and fifteenth centuries were beset by famine and plague, beginning with the Black Death of 1347 to 1350. Peasant revolts were widespread, and the Church split in the Great Schism, with election of rival popes for Avignon and Rome. At the same time, however, more commoners were becoming educated, challenging the domination of the literate clergy. The birth of the modern Western worldview was imminent, awaiting only the Renaissance, the Reformation, and the Scientific Revolution.

## Renaissance, Reformation, and Scientific Revolution

The end of the Middle Ages came with the rise of Humanism in Italy. One key element of Humanism was secular and widespread education. This period, named "the Renaissance" by the Humanists themselves, lasted roughly during the fifteenth and sixteenth centuries. The Humanists viewed the medieval period as "dark ages" and sought to "revive" classical thinking and culture. This included a revival of the languages of antiquity. The rhetorical works of Italian Humanists, including Vico, are discussed in chapter three. During the Renaissance, kings asserted their absolute sovereignty throughout the North. Also, the Europeans became aware of the New World and began plundering its riches and, in some cases, enslaving its native populations. The period was not one of dramatic growth, however, as the plagues continued into the fifteenth century, as did an economic slump. Further, the Catholic Church had become both decadent and corrupt, with ecclesiastic conspiracy and intrigue the norm. However, this period also saw the rise of powerful cities, including Antwerp, Lisbon,

London, Lyons, and Augsburg. It was a time of religious mysticism as well as technological invention, among the most important of which was the movable type.

The second significant movement of the period following the Middle Ages was the Reformation, which began in 1517 when Martin Luther posted ninety-five theses against indulgences (remissions from punishment of sin, which were sold to believers) on a church door. During the next fifty years, a handful of religious individuals shattered the unity of Western Christendom, denied the authority of Rome, and founded new "Protestant" churches and sects. In the process, the papacy itself was saved by internal reforms. One of the tenets of the new Protestantism was individual access to the Bible, for the believer could find salvation only through the Holy Scripture, not by the intervention of the Catholic Church. Tarnas elaborates:

> Protestantism's reclamation of the unalterable Word of God in the Bible thus fostered in the emerging modern mind a new stress on the need to discover unbiased objective truth, apart from the prejudices and distortions of tradition. It thereby supported the growth of a critical scientific mentality. . . . But in time, the Word itself would become subject to that new critical spirit, and secularism would triumph.[3]

The Scientific Revolution began with Copernicus, who called into question the Church-blessed prevailing view of the solar system by suggesting a sun-centered universe. Although little immediately became of this idea, the new Gregorian calendar adopted by the Church was based on Copernicus' ideas. Later, however, opposition mounted, beginning with Protestant reformers who argued that the theory contradicted Scripture. Soon it was deemed a threat to the entire Christian view of the cosmos. When Galileo constructed a telescope and added his astronomical observations to the other evidence supporting the Copernican theory, he published his findings. The response was severe. The book was banned, Galileo was forced to recant, and he was placed under house arrest. Those who espoused the Copernican view were deemed atheists and were dismissed from their posts and banished. However, Galileo's writings were smuggled out of Italy and into the northern part of Europe, where the next stage of the Scientific Revolution would occur.

In England and France, new ideas radically altered the Western intellect. Skeptical of mathematical and Aristotelian syllogistic logic, Francis Bacon proposed an inductive logic, which started from the analysis of data and moved to general conclusions. Deductive reason, he argued, imposed the biases of accepted general premises upon observation; however, induction allowed for unbiased observations, thus creating the potential for new empirical discoveries. Rene Descartes, whose discovery of the *cogito* was discussed in chapter seven, took the opposite position from Bacon, arguing that mathematics could be used to reason from self-evident principles. Only by that means could one reach absolute certainty. The self-evident proposition is the existence of the *cogito*, the "first principle and paradigm of all other knowledge."[4] From this point, Descartes reasoned to God's existence, then to the existence of the objective world, guaranteed by God. Although Descartes privileges deduction, by moving from human reason to the existence of God rather than the other way around, he freed science from religious dogma. Finally, Isaac Newton combined the ideas of Descartes, Galileo, and Johann Kepler (who posited laws of planetary motion) and identified gravity as a universal force. Thus, as a result of the Scientific Revolution, humans could study and comprehend the workings of an orderly universe, using that knowledge for their own betterment. In this universe, human intelligence was the centerpiece of creation. Upon this foundation was the Enlightenment born.

## Enlightenment

The Enlightenment, roughly covering the period of the seventeenth and eighteenth centuries, built upon the Scientific Revolution by using reason to discover knowledge useful to human society. A variety of thinkers, including John Locke, David Hume, Adam Smith, Immanuel Kant, Voltaire, and Benedict de Spinoza, were the first of the modern age, and they added philosophical, political, and economic ideas to the scientific understandings developing in the wake of the Scientific Revolution. This intellectual development paralleled technological and social changes, as well as industrial and democratic revolutions, that mark the beginning of the modern Western mind. This intellectual transformation, beginning in classical Greece and extending to the contemporary West, would not have been possible, however, without the development of communication technologies.

## Communication Technologies

In one sense of the word, all communication requires technology. Oral communication requires certain human organs to create and interpret sounds. Writing, printing, and electronic media, however, more frequently are cited as communication technologies. These technologies have had a significant impact on the development of the

Western state of mind. The influence of writing technology on human communication and society was discussed in Part Two of this text as well as in chapter seven. In this section, the influences of all these technologies are reviewed, including the electronic media that have made possible Marshall McLuhan's "global village."

## Pictorial Representations

The first visual encoding significantly predates writing. Although isolated examples are much older, so far as we know at present, visual representations began to be common in Africa, Europe, Australia, and Asia approximately 40,000 years ago. These included engravings or carvings on bone and ivory. About 25,000 years ago, painting and drawing skills are identifiable from archeological findings; figurines, clay sculptures, and tokens were common in groups living approximately 15,000 years ago. These visual representations do not seem to be a necessary consequence of oral language, although the development of language is a necessary precedent for development of pictorial representations. Further, pictorial representations apparently are not necessary and sufficient precursors of writing, as about only one language in ten ever had a written form; in other words, many societies which developed pictorial representations did not develop writing.

Scholars believe that pictorial representations developed in relationship to the ceremonial and mythological life of a group; the images apparently have great religious significance. Merlin Donald argues that the pictures are not truly symbolic. He suggests that number signs were among the first truly visual *symbols*, as they display the element of arbitrariness that, for example, a carving of a human figure does not.[5] Only with the development of writing does the new form of human consciousness discussed in chapter seven develop.

## Writing

Writing is such a powerful change in a society that, at its development, frequently humans regard it with awe or ascribe to it magical powers. In some societies, only special groups, such as the clergy, are allowed to learn to write. As writing becomes more widespread but not universal, literacy is a craft practiced for compensation.[6]

Writing extends human communication across geographical area and time, giving a permanence to the spoken word. Whether the writing is etched in stone, on paper, or some other material, the fixedness of communication allows for the development of a very different society than one dependent upon the communication technology of the human voice. Although writing is not, as some claim, necessary for civilization, writing clearly is necessary for industrial, bureaucratized society.[7] Historically, the appearance of writing is simultaneous to significant development in transportation, arts, commerce, and government in most societies. Mesopotamian urban civilization relied on writing on clay tablets. The monarchies of Egypt and Persia were made possible by writing, as was the Roman Empire. The Chinese civilization, medieval Europe, and the nineteenth-century Fulani kingdoms in West Africa also depended upon writing. Certainly modern industrial nations would not be possible without writing technology.[8]

With writing, although not immediately and not inevitably, comes a host of societal changes. Among these are economic development, as writings are critical for commerce; the rising power of secular and religious leaders, who can document their right to power and issue edicts over large areas; the creation of institutions of education, which supplant the teachings of the minstrel; the beginning of history, as the permanence of writing lends stability to stories about the past; the growth of science, as observations can be recorded, compared, and shared; and the development of abstract reasoning.

The process of writing forces attention on language. Although oral societies may have some visual means of permanently encoding information, such as pictorial representations, such means do not focus attention on language. Writing changes the very nature of language. When language is written down, humans can separate it from themselves and think about it. Once humans develop writing, language can become an object of study; individuals can categorize such things as grammar, syntax, and other linguistic elements.[9] As a result of distancing oneself from language, human consciousness is heightened.[10]

A related effect of writing is that, unlike oral-communication technology (which is a social event), writing isolates. Both the act of writing and the act of reading are solitary, individual events. This also aids the development of self-consciousness; the individual focus is internal—thinking about what one will write and how and analyzing what one has read. As Ong notes, writing is a "solipsistic operation."[11]

On the other hand, memory becomes largely external to the individual. As noted in chapter five, oral people had prodigious memories. Literate individuals rely on external, semi-permanent records for memory. This shift is reflected in the change in rhetorical instruction. In ancient Rome, instruction in rhetoric involved five canons—invention, disposition, style, delivery, and memory. By the sixteenth century, rhetorical textbooks listed only four, omitting memory.[12] By writing down ideas, humans preserved them in the public record; at a later date, these ideas could be improved or refined. Only because of writing, for example, were the ideas of the classical Greeks preserved for modern civilization.

Writing also may be a necessary precursor to what Donald calls the "theoretic culture." He argues that the human mind, freed by external memory devices and self-consciousness, now could reflect upon its own representations and modify them. The first "devices" in the development of theoretic culture were analogs, that is, models of things such as astronomical cycles, time, and space. Stonehenge in England is such an analog. Some of these analogs predate writing, but they are very early *systems* of knowledge. Once writing developed, these early systems evolved into deliberate and analytic uses of symbolic thought.[13]

The development of so-called "learned" languages also resulted from writing. In oral societies, individual groups developed dialects and offshoots of languages. Writing cannot represent each idiosyncratic dialect; one is chosen, privileged, and becomes the standard or learned language. In the case of Latin, vernaculars—the early forms of Italian, Spanish, French, and other Romance languages—existed in various parts of Europe around 550 to 700. Written Latin, however, was the learned language—preserved by the Catholic Church, the state, and the schools. Most individuals in Europe were not literate, thus had no access to learned Latin. Instead they spoke one of the many dialects of the emerging Romance languages or a Germanic, Slavic, or non-Indo-European language. Only those who attended school, which limited education by and large to males, had access to the language of science and industry. Writing controlled learned Latin while new languages proliferated orally from a Latin base. Ong notes the results:

> Learned Latin was a striking exemplification of the power of writing for isolating discourse and of the unparalleled productivity of such isolation. . . . [It] effects even greater objectivity by establishing knowledge in a medium insulated from the emotion-charged depths of one's mother tongue, thus reducing interference from the human lifeworld and making possible the exquisitely abstract world of medieval scholasticism and of the new mathematical modern science which followed on the scholastic experience. . . . Modern science grew in Latin soil, for philosophers and scientists through the time of Sir Isaac Newton commonly both wrote and did their abstract thinking in Latin.[14]

Ruth Finnegan argues that writing has so permeated the West that individuals in Western culture are preoccupied with written forms, and that this preoccupation colors notions of education, art, and scholarship. Among the resulting beliefs are that something which is written has more value than something oral, which is not worthy of scholarly study. Even music, she argues, is associated in the West with the written form. Thus music that is not inscribed is not serious music. Ask members of a choir or orchestra if they "have 'their music,' " and they will assume you mean the sheets of printed notated text.[15]

The importance of writing to the development of human culture is hard to overestimate. Orality can produce memory, narratives, and forms of understanding unavailable to literate people. However, the evolution of human consciousness requires both orality and, from it, the growth of literacy. The importance of writing comes not with what writing does to individuals but what individuals do with writing.[16] Writing is just the beginning; it is the necessary but not sufficient condition of these changes. Among the other necessary conditions is the change in consciousness associated with literacy, as discussed in chapter seven. In addition, none of the above changes attributed to writing likely would have occurred without the development of printing technology; only with print does widespread literacy become possible.

## Printing

The invention of printing spawned another communication and information revolution. In the Far East, block printing was invented in the eight century, and by the ninth century it was used for printing books. Since Chinese script is based on signs for words (ideograms), block printing was much more feasible in the Near East. The base unit of the alphabet, the letter, is so small that it is difficult to carve on blocks, thus making block printing a less useful technology in the West. Therefore, only with the invention of movable type by Johann Gutenberg in the fifteenth century did printing become a significant technology in the West.[17]

The invention of a lightweight material upon which to print was as important to the development of printing as block or movable type. In the West, parchment preceded paper, but it was too expensive for printing books in quantity. Each copy of an early Bible would have required the skin of three-hundred sheep. Although the Chinese invented paper in approximately 105, its use and manufacture did not come to Europe until the twelfth century and not to England until the fifteenth.[18] Only with the availability of paper was the potential for printing by movable type truly realized.

When printing arrived, it moved human culture from the reliance on script to text. One of the most significant things about printing is the repeatability of the text, allowing many copies of the same work. Further, those copies, unlike painstakingly hand-written copies, are guaranteed to be the same. In addition, printed texts are easier to read. Thus, the increased availability of accurate, easy-to-read texts was a significant cause of the spread of literacy among the masses and the rise of the middle class. As a result, the print revolution affected far more people than did the writing revolution; literacy no longer was the monopoly of rulers, priests, or the privileged.

The Reformation is linked to printing, as the presses made possible the wide availability of the Bible. Elizabeth Eisenstein suggests that the relationship between the development of printing and Protestantism was a mutual one. Certainly the availability of Bibles aided in the Lutheran revolt; however, she argues that the drive to "spread the Gospel and to convert the infidel" created a need for printed materials that spurred the development of printing presses.[19] The presses also changed the economic system, as markets and trade networks developed. Eisenstein claims that printing changed fundamental human understandings, developing tolerant and ecumenical points of view—views that were characteristic of the Enlightenment. Thus were orthodoxy and society changed forever by the printing press.[20]

Many aspects of the modern world resulted from printing. According to McLuhan, until 1700, more than half of all printed books were works from ancient or medieval times. The printing press shifted boundaries of culture, encouraging writers and enabling the creation of new information. The notion of an author was boosted, as the author's works now could be widely available. McLuhan also argues that printing led to nationalism, as unifications of populations were "unthinkable before printing turned each vernacular into an extensive mass medium."[21] The social result of printing, he claims, is uniformity. This drive for uniformity comes in many varieties—language, experience (as larger groups of people experience the same music, literature, and information), and beliefs.

Many other developments accompanied printing, For example, dictionaries were created, which led to an emphasis on correctness in language. Print created a sense of ownership in words, leading to copyright laws and printing monopolies. Availability of print made ideas powerful and subversive, so governments created systems of censorship to keep certain "dangerous" ideas away from the public. Further, as reading is a solitary activity, print also led to the need for personal space and privacy. In addition, print furthered the development of self. Ong argues that print "encouraged human beings to think of their own interior conscious and unconscious resources" as things and to think of mind as a sort of mental space.[22] He goes so far as to argue that knowing orally is different from knowing through print. Print isolates information on a page, making knowledge seem definitive and confined. It gives a sense of closure.[23] David Payne argues that the literacy generated by print leads to a particular way of viewing the world:

> [T]he events of literacy are necessarily individual, psychological, and interior. The permanence of the written word and piety toward "The Word" could facilitate development of a kind of "gyroscope" in one's inner, privately experienced character. In Western culture, literacy culminates in the individual's ability to experience the word of God directly, rather than through an outer institution or the oral transmission of a priest. Literacy leads to individual access to science and discovery, and it fosters the kind of independent moral substance presumed in modern notions of democracy. The experience of knowing through literacy is private, personal, and involves the internalization of knowledge within the individual consciousness. Literate consciousness is one in which individual responsibility (through guilt) could insure the common mores and participation of diverse people disconnected in time and space.[24]

The technology of printing likely is the essential key to the modern Western mind. Eisenstein argues that printing allowed various texts to be considered "side by side"; it ensured that texts could be studied without the necessity of transcription; it widened enormously the range of available material for study; and it broadened the data pool, as "identical images bearing identical labels" could be issued to widely scattered observers. Thus, printing was essential to the Scientific Revolution. With printing, "[t]he closed world of the ancients was opened, vast expanses of space (and later of time) previously associated with divine mysteries became subject to human calculation and exploration."[25] Whether the changes resulting from electronic communication technologies will eclipse those resulting from printing remains to be seen.

## Electronic Media

The effects of the electronic media on the world and the Western mind are significant. From radio to the latest communication technologies, electronic media have changed many things, including the ways in which humans interact with each other, the nature of Western culture, and perhaps even the ways in which we think. These and other effects may determine the nature of the Western mind in the twenty-first century.

The development of radio marks the beginning of the electronic era. Radio combines the extension of communication, which began with print, with the oral situation. Thus, the size of an audience listening to a speaker is extended from the range of the speaker's voice to the globe and beyond. As Havelock notes, the "potential of the oral spell had been reasserted after a long sleep."[26] Radio developed rapidly during World War I; however, its impact on the public was most notable during World War II, when Franklin Roosevelt's "fireside chats" and Adolf Hitler's speeches exerted powerful influences over widespread audiences. McLuhan also argues that radio technology, which is acoustic (designed for the ear), revived some of the oral aspects of communication from nonliterate cultures. McLuhan's ideas are based on his famous but frequently criticized statement, "the medium is the message," by which he means the technology of communication influences in significant ways the content of what is communicated and its effect on humans. McLuhan notes, "the 'message' of any medium or technology is the change of scale or pace or pattern that it introduces into human affairs."[27]

Television reintroduced the visual into long-distance, nearly instantaneous communication. With television, political activity has come full circle from the Athenian democracy, which relied on debate and oratory before large audiences; to the print era, in which pamphlets and newspapers carried reports of political activity to the most distant boundaries of a country, where citizens had never seen nor heard politicians and government officials; to the electronic era, in which Presidential candidates debate before national television audiences, and C-SPAN carries live, gavel-to-gavel congressional debate and deliberation. Unlike the Athenian model, however, the electronic audience is freer to wander, both mentally and physically, and changing a channel is much easier than leaving a crowded forum. Thus, the modern television era is the era of the sound bite, of performers and performances, and of entertainment.

Further, radio and television are not the only electronic media. Just as significant in the last decade of the twentieth century are computers, VCRs, fax machines, multimedia, and many other communication technologies. Computers, like print, rely on the visual, and they isolate the individual from human contact. Unlike print, however, they are interactive, allowing intellectual contact by means of words on a screen, creating a dialogue rather than the monologue inspired by print. Interactive video may be available to most Western individuals in the near future. Fax machines add incredibly rapid transmission of a facsimile nearly equivalent to a printed copy. As Stewart Brand notes, "A global computer is taking shape, and we're all connected to it."[28]

The effects of these and other communication technologies are many. During the Gulf War, Saddam Hussein, along with the rest of the world, followed the progress of the bombing of Baghdad by watching CNN.

During demonstrations in Tiananmen Square, Chinese student dissidents communicated with the world by means of fax machines. No longer can a country remain isolated nor its citizens remain unaware of activities elsewhere in the world; the electronic media know no geographical nor political boundaries. Perhaps the most famous discussion of this phenomenon is by McLuhan, who argues that technology, particularly electronic media, has created a "global village." Human beings are made aware not only of the existence but the lifestyles and ideas of humans literally around the globe. Just as print encouraged larger groupings of people, so electronic media encourage globalization, according to McLuhan:

> The immediate prospect for literate, fragmented Western man encountering the electric implosion within his own culture is his steady and rapid transformation into a complex and depth-structured person emotionally aware of his total interdependence with the rest of human society. . . . Fragmented, literate, and visual individualism is not possible in an electrically patterned and imploded society.[29]

Although the world is "shrinking," as McLuhan suggested, events in Eastern Europe and the former Soviet Union during the early 1990s did not follow his predicted pattern—the global community will not necessarily be harmonious, as nationalistic tendencies and religious animosities certainly have not disappeared.

Further, electronic media have changed the nature of community in ways not predicted by McLuhan. Historically, community is defined geographically. However, in the electronic era, professional communities develop, linked by telephone, professional journals, computers, audio and video recordings, and other technologies allowing communication or common cultural experiences.[30] These groups, which Melvin Webber calls "cosmopolites," are communities that transcend space: "[t]hey share a particular body of values; their roles are defined by the organized structures of their groups; they undoubtedly have a sense of belonging to the groups; and by the nature of the alliances, all share in a community of interests."[31] Alvin Toffler predicts, in *The Third Wave*, that the costs of electronic media soon will be less than the costs of commuting, resulting in individuals working from their homes, recreating a geographical community.[32] Gary Gumpert, however, disagrees, suggesting that Toffler's "electric cottages" may produce isolated individuals who, although committed to McLuhan's global community, have little contact with or commitment to the neighborhood community.[33]

Electronic media also have influenced Western culture. One aspect of early radio and television that was very different from printing was the loss of control by the audience. A reader can read at her or his convenience. Without VCRs, the television audience is limited to the schedules of programmers. With the advent of VCRs, a new phenomenon has resulted—the "collectible performance." Gumpert explains:

> What is novel is the collection of audio/visual *performances*. . . . Whereas, at one time, only symbolic representations of a performance existed in the form of scripts and scores, now the performance itself is reproducible. The collectible performance began with the phonograph record. While motion picture film was used to record performances, as well as being an artistic performance in its own right, it had not become part of each home's entertainment, educational, and intellectual repository. It is only now as motion pictures are being stored in video cassettes that renting, borrowing, or buying a film has become commonplace.[34]

Thus performances that formerly existed only in the memory of those who had viewed them now can be "brought to life" at will.

A related cultural effect of electronic media is that economics drives culture. When the electronic media are privately owned, ratings determine what information and entertainment gets produced. Some argue that the result is a leveling effect; predictability is favored over uniqueness as networks and stations are unlikely to risk profits on new, unproven formats. The result is what scholars are calling "mass" or "popular culture," which is distinguished from "high" culture such as opera, ballet, and museums. High culture historically has been associated with the elite; mass culture may be a democratizing influence. Dwight MacDonald notes:

> Like nineteenth-century capitalism, Mass Culture is a dynamic, revolutionary force, breaking down the old barriers of class, tradition, taste, and dissolving all cultural distinctions. It mixes and scrambles everything together, producing what might be called homogenized culture, after another American achievement, the homogenization process that distributes the globules of cream evenly throughout the milk instead of allowing them to float separately on top. It thus destroys all values, since value judgments imply discrimination. Mass culture is very, very democratic: it absolutely refuses to discriminate against, or between, anything or anybody. All is grist to its mill, and all comes out finely ground indeed.[35]

On the other hand, electronic media have made high culture available to the masses, should they choose to view an opera on public television, listen to classical music on public radio, or purchase their own compact disc or videocassette of some performance. Thus, individuals who are unlikely to attend such performances in large concert halls have access to them in a mediated form.

The result is that individuals, in the privacy of their own homes and sometimes simultaneously, experience the same cultural events, whether they are deemed "high" or "popular." Thus a common experience is available to those who do not know each other, an experience that transcends political and geographical boundaries. This phenomenon extends beyond the United States and, indeed, beyond the West. As the United States is a major exporter of television programming, the charge of cultural imperialism follows the worldwide clamor for American music, fast food, and clothing—a demand created in part by the electronic media.

Yet another cultural effect of electronic media may be the elimination of distinctions among groups of people. Social groups, divided by age, status, and situation, formerly had different worldviews. Joshua Meyrowitz argues that this resulted from reading different literatures, thus having different intellectual experiences. Further, in face-to-face interactions, social groups tend not to integrate, thus giving different groups different experiences. In the electronic age, however, the experiences of social groups overlap, particularly as a result of television. He notes, "restructurings of social arenas and social performances are at least a partial reason for recent social trends, including the blurring of conceptions of childhood and adulthood, the merging of notions of masculinity and femininity, and the lowering of political heroes to the level of average citizens."[36]

Some writers suggest that this social restructuring is leading to the disintegration of U.S. society. Chapter one features Kenneth Burke's definition of a human being, including the phrase "goaded by the spirit of hierarchy."[37] Richard Weaver, whose rhetorical theory is discussed in chapter three, agrees that hierarchies are central to human existence but argues that Western society ought to be based on particular hierarchies.[38] He argues that piety, the respect for others demonstrated through discipline, must play an important role in human life. According to Weaver, this piety involves acceptance of one's rightful place on the hierarchy. Distinctions are so important to Weaver that he challenges the very notion of equality, arguing that it is a "disorganizing concept" that "attempts a meaningless and profitless regimentation of what has been ordered from time immemorial by the scheme of things."[39] For example, he challenges the "foolish and destructive notion of the 'equality' of the sexes."[40] Weaver likewise believes in distinctions between classes and among professions, for people interact best when "they know their position."[41] If all this is a result of the electronic media, then communication technologies are causing what Weaver calls "flight from center," the disintegration of society that results from abandoning a cultural vision based on distinction. Thus would he criticize the democratic tendencies of electronic media noted by MacDonald, Gumpert, and others.

The electronic media also may be changing our fundamental conceptions of the world. This relates, in part, to the democratizing effects, particularly of television. Meyrowitz notes that media have different access codes. Audiences for print are limited by literacy and level of education and reading ability, as books and periodicals vary in language difficulty. On the other hand, television by and large is accessible to people of all ages and backgrounds. Although they may interpret televised messages in different ways, both oral and literate individuals have access to the medium.[42] As a result, television can bring information to everyone who is watching.

The electronic media also may shape our views of particular groups, such as women, the elderly, minorities, or the police. Further, these media may desensitize individuals to violence or may be responsible for inculcating particular societal values. As Richard Harris notes, "Media affect our minds—they give us ideas, change our attitudes, tell us what the world is like. These mind-changes, that is, our perceived reality, then become the framework around which we interpret the totality of experience. Thus media consumption is basically a cognitive phenomenon."[43]

Many scholars have suggested other possible effects of television. For example, Kathleen Jamieson and Karlyn Campbell suggest that television concentrates the power that comes from controlling information in the hands of an anonymous few.[44] Further, news coverage now shapes events; political demonstrations in a far corner of the earth will be orchestrated solely to make the evening news in a Western country, particularly the United States. Some scholars charge that the electronic media are obliterating common-sense distinctions of time and space. Gumpert argues that reality becomes relative. The audience often is not told whether an event is broadcast live or taped; in addition, the distinction between "reality" and dramatization also is fuzzy. Indeed, even reality which is edited becomes a different experience from an unedited version. Unlike print, in which the activities of author and editor are apparent, in television, both are hidden from view. "The lack of apparent concern over this specific issue suggests the degree to which we have abdicated sensory responsibility."[45]

Another effect of the electronic media is the decreasing ability of political authorities to control knowledge. When the newest technology is writing, scribes cannot copy many books. Thus, control of the information flow is relatively easy, as subversive information is reduced to whispers. Attempts to control information when radio and television signals know no boundaries, when satellites can beam messages anywhere in the world, when telephone lines can carry text and link computers, is nearly impossible. The masses have gained unprecedented access to information. "Computers, telephones, radio, and satellites," notes Ithiel De Sola Pool, "are technologies of freedom."[46]

They also may be technologies challenging individual privacy. As research methods employed by marketing and advertising firms become more sophisticated, subliminal tyrannies become more likely. The new technologies also are allowing data collection to grow at an alarming rate. Tremendous amounts of personal information about your family, your credit history, your academic records, your reading and video watching habits, and other details are widely available in some electronic form. Individuals cannot hide in the global village, and the West faces immediate challenge not only from "uncontrolled excesses" of communication technology but also the "unholy alliance" between the electronic media and private corporations.[47]

Thus, influence of electronic media in the late twentieth century remains to be finally evaluated. However, the conquering of political boundaries, the blurring of social and educational distinctions, the creation of new ways of seeing the world, and the challenge to censorship are among the significant effects. Further, these effects vary; the media influences are different in, for example, developing countries than in the West.[48]

## Summary

The evolution of the modern Western mind resulted from a combination of things. Classical Greek thinking was preserved for the modern West by various groups and institutions, including the Arabs in Alexandria, scribes in Church monasteries, Alexander and Constantine, and the development of Christianity. The rise of science and the teachings of Protestantism also had profound effects on Western thought. The development of communication technologies was both concurrent with and necessary to these historical events. Just as writing changed human consciousness from the state of mind in oral society, print allowed common people to have access to ideas, and it challenged the intellectual authority of both church and state. The effects of the electronic media remain to be fully understood; however, the challenges to culture, individual privacy, and geographical community are balanced by the potential for global interaction and understanding and unparalled access to information.

Not all ideas have such a profound impact on society as those described in this chapter, and not all effects of new ideas and technologies are beneficial. In the film, *The Gods Must Be Crazy*, by South African filmmaker Jamie Uys, a coke bottle is tossed from an airplane and lands in the very isolated village of a Bushman tribe. The unique object causes a stir in the village; it also brings jealousies and conflict into what was a harmonious and giving society. To avoid further harm from this new object, Xixo, a tribesman, takes the bottle and begins a long walk to "the end of the world," to throw the bottle over the edge.

Thanks in part to communication technologies, the Greek ways of viewing the world and the further developments of the mind wrought by the Reformation and the Scientific Revolution are still present in Western society. Although these ideas are expressed in all aspects of life, they are seen no more clearly than in our Western modes of thought.

## Endnotes

1. Elise Boulding argues that the year 200 B.C. is the dividing line between the oppression of antiquity and the more open societies of Europe. Among the liberating influences, she claims, is the early Christian movement. Elise Boulding, *The Underside of History: A View of Women through Time* (Boulder, CO: Westview, 1976) 340.
2. Richard Tarnas, *The Passion of the Western Mind: Understanding the Ideas That Have Shaped Our World View* (New York: Harmony, 1991) 168.
3. Tarnas 242.
4. Tarnas 277.
5. Merlin Donald, *Origins of the Modern Mind: Three Stages in the Evolution of Culture and Cognition* (Cambridge, MA: Harvard UP, 1991) 280–87.
6. Walter J. Ong, *Orality and Literacy: The Technologizing of the Word* (New York: Methuen, 1982) 93–94.
7. Gelb claims, "Writing exists only in a civilization and a civilization cannot exist without writing" (emphasis omitted). I. J. Gelb, *A Study of Writing*, rvd. ed. (Chicago: U of Chicago P, 1963) 222.
8. Ruth Finnegan, *Literacy and Orality: Studies in the Technology of Communication* (New York: Basil Blackwell, 1988) 18.
9. Eric A. Havelock, *The Muse Learns to Write: Reflections on Orality and Literacy from Antiquity to the Present* (New Haven: Yale UP, 1986) 112–13.
10. Ong 82.
11. Ong 101.
12. Ong 116.
13. Donald 339–43.
14. Ong 113–14.
15. Finnegan 124–25.
16. David R. Olson, "Introduction," *Literacy, Language and Learning: The Nature and Consequences of Reading and Writing*, ed. David R. Olson, Nancy Torrance, and Angela Hildyard (New York: Cambridge UP, 1985) 15.
17. Finnegan 26–27.
18. Thomas Francis Carter, *The Invention of Printing in China and Its Spread*

*Westward*, 2nd ed. (New York: Ronald, 1955) 132–38.

19. Elizabeth L. Eisenstein, "On the Printing Press as an Agent of Change," *Literacy, Language, and Learning: The Nature and Consequences of Reading and Writing*, ed. David R. Olson, Nancy Torrance, and Angela Hildyard (New York: Cambridge UP, 1985) 27.

20. Eisenstein 29.

21. Marshall McLuhan, *Understanding Media: The Extensions of Man*, 2nd ed. (New York: New American, 1964) 155–61.

22. Ong 131–32.

23. Ong 133–34.

24. David Payne, "Characterology, Media, and Rhetoric," *Media, Consciousness, and Culture: Explorations of Walter Ong's Thought*, ed. Bruce E. Gronbeck, Thomas J. Farrell, and Paul A. Soukup (Newbury Park, CA: Sage, 1991) 227–28.

25. Elizabeth L. Eisenstein, *The Printing Press as an Agent of Change: Communications and Cultural Transformations in Early–Modern Europe*, vol. 2 (Cambridge: Cambridge UP, 1979) 685–87.

26. Havelock 31.

27. McLuhan 24.

28. Stewart Brand, *The Media Lab: Inventing the Future at MIT* (New York: Viking, 1987) 33.

29. McLuhan 59.

30. Gary Gumpert, *Talking Tombstones and Other Tales of the Media Age* (New York: Oxford UP, 1987) 179.

31. Melvin M. Webber, "The Urban Place and the Nonplace Urban Realm," *Explorations Into Urban Structure* (Philadelphia: U of Pennsylvania P, 1964) 109–10.

32. Alvin Toffler, *The Third Wave* (New York: William Morrow, 1980) 210–11.

33. Gumpert 185–89.

34. Gumpert 27.

35. Dwight MacDonald, "A Theory of Mass Culture," *Mass Culture: The Popular Arts in America*, ed. Bernard Rosenberg and David Manning White (Glencoe, IL: Free Press, 1957) x.

36. Joshua Meyrowitz, *No Sense of Place: The Impact of Electronic Media on Social Behavior* (New York: Oxford UP, 1985) 5.

37. Kenneth Burke, *Language as Symbolic Action: Essays on Life, Literature, and Method* (Berkeley: U of California P, 1960) 15–16.

38. Indeed, Weaver argues for specific hierarchies that likely were impressed upon him by his childhood in the old South. He claims that "[t]he American South not only had cherished the ideal but had given it an infusion of fresh strength, partly through its social organization but largely through its education in rhetoric and law." Richard M. Weaver, *Ideas Have Consequences* (1948; rpt. Chicago: U of Chicago P, 1976) 55.

39. Weaver 42.

40. Weaver 177.

41. Weaver 43.

42. Meyrowitz 74–81.

43. Richard Jackson Harris, *A Cognitive Psychology of Mass Communication* (Hillsdale, NJ: Lawrence Erlbaum Associates, 1989) 246.

44. Kathleen Hall Jamieson and Karlyn Kohrs Campbell, *The Interplay of Influence: News, Advertising, Politics, and the Mass Media*, 3rd ed. (Belmont, CA: Wadsworth, 1992) 8.

45. Gumpert 53.

46. Ithiel de Sola Pool, *Technologies of Freedom* (Cambridge, MA: Harvard UP, 1983) 226.
47. N. D. Batra, *A Self-Renewing Society: The Role of Television and Communications Technology* (Lanham, MD: UP of America, 1990) 36.
48. Meyrowitz 69.

# Chapter Nine

# The Rational Paradigm

The notion of Western rationality, like most other aspects of the Western mind, has roots in classical Greece, particularly in Aristotle. Upon that basis, philosophers and argumentation scholars have developed rules that describe and prescribe the use of language to arrive at conclusions. This study of reasoning historically was known as logic and was divided into two major categories—deduction and induction. More recently, some scholars have limited the term *logic* to formal logic, that is, to deduction, which focuses on validity and certain conclusions and eschews notions of probability. Induction, the method of science, is concerned with identifying the most likely conclusions rather than with validity or mathematical certainty. Also, some scholars have challenged the application of traditional logic to practical reasoning, resulting in the development of argumentation theory. Thus, the study of rationality no longer is limited to formal logic.

Although a complete analysis of deduction, induction, and argumentation is beyond the scope of this text, a basic understanding of these topics is useful in the study of rhetoric and its relationship to the contemporary Western worldview.[1] The chapter begins with a section on the so-called *laws of thought* at the foundation of Western rationality and with a taxonomy.

## Foundations of Western Rationality

For centuries, logicians have posited three laws as the basis of rationality. These laws rely upon the notion of a *concept*, which is defined as the mind's abstracted notion of objects in reality. Thus, the concepts of the mind range from nouns (*tree, poem, worldview*) to verbs (*run, study, contemplate*). The concept in question might be either a *particular*, such as *Hannah Arendt*, or a *universal*, such as all *women*. The relationship among concepts, according to the fundamental laws of thought, follow the laws of identity, noncontradiction, and excluded middle.

The *law of identity* is expressed as "A = A." This law holds that a concept has some unchangeable essence at its core which allows particular instances of the concept to have identity. Thus, an "apple is an apple"; a "game is a game"; and a "woman is a woman." In the Western tradition of rationality, were these concepts not somewhat constant, then communication and reasoning would not be possible.

The *law of noncontradiction* holds that "something cannot be both A and not A." This law is a correlative to the law of identity—for one concept to have identity with another, it cannot, at the same time, be something contradictory to that concept. Thus this law is an "axiom of consistency."[2]

The *law of the excluded middle* says that a concept must be one thing or not that thing—no middle ground existing. This is expressed as "everything is either A or not A." Thus, an object either is a horse, or it isn't a horse; it either is alive, or it isn't.

Modern Western logic and rationality are based on these three laws. Further similarities in contemporary theories of deduction, induction, and argumentation are the terms that are shared by these fields. Understanding the basic terms provides a foundation for the study of logic and practical reason.

A *proposition* is a statement about some state of affairs. It is an assertion, denial, or the like, that is, a statement that something "is the case." Thus, propositions have the potential to be established as true or false. Following are examples of propositions: 1) *All humans have the potential for language*; 2) *Some histories exclude women*. Propositions involve not the words of a sentence but the meaning of those words. Therefore, the following two sentences express the same proposition: 1) *All humans are mortal*; 2) *All humans will die eventually*. Similarly, propositions are not specific to a language. The following sentences express the same proposition: 1) *La mesa es verde*; 2) *The table is green*. Propositions can be true or false. If, in the example above, the table in question is red, the statement is, nonetheless, a proposition; it is a false proposition.

An *inference* is the process of arriving at a proposition on the basis of one or more other propositions. One infers that *Allesandro has a cold* (a proposition) based upon another (*Allesandro sneezed*). If *Carmela is a human being*, and since *human beings are mortal* (two separate propositions), you can infer that *Carmela will die eventually* (a third proposition).[3] A major concern of logic and theories of rationality is identifying rules for determining whether such inferences are warranted.

An *argument* is two or more propositions, some of which are given as grounds for concluding another. Those propositions serving as the basis for the conclusion are called, variously, *premises*, *data*, or *grounds*. The *conclusion* or claim is based on these. The *premises* of an argument are the bases upon which an inference is made. A *conclusion* is that proposition, or that portion of an argument, which one is asked to infer. Certain words may indicate or introduce a conclusion: *therefore, hence, consequently, then, thus, so*. An argument made by those who oppose the death penalty is:

> Taking the life of another human being is immoral.
> The death penalty involves taking the life of another human
>   being.
> Therefore, the death penalty is immoral.

The latter proposition, the conclusion, is based upon the former propositions, the premises.

*Probability* concerns the chances that something is true. The chances of heads appearing on any flip of a coin involves questions of probability. Aristotle argued in the *Rhetoric* that human affairs were in the realm of the contingent or the probable; therefore, rhetoric was useful in determining probable truth in policy, law, and other realms of human activity.[4]

Although the terminology is similar in discussions of both deduction and induction, the nature of the reasoning process is distinct. In the next sections, discussions of deductive logic and inductive reasoning suggest, in broad outline, the nature of both forms of reasoning.

## Deduction

A deductive argument involves a conclusion which is entailed in the premises, that is, the conclusion is derived directly from information already present in the premises. Deductive arguments, if valid and if based on true premises, are always true. A deductive argument is valid if it follows particular rules for its form.

### Syllogism

Deductive arguments may be expressed as syllogisms, with the *categorical syllogism* commonly used as illustration. The following categorical syllogism is the classic, overused, and sexist example:

> All men are mortal.
> Socrates is a man.
> Therefore, Socrates is mortal.

Other types of deductive syllogisms exist. For example, a syllogism can be disjunctive:

> Either the sun will come out or Ian will not go skiing.
> The sun did not come out.
> Therefore, Ian will not go skiing.

A syllogism also can be conditional:

> If Lisa does not pass this course, she will not graduate.
> Lisa did not pass this course.
> Lisa will not graduate.

Arguments that are syllogistic in form are not always expressed completely. For example, when Geraldine Ferraro was selected by the Democrats to run for Vice President with Walter Mondale, some editorial writers made the following claim during the campaign: "Ferraro should not be elected Vice President because she made a mistake on her income tax return." When completely expressed, the argument is a syllogism:

> No person who makes a mistake on his or her income tax return
>   should be elected Vice President.
> Ferraro made a mistake on her income tax return.
> Therefore, Ferraro should not be elected Vice President.

Aristotle calls arguments in syllogistic form that use implied premises held by the audience *rhetorical syllogisms* or *enthymemes*.[5]

Logicians, over the centuries, have devised rules to determine the validity of deductive arguments. These rules are based on the form of the syllogism; if the form is correct, the deductive inference will be warranted. These rules take several forms and are expressed in a variety of ways. If certain forms, that is, relationships, are present, then the reasoning is valid. For a deductive conclusion to be true, the premises must be true *and* the syllogism must be valid. Because the following syllogism does not follow the rules for validity, true premises do not lead to a true conclusion:

> Some men are feminists.
> Some feminists bear children.
> Therefore, some men bear children.[6]

One criticism of deduction is that it does not lead to new conclusions—the information in the conclusion is contained in the premises. British logician Stephen Toulmin described this problem with the following syllogism:

> Anne is one of Jack's sisters;
> All Jack's sisters have red hair;
> So, Anne has red hair.[7]

Deductive premises must be true for the conclusion to be true. In order to know that these premises are true, either the sisters must be in sight of the arguer or the arguer must already know that Anne has red hair, making the exercise of argument a bit silly. That is Toulmin's point: the rules for formal logic cannot be applied to anything but analytic statements, which are rare in practical argument. Francis Bacon,[8] in the late sixteenth and early seventeenth century, and John Stuart Mill,[9] in the nineteenth century, made similar points, arguing that deduction does not involve reasoning to new premises and therefore is unsuitable for scientific reasoning and for making discoveries about nature. Induction, on the other hand, allows an inference from certain propositions or data to a conclusion that goes beyond the premises; induction thus leads to new knowledge.

## Induction

Induction came to prominence in the late sixteenth century, with Bacon and Mill providing leadership in developing inductive methods. Induction is the method of science—reasoning from known facts or premises to a conclusion that goes beyond, or is more general, than the premises. To borrow Toulmin's example, if you know that Jack's sister Anne has red hair, and that his sister Theresa has red hair, and that his sister Colleen has red hair, you might, by inductive reasoning, arrive at the conclusion that all of Jack's sisters have red hair. General propositions are inferred from particular facts and observations. A scientific hypothesis is nothing more than a proposed conclusion, which is tested. When a large enough number of observations without relevant negative instances are obtained, then the conclusion is put forward as probably true.

For Bacon, reasoning includes inventing or discovering arguments, judging arguments, memorizing arguments, and communicating arguments.[10] If reasoning begins with the facts of experience, it is inductive. To invent, he argues, is "to discover that we know not, and not to recover or resummon that which we already know" (which is the method of deduction).[11] To reason inductively, he suggests a scientific method that collects and "present[s] to the understanding all the known instances which agree in the same nature" and also presents to the understanding negative instances, that is, "instances which do not admit of the given nature." His method then involves comparison, experimentation, and questioning, allowing probable conclusions to be drawn.[12] Thus, with Bacon, arrives a change in the conception of knowledge and rationality; the former emerges from a methodical investigation of nature and the latter involves reasoning based on something other than proofs from preexisting "knowledge."

To understand inductive reasoning, one can review some of the types of inductive arguments. A significant amount of everyday reasoning is inductive; indeed, many of what we deem "deductions" by Sherlock Holmes actually were inductions. Among the types of inductive arguments common in practical reasoning are argument by analogy, argument from example or enumeration, and argument from cause or effect.

An argument by *analogy* involves comparison of one situation, about which we have certain information, to another situation, arguing that the two are analogous; therefore, the information which is true in the first situation likely will be true in the second. For example, if I argue that Canada has a system of socialized health care that is beneficial to Canadian citizens, therefore a similar system in the United States would be beneficial to U.S. citizens, I am arguing by analogy. The conclusion of such an argument does not have the certainty of a deductive conclusion. Instead, it is more or less probable. Argument by analogy also may proceed by means of metaphor, as when, in "The Study in Scarlet," Dr. Watson discovers, to his chagrin and amazement, that the brilliant Sherlock Holmes knows nothing about literature, philosophy, or astronomy, and very little about politics. Holmes' defense:

> [A] man's brain originally is like a little empty attic, and you have to stock it with such furniture as you choose. A fool takes in all the lumber of every sort that he comes across, so that the knowledge which might be useful to him gets crowded out, or at best is jumbled up with a lot of other things, so that he has a difficulty in laying his hands upon it. Now the skilful workman is very careful indeed as to what he takes into his brain-attic. He will have nothing but the tools which may help him in doing his work, but of these he has a large assortment, and all in the most perfect order.[13]

Analogy is a frequent means of inference. For example, when we buy particular brands of automobiles or shoes because of the performance of a different automobile or pair of shoes of the same brand, we likely are reasoning by analogy. Similarly, individuals who avoid relationships because they were hurt in a prior relationship are basing their behavior on analogical reasoning.

Just as the conclusions of analogical arguments are not claimed to be absolutely true, so the tests of such arguments are not absolute. However, the likelihood or probability that an analogical argument leads to true conclusions may be tested by asking—are the two situations really analogous? That is, are the number of relevant similarities in the two situations high and significant as compared to the relevant dissimilarities?

An argument from *example* or *enumeration* involves a list of items which have certain characteristics in common. The conclusion of such an argument is that the characteristic will always be found in such an item. For example, if you meet Anne, Theresa, and Colleen, Jack's sisters, and see that they all have red hair, you may conclude that all of Jack's sisters have red hair. Or, after biting into five apples out of a bag, you may claim that all the apples in the bag are rotten. In "The Red-headed League," Holmes inferred that a man had been in China based on the fish tattooed above his right wrist, which was stained in a manner peculiar to China, and on the Chinese coin hanging from his watch chain.[14]

The tests of conclusions based on examples or enumerations are: 1) is the sample size sufficient?; 2) are the samples representative?; and 3) are negative instances accounted for? In other words, if you take three apples, coming from the top, middle, and bottom of a medium-sized grocery bag, and then take two more, all of which are rotten, you reasonably may conclude that all the apples in the bag are bad. If you visit Jack's house and see three red-headed women and one blonde, but you learn that the blonde is a friend of Jack's sister Colleen, you have accounted for the negative instance, thus making your conclusion that all of Jack's sisters have red hair a probable one.

*Cause and effect* arguments involve the notions of necessary and sufficient conditions. A necessary condition means that a certain item or situation must exist before something else can exist. If a jar of milk is knocked off the table, it is necessary that some external force was applied to the jar—be it the wind, the cat, little Susie, or whatever. Not all necessary conditions, however, are sufficient conditions. For example, it is a necessary condition for snow to fall that the temperature be near or below freezing. However, that is not a sufficient condition for snow, as many very cold days are bright and without precipitation. We use the term *cause* in both instances, which confuses the very distinct causal notions of necessity and sufficiency. In "The Adventure of the Blue Carbuncle," Holmes attempts to determine why a gentleman ran away from a policeman. The gentleman, who was walking along a city street carrying a plucked goose over his shoulder, was set upon by ruffians. When he raised his walking stick to fend them off, he accidentally smashed a shop window. When a policeman rushed up to assist him, the man fled, leaving his goose and his hat. Holmes was not satisfied that breaking the window would cause the man to flee the policeman. However, when he discovered a stolen diamond lodged in the body cavity of the goose, Holmes knew he had discovered the cause of the man's flight.[15]

Some conclusions about cause and effect are based on repeated observations. If the presence of X brings about Y repeatedly, in a variety of circumstances, at some point, a conclusion is warranted that X causes Y. Mill criticized this method of inferring causes, suggesting instead what has come to be known as "Mill's Methods of Inductive Inference." These five methods, in very simplistic terms, experimentally vary the circumstances of observation in order to determine whether the purported cause appears, disappears, and varies in intensity in conjunction with the phenomenon.[16] A hypotheses thus can be tested to confirm or deny the causal relationship it asserts.

Inductive arguments are useful to the discovery of new knowledge. Although scientific principles, which are the product of induction, are only probably true, if the number of observations upon which they are based are many, and so long as we notice no negative instances, we behave as if such principles were true. Many scientific hypotheses, however, are not directly verifiable, for they involve unobservable entities and highly speculative notions.[17] That which "disproves" a scientific conclusion frequently is the identification of anomalies—phenomena unpredictable or unexplainable by the scientific hypothesis or theory.[18]

Some modern philosophers have attempted a calculus of induction, based upon the notion of probability, which is designed to give to some forms of induction a systematic formality akin to deduction.[19] Although probability defined as frequency makes such calculations possible, the unpredictable nature of scientific discovery and inductive reasoning concerning things other than regularly occurring instances (such as a coin toss or roll of the dice) likely always will distinguish induction from deduction. Further, mathematical formulations of either deductive logic or inductive reasoning are not useful in describing everyday argument. For Bacon, you will recall, the art of inductive logic involved communicating (that is, elocution, which includes the arts of grammar and rhetoric) as well as inventing arguments. This acknowledgement of the role of rhetoric in rationality is precursor to the modern view of argumentation.

## Argumentation

Argumentation theory attempts to describe practical argument and set standards for evaluation in ways that avoid the dilemma of the absolutism in formal logic on the one hand and complete relativism on the other. The field has become "the study of the logical forms underlying ordinary language claims, disputes, and debates."[20] In addition, it has grown to include not only "argument-as-product" but "argument-as-process."[21]

Although a number of scholars, including Mill and C. S. Peirce, have contributed to this discussion, scholars who have significantly influenced argumentation theory are Stephen Toulmin and Chaim Perelman. Toulmin's work is an effort to extend some of the rigor of formal logic to arenas in which argument is not so certain, such as law, science, and moral choice—the arenas of human understanding. He attempts to create a logic of Aristotelian probabilities, which he calls "substantial" logic, that acknowledges the role of context in practical argument. Whether arguing in the legislature about appropriate policy, in the courts about questions of fact, or in public concerning questions of value, such arguments require an inference from data to claim.

Perelman and his associate, Lucie Olbrechts-Tyteca, focus on the techniques of persuasion involved in argumentation, which is why they call their argument theory a "new rhetoric." According to them, a theory of argument should be "the study of the discursive techniques allowing us to induce or to increase the mind's adherence to the theses presented for its assent."[22] They argue that formal logic is insufficient to explain practical reasoning. One of the distinctions they cite between demonstration and argumentation is that the latter is concerned with an audience. Math and formal logic ignore context; argumentation does not. As they suggest, "[t]o engage in argument, a person must attach some importance to gaining the adherence of his interlocutor, to securing his assent, his mental cooperation," for facts do not speak for themselves.[23] Thus, a significant distinction between contemporary argumentation theory and the theories of induction and deduction reviewed previously is the attention given to context, specifically to audience and to argument fields.

## Audience

Perelman and Olbrechts-Tyteca contextualize their theory of argument by emphasizing audience. They identify audiences that transcend those physically present at a rhetorical event. Instead, they define an audience as "the ensemble of those whom the speaker wishes to influence by his argumentation."[24] This audience is a mental construct of the speaker rather than actual auditors either present for a speech or reading a text. Perelman and Olbrechts-Tyteca specifically identify the *particular audience*, which is the group of people a speaker is trying to persuade. The particular audience may be the audience gathered before an orator, if that is whom he wishes to persuade. On the other hand, a speaker may be attempting to influence those not present, in which case the wider group would comprise the particular audience. For example, Newt Gingrich and other members of Congress used to give late-night fiery speeches before an empty chamber, knowing C-SPAN was carrying the proceedings live. The particular audience was the people watching television, unaware the speaker was addressing empty chairs. An essayist may be writing for posterity rather than those who will read her work in the near future. Further, a speaker before a generally hostile audience may be trying to influence only those who have not made up their minds on the issue. In that case, the particular audience is a subset of the persons present. The speaker or writer chooses the particular audience he or she wants to influence. The key to argumentation is the audience, for the adherence of the audience is the aim of practical argument: "Every argumentation is addressed to an audience, large or small, competent or less competent, which the speaker seeks to persuade."[25]

## Fields

Toulmin's discussion of contexts relates not to audience but to argument fields, that is, the arena in which the argument functions. What counts as a good argument may differ significantly between, for example, the field of religion and the field of politics. When examining practical argument, Toulmin suggests we distinguish between items that are *field dependent* and those that are *field invariant*. Formal logic suggests that all aspects of argument are field invariant, a claim Toulmin challenges. Instead, in his substantial logic, he identifies structure as a field-invariant aspect of argument and other items, such as criteria of modal qualifiers, as field dependent.

**Field Invariant**.   A significant field-invariant aspect of argument is its structure. Toulmin's best-known contribution to modern argumentation theory is his *layout of argument*, in which he identifies the parts of any practical argument, that is, the parts of substantive justifications for claims. The six potential parts of any substantive argument are: data, warrant, claim, modal qualifier, rebuttal, and backing for warrant.[26]

The two most basic parts of any argument are the *data* and the *claim*. The claim is the conclusion of the argument or that which is being argued. The data are the foundation for the claim, that which leads to the conclusion.[27] When an attorney argues to a jury that her client should be found not guilty, she may use as data that the prosecution has failed to prove its case, that the evidence against her client is only circumstantial, that the witness giving the client an alibi is more believable than the prosecution's witness, who places the defendant at the scene of the crime, and so on. All of these could serve as data for the claim that the defendant is not guilty of the crime charged.

The next field-invariant structure in argument is a *warrant*. The warrant is that portion of an argument which connects the data to the claim, that is, it "warrants" the inference of the claim from the data. Toulmin says that warrants "correspond to the practical standards or canons of argument";[28] in other words, warrants may state rules of inference or logical entailment. In the example above, if the attorney argued that her client was not guilty of the crime charged because a witness placed him in another city at the time of the crime, the warrant between this data and claim is implicit—one person cannot be in two places at the same time. If a legislator argues in favor of his tax-reform bill because it eliminates unfairness in the existing tax code, the implicit warrant is that we should support policies which are fair over those which are unfair. Toulmin's example is: Based on the data that Harry was born in Bermuda, one can claim Harry is a British citizen because of the warrant that a man born in Bermuda will be a British subject.[29]

Although data are appealed to explicitly, warrants frequently are implicit. A warrant is the point at which an argument is evaluated; as Toulmin notes, "unless, in any particular field of argument, we are prepared to work with warrants of *some* kind, it will become impossible in that field to subject arguments to rational assessment."[30] Although data can be challenged as untrue, the crux of an argument is the warrant, which links the data to the claim. As the warrant becomes the "inference ticket," a challenge to the warrant will determine the acceptability of an argument. In the examples above, if fairness is not a reason to change policies, then the legislator's argument fails. If persons could be in two places at the same time, the attorney's argument fails. If people born in Bermuda are not British citizens, the argument in Toulmin's example fails.

Because warrants allow various force to inferences, the next aspect of the structure of practical arguments is a *modal qualifier*. Modal qualifiers are words that state, or attenuate, the strength of a particular claim. Warrants, says Toulmin, are of different sorts. Some warrants may make a claim necessary or unequivocal while others make a claim only probable or likely. The attorney arguing for her client may say "you *must* find my client guilty," or she may say, "therefore, my client is very *unlikely* to have committed the crime." These two claims have different modal qualifiers, which means the data confer a different force upon the claim by virtue of the warrant. Words such as *always*, *sometimes*, *certainly*, *frequently*, and so on, operate as modal qualifiers in practical arguments.

As claims may not hold in all cases, Toulmin identifies *rebuttals* as the next part in the layout of practical argument. Rebuttals are conditions for exception of a claim, that is, the instances in which the claim does not hold. For example, in Toulmin's argument about Harry's citizenship, the qualifier, claim, and rebuttal might be: "So, presumably Harry is a British subject unless he has become an American citizen." Although attorneys are not in the habit of offering rebuttals to their claims in closing arguments, our defense counsel could argue, "Therefore my client most likely is not guilty unless the crime was committed at a time different than what the police claim." In a more likely scenario, if you are driving down the street, you might use the following argument: "Because I hear a thumping noise, I probably have a flat tire, unless something is going wrong with the engine." This sentence explicitly contains data, qualifier, claim, and rebuttal. The warrant is implicit—tires make this sort of thumping noise when they are going flat.

The sixth and final aspect of Toulmin's layout of practical argument is *backing for warrants*. Warrants are not applicable in all cases; therefore, an arguer may need to justify the applicability of a particular warrant to the argument at hand. Certainly, if someone challenges a claim by challenging the applicability of the warrant to the case, that position will weaken an argument severely if the challenge is not met. In Toulmin's example, backing for the warrant that a man born in Bermuda generally will be a British subject would be citation of the relevant British law establishing that claim. Some warrants are less challengeable, such as the warrant that a person cannot be in two places at the same time. On the other hand, other warrants, although accepted in a particular field, may contradict. In the tax-reform example, although making public policy fair is one value upon which a warrant can be based, fairness is not always championed, particularly when it comes at the expense of other values, such as simplicity of the legal code, adequate government revenue, or cost. When a warrant is challenged and backing becomes necessary, another argument may ensue, with the warrant becoming the claim, the backing functioning as data, and so on.

This layout of argument is field invariant. Although particular arguments may not have all six parts, arguments in any field will have an explicit claim, almost always explicit data and implicit warrant, and a potential for qualifiers, rebuttal, and backing. Thus, the layout of practical argument is applicable to any field of argument.

**Field Dependent**. Those aspects of argument which are field dependent vary from argument field to argument field. Among the field-dependent aspects of practical argument include the degrees of formality and precision required in an argument, modes of resolution, the goals of argumentation,[31] and the criteria of the modal qualifier.[32]

The *degree of formality* of arguments refers to the formality and style required in a particular field. The formality required in arguments over what to have for supper is very different from the formality required in an argument over competing scientific theories, carried out in scholarly journals. Similarly, an argument made in a campaign speech is less formal than those made in the complaint and response of legal pleadings, both of which are more formal than arguments between siblings.

The *degree of precision* of arguments is the exactitude or preciseness specified by or necessary to the field. For example, an argument made about theoretical chemistry or the design of a space shuttle or the tolerance of metal for bridge supports requires a very high degree of precision. Similarly, legal arguments over property boundaries in an easement dispute or over historical water usage in a water appropriation case in a western state, or details about the chain of custody in an evidence challenge require a significant degree of precision. Less than these examples is the precision required in haggling over a bill at the auto repair shop or advertising copy trumpeting the virtues of one laundry soap over another. Very little precision is required in arguments concerning assignment of household tasks or interpersonal relationships.

*Modes of resolution* differ dramatically among argument fields. When young children argue, frequently resolution comes either with the older or stronger child prevailing or when parents intervene to make a decision. In the political arena, authority sometimes resolves arguments. Arguments concerning licenses to broadcast are settled by various administrators at the Federal Communications Commission, whose decisions frequently are appealed to the federal courts. In the federal court system, the final resolution is made by the Supreme Court—which either decides a case or refuses to hear it, allowing the decision of the lower court to stand. In the Supreme Court, a vote is taken and the majority prevails in most instances.[33] Individuals and families develop unique modes of resolution. Dominant family members may develop a tactic of "wearing down" less dominant members, so that the latter eventually "cave in." The U.S. Congress has both official and unofficial modes of resolution. Officially, certain numbers of votes, either a majority for most business or two-thirds majority to override a presidential veto, are necessary to resolve a dispute. However, the committee structure and the power of seniority may resolve disputes unofficially, while officially, a vote is taken. In addition, arguments in some fields are resolved by one side winning and the other losing, such as a court proceeding. In other fields, compromise or consensus may end a dispute.

The *goals of argumentation* in a given field "depend on *what is at stake*."[34] A goal of argumentation may be that justice prevail; such is the goal of the criminal law. On the other hand, the goal may be cessation of a dispute; such is the goal of the civil law. The medical field is interested in coming to decisions of the most utility and scientific predictability. Toulmin, Richard Rieke, and Allan Janik illustrate the various goals of argumentation by the following claim: "Jack is insane." This claim is very different if made by Jack's physician, whose goal is an accurate diagnosis and proper treatment of Jack, than if made by an attorney representing Jack's wife, whose goal is obtaining power of attorney over Jack's financial affairs.[35]

Finally, the *criteria for the modal qualifier* are field dependent. The criteria of a modal qualifier are the standards or reasons by which we decide the use of that term is appropriate in the present context. Toulmin explains:

> We say, for instance, that something is physically, mathematically or physiologically impossible, that it is terminologically or linguistically out of order, or else morally or judicially improper: it is to be ruled out, accordingly, *qua* something or other. And when we start explaining "*qua* what" any particular thing is to be ruled out, we show what criteria we are appealing to in this particular situation.[36]

For example, to say, "it is impossible to find a rational number that is the square root of 2," involves the modal qualifier *impossible*. The criteria for impossibility comes from the field of math. Likewise, one might say, "it is impossible to eat just one potato chip." The criteria for the term is much different in this field of interpersonal conversation than in the field of mathematics. Similarly, if a judge announced, in a courtroom, "It is impossible for me to sentence this defendant to life in prison, as I would like to do," the criteria for impossibility is found in the law, which sets the limits on prison sentences for particular crimes.

The aspects of practical argument that are field dependent are ignored by traditional logic, which assumes that everything is field invariant. Toulmin's contribution is to force consideration of context by identifying the potential for field-dependent aspects of argument, and Perelman and Olbrechts-Tyteca bring consideration of the audience to discussion about reasoning. Upon this basis of context, these scholars attempt to construct logics of practical reasoning. Toulmin's system is described above and includes his field-invariant layout and various field-dependant aspects of argument. Perelman and Olbrechts-Tyteca attempt to redescribe what historically were known as inductive and deductive arguments as argumentative strategies.

## Argumentative Strategies

Perelman and Olbrechts-Tyteca suggest several strategies for argumentation, including using argumentative starting points that have audience agreement, making arguments "present" for an audience, converging arguments, and using particular argumentative techniques.

**Starting Points of Arguments**. Some practical arguments, according to Perelman and Olbrechts-Tyteca, begin from premises, much like deductive arguments. They refer to these premises as *"starting points of argument"* and suggest that argumentation is most persuasive when the arguer begins from starting points with which the audience agrees. Starting points can be facts or general truths that the society accepts as true, presumptions, which are believed true until refuted, or values or preferences that the particular audience holds. Argumentation then becomes the process of transferring the agreement accorded the starting points to the argumentative claim.

**Presence**. Although facts, truths, presumptions, values, and preferences exist despite the rhetor, by choosing those to be used as potential starting points, the rhetor gives to them *presence*, that is, she directs the sensibilities of the audience by her choice. The audience is moved to sympathy by media descriptions about starving children in one country, while they have no emotion about the starving children in another country, about whom they know little. That which is present to the consciousness of the audience is that which will be considered by them, which will preoccupy their minds, which will persuade them. During the 1984 Presidential campaign, the Republicans aired the now-famous Willy Horton advertisements. Horton was released from prison under a Massachusetts early-release program initiated by Dukakis, and he promptly committed a heinous crime. This advertisement created presence for voters, who focused on Horton rather than all the successful releases in the program or, for that matter, other good actions by Dukakis while governor of Massachusetts. Rhetors also are able to suppress presence. Ronald Reagan was dubbed the "teflon President" because negative charges against him did not remain present in the minds of the public.

**Interaction of Arguments**. The persuasiveness of arguments also is affected by their placement in discourse and by either ignoring or acknowledging and countering the opposing arguments. One can weaken an opponent's argument by making it seem routine, unimportant, silly, or overstated. One's own argument can be made stronger if portrayed as bold and important or, in contrast, balanced and obvious. In addition, claims are accepted as more probable if reached from a variety of starting points, an interaction Perelman and Olbrechts-Tyteca refer to as *convergence*. If two compelling arguments are available to reach the same claim, although the shorter would be the "more elegant" and all that would be necessary in formal logic, in argumentation, conclusions are buttressed by multiple arguments.[37]

**Techniques of Argumentation**. Finally, the method of arguing is described by Perelman and Olbrechts-Tyteca. Rather than describing this process as induction or deduction, they categorize the methods of getting from starting points to conclusions as liaison or dissociation. *Liaison* is a process of linking the starting point and the claim. *Dissociation* distinguishes between starting points and claims, to separate a starting point which the audience does not value from the speaker's claim. The point of such break is to give a solution for incompatibilities arising when one idea is linked to another. Pro-choice advocates must dissociate the notion of abortion from that of murder, which is a liaison created by the arguments of abortion opponents.

**Standards for Judgment**. Formal logic has specific standards of validity, and induction has particular tests for various types of argument. Perelman and Olbrechts-Tyteca's proposal for standards of judgment is, like the rest of their scheme, audience centered. For this purpose, they posit the notion of the *universal audience*, which is the speaker's idea of all reasonable people. As Cox and Willard note, the universal audience "is a construction of particular audiences and of the culture or historical epoch in which an audience participates."[38] Without the absolutes of formal logic, we must find another way to distinguish good arguments from bad ones. The universal audience fulfills that role. A particular audience may be persuaded by a poor argument; however, the universal audience, by definition, is persuaded only by good arguments and, therefore, sets the standard for practical rationality. As Perelman and Olbrechts-Tyteca note, "*agreement of a universal audience is thus a matter, not of fact, but of right.*"[39] The quality of an argument thus becomes audience-centered. If all individuals competent to make such a decision agree that a conclusion is true, that is the criterion of truth available in human society.

The role of language in these argumentation theories is significant and makes of argumentation something more human than mathematical. As Perelman and Olbrechts-Tyteca note:

> All language is the language of a community, be this a community bound by biological ties, or by the practice of a common discipline or technique. The terms used, their meaning, their definition, can only be understood in the context of the habits, ways of thought, methods, external circumstances, and traditions known to the users of those terms.[40]

Thus, argumentation, based in language, is a process not of logical demonstration but of discussion and deliberation about the probable, designed to persuade an audience in a particular argument field, and judged, ultimately, by general audience adherence. These scholars have set out to describe the process whereby such discussion and deliberation occur.

## Summary

The modern Western worldview is rooted in the principles of rationality described in this chapter. Many of these principles harken back centuries. In Umberto Eco's novel, *The Name of the Rose*, which also was made into a motion picture, these principles were used by an English Brother, William of Baskerville, who travels to an Italian Franciscan abbey in 1327 to investigate heresy and, upon his arrival, a series of murders. As he and a novice near the abbey, they meet a band of monks and servants, to whom William explains that Brunellus, the horse for which they are looking, can be found down a particular path. As he had seen neither these men before nor any horse, his conclusions amaze everyone. He then explains the series of observations and guesses that allowed him to reason to this correct conclusion, demonstrating the same keen powers of observation and reason as the centuries-later detective, Sherlock Holmes.

The power of reasoning is valued highly in Western society. Indeed, the dominant paradigm in modern Western society is based upon principles of formal logic exemplified in deduction and mathematics and the principles of reasoning to probable conclusions exemplified in induction. Even when these processes are redescribed and contextualized by Toulmin and Perelman and Olbrechts-Tyteca, they remain firmly rooted in Aristotelian notions of rhetoric and probabilities. As these models of rationality suggest, the dominant Western paradigm is critical—questioning conclusions and looking for negative instances; it is a "rational paradigm."

What is not made clear by Toulmin or Perelman and Olbrechts-Tyteca, nor by discussions of induction and deduction, is the relationship between nature, or reality, and the language used to talk and argue about reality. That question is at the heart of postmodern challenges to the "rational" or dominant paradigm.

## Endnotes

1. The focus on Western modes of thinking in no way implies superiority over ways of thinking or forms of rationality that have developed in other parts of the world. This section describes what has become the dominant paradigm in the modern West in order to understand the effects of that paradigm on those who live within it. For discussion of the development of non-Western logics, see Anton Dumitriu, *History of Logic*, trans. Duiliu Zamfirescu, Dinu Giurcăneanu, and Doina Doneaud, vol. 1 (Tunbridge Wells, England: Abacus, 1977) 12–65.
2. John Grier Hibben, *Logic: Deductive and Inductive* (New York: Charles Scribner's Sons, 1905) 100.
3. John Stuart Mill argues that *inference* involves moving from premises to conclusions not entailed thereby, thus making the term *inference* not appropriate to deductive logic. John Stuart Mill, *A System of Logic Ratiocinative and Inductive: Being a Connected View of the Principles of Evidence and the Methods of Scientific Investigation*, ed. J. M. Robson, vol. 1 (1974; rpt. Toronto: U of Toronto P, 1981) II i 2–4. However, not all scholars make this distinction. See, for example, Irving M. Copi, *Introduction to Logic*, 7th ed. (New York: MacMillan, 1986) 5.
4. Aristotle, *On Rhetoric: A Theory of Civic Discourse*, trans. George A. Kennedy, (New York: Oxford UP, 1991) 1 2 1357.
5. Aristotle 1 2 1356b.
6. This syllogism violates the rule that a valid deductive syllogism cannot have two particular premises.
7. Stephen Edelston Toulmin, *The Uses of Argument* (1958; rpt. London: Cambridge UP, 1974) 123–24.
8. Francis Bacon, "Preface," *Novum Organum, Great Books of the Western World*, ed. Robert Maynard Hutchins, vol. 30 (Chicago: Encyclopedia Britannica, 1952) 105–06.
9. Mill II iii 5.
10. Francis Bacon, *Advancement of Learning, Great Books of the Western World*, ed. Robert Maynard Hutchins, vol. 30 (Chicago: Encyclopedia Britannica, 1952) 2 XIII.
11. Bacon, *Advancement of Learning* 2 XIII 6.
12. Bacon, *Novum Organum* 2 11–12.
13. Sir Arthur Conan Doyle, *The Complete Sherlock Holmes* (Garden City, NY: Doubleday, 1930) 21.
14. Doyle 177.
15. Doyle 244–49.
16. Mill VIII 1–7.
17. Copi 483–84.
18. This process is discussed at length in Thomas S. Kuhn, *The Structure of Scientific Revolutions*, 2nd ed. *International Encyclopedia of Unified Science*,

vol. 2, no. 2 (1970; rpt. Chicago: U of Chicago P, 1974).

19. See discussion in Dumitriu, vol. 3, 99–111.

20. J. Robert Cox and Charles Arthur Willard, "Introduction: The Field of Argumentation," *Advances in Argumentation Theory and Research*, eds. J. Robert Cox and Charles Arthur Willard (Carbondale, IL: Southern Illinois UP, 1982) xxi (emphasis omitted).

21. Joseph W. Wenzel, "Three Perspectives on Argument: Rhetoric, Dialectic, Logic," *Perspectives on Argumentation: Essays in Honor of Wayne Brockriede*, ed. Robert Trapp and Janice Schuetz (Prospect Heights, IL: Waveland, 1990) 11.

22. Chaim Perelman and Lucie Olbrechts-Tyteca, *The New Rhetoric: A Treatise on Argumentation*, trans. John Wilkinson and Purcell Weaver (1969; rpt. Notre Dame, IN: U of Notre Dame P, 1971) 4 (emphasis omitted).

23. Perelman and Olbrechts-Tyteca 16.

24. Perelman and Olbrechts-Tyteca 19 (emphasis omitted).

25. Chaim Perelman, *The Idea of Justice and the Problem of Argument*, trans. John Petrie (1963; rpt. Atlantic Highlands, NJ: Humanities, 1977) 101.

26. Toulmin 94–145.

27. In another text, the term *grounds* is substituted for *data*. Stephen Toulmin, Richard Rieke, and Allan Janik, *An Introduction to Reasoning*, 2nd ed. (New York: MacMillan, 1984) 32–39.

28. Toulmin 98.

29. Toulmin 99.

30. Toulmin 100.

31. Toulmin, Rieke, and Janik 113–28.

32. Toulmin 36.

33. In the instance of argument on whether to hear cases, the Court will issue a *writ of certiorari*, which is necessary for the Court to hear most appeals, based on the "rule of four," meaning that approval of four of the nine justices will result in a case being heard.

34. Toulmin, Rieke, and Janik 274.

35. Toulmin, Rieke, and Janik 274–75.

36. Toulmin 30.

37. Perelman and Olbrechts-Tyteca 474.

38. Cox and Willard xxiv.

39. Perelman and Olbrechts-Tyteca 31. See also, Chaim Perelman, *The Realm of Rhetoric*, trans. William Kluback (Notre Dame, IN: U of Notre Dame P, 1982) 17 and *The Idea of Justice* 87, 155.

40. Perelman and Olbrechts-Tyteca 513.

# *Part Four*
# **Challenges to the Rational Paradigm**

A key element in the modern worldview was belief in progress, of movement toward truth in all areas of life; knowledge could be standardized and social orders planned. Modernism thus was "positivistic, technocentric, and rationalistic."[1] Modern Western societies elevated the study of science to a position of preeminence. The modern scientific premise was that the world could be controlled and ordered if only we could understand and describe it. Finding this correct representation was to be, as David Harvey explains, "the means to Enlightenment ends."[2] However, in the twentieth century, when the promise of modernity failed to be realized and when oppression of peoples around the world continued, these modern assumptions began to be challenged.

Among the first challenges was the recognition that to describe the world in a single representation or discourse was impossible. Human understandings involve multiple perspectives. Modernism thus began to edge toward perspectivism and relativism, that is, toward realization that single explanations are not functional ways of knowing. The modern worldview, however, refused to give up its belief in truth or in the eventual possibility of true knowledge of an admittedly complex reality.

Contemporary theories of rhetoric, such as those espoused by Richards, Weaver, and Burke, and contemporary theories of argument, such as those of Toulmin and Perelman, are examples of the loosening of the modern worldview and its adherence to the so-called rational

**171**

paradigm, a paradigm in which humans are set apart from the world and, by dialectical and rhetorical means, modify their understandings to match reality more closely. Instead, as these theorists suggest, language may be epistemic; that is, language may function as a human means for determining or creating rather than discovering truth. Many ideas about language appearing in the last third of the twentieth century adopt this perspective and analyze the import of claiming that rhetoric creates truth.

Other theorists in the twentieth century challenge the rational paradigm more directly. With imposing names such as *poststructuralism*, *deconstruction*, and *postmodernism* and even more daunting vocabularies and descriptions, these theories rest upon a common base—that language plays the central role in shaping culture and individuals. In this section, some of the major themes that challenge the rational paradigm are reviewed. Feminist and minority voices, raised to challenge the modern Western worldview, also are detailed.

## Endnotes

1. David Harvey, *The Condition of Postmodernity: An Enquiry into the Origins of Cultural Change* (1990; rpt. Cambridge, MA: Basil Blackwell, 1992) 9.
2. Harvey 27.

# Chapter Ten

# Contemporary Theories of Discourse

Among the central challenges to the rational paradigm are two contemporary theories of discourse—the poststructuralism of Michel Foucault and deconstruction, which largely is credited to the writings of Jacques Derrida. These contemporary theories of discourse begin with the premise that discourse creates human understanding and move variously to explain how systems of signs and linguistic codes operate, what role remains to humans under such conditions, and how to understand and read texts. In this chapter, these two theories of discourse are discussed in the context of their intellectual precursor, structuralism.

## Structuralism

An understanding of structuralism is an important gateway to poststructuralism and deconstruction. Structuralism is a method of investigation that seeks to explain cultural phenomena ranging from language to myths to restaurant menus; these phenomena are viewed as manifestations of underlying systems of signification, as codes composed of interrelated signs. Language serves as the paradigm case—that is, the standard sign system upon which the structuralist method is based. The basic principles of structuralism are found in the work of Ferdinand de Saussure, whose ideas on language gave birth to the modern discipline of linguistics. Claude Lévi-Strauss adopted structuralism as his method for anthropology. Identifying other scholars in the structuralist tradition is difficult, for many who share a structuralist taxonomy or approach specifically deny the label. As John Sturrock notes, "These 'structuralists' may lack a common programme but they do not lack a common ancestry. It is principally in the genealogy of their ideas that one should look for evidence of their kinship. This common ancestry is very much a matter of vocabulary."[1] The common vocabulary of structuralism comes directly from Saussure.

## Ferdinand de Saussure

Saussure, as discussed in chapter two, identified two components of every sign—the signifier (sound image) and the signified (concept). The significance of this two-part distinction is that objects in the world, the "referents" in I. A. Richards' semantic triangle, are ignored. That which is signified is not preexisting reality but rather a human construct. Furthermore, the signifier and signified are separable only in theory, as both are necessary for signification. As Sturrock explains, "there can be no signifier without a signified; correspondingly, no concept can be said to exist unless it has found expression . . . either inwardly as a thought or outwardly in speech—there can be no signified without a signifier."[2]

Despite this inseparability, however, structuralists make much of the *theoretical* distinction between signifier and signified. Indeed, the distinction is part of the common vocabulary of structuralism and poststructuralism. Theorists acknowledge that meaning is a human construction, and the nature of messages is conditioned by the culture of sender and receiver. This conditioning occurs by means of the codes of the culture. Although messages are individual and intentional, the linguistic code is collective, anonymous, and unconscious. Every culture has a vast number of codes, the study of which is known, in Europe, as *semiology* and, in the United States, as *semiotics*.

Most linguistic studies prior to Saussure were diachronic; they studied the evolution of language through time. Structuralism, on the other hand, is synchronic, as it studies systems of signs ahistorically. Further, the study is of the system or structure of language (*la langue*) rather than specific utterances (*parole*); the former gives structure to and thereby controls the latter. Based upon Saussure's claim that *la langue* is arbitrary, the structure or system of language is of tremendous importance for structuralism. Signifieds are arbitrary; the system of language and various codes create a meaning that has no necessary relation to an external reality and, thus, no relation to an absolute and abiding truth. At the same time, linguistic and other codes are stable and relatively immutable to intentional change; therefore, they have enormous influence over human action and understanding. In other words, the units of language have a conventional meaning but depend for that meaning upon other units. Without the other units, without the linguistic system, no meaning is possible. In short, meaning is not a preexistent thing; it is not the referent in Ogden and Richards' semantic triangle. Meaning is a *function* of the differences among signs registered in human understanding.

Structuralism uses Saussure's theory of language to understand other cultural activities and other codes of signification that create meaning. By this means, language becomes, for most of the twentieth century, "both paradigm and obsession."[3]

## Others Who Use the Structuralist Vocabulary

Lévi-Strauss, a French anthropologist, was perhaps most influenced by Saussure. He argues that specific myths and cultural systems (totemic, kinship, and so on) of primal populations can be reduced to certain universal structures—that is, to a limited number of basic themes. In a sense, he identifies a grammar of myth. Among his claims is that he has identified a primordial logic common to all human minds ("*la pensée sauvage*") in the logic of myths. When Lévi-Strauss studied myth, he saw not its narrative content but rather the universal operations of the human mind. These structures represent the possible ways in which reality can be ordered within a society using the mythic code. Human understanding within that society is constrained by the structures of myth, which dictates meaning to individuals.

An important result of viewing myths structurally is that one moves away not only from reality, as did Saussure with his two-part sign, but beyond the individual human subject. Although myth needs individuals to exist, it transcends an individual subject. As myth has a logic of its own, people who retell and listen to the retelling of myth understand ("see") the world through this logic, through the structures of the myth. As Terry Eagleton explains:

> One result of structuralism, then, is the "decentering" of the individual subject, who is no longer to be regarded as the source or end of meaning. Myths have a quasi-objective collective existence, unfold their own "concrete logic" with supreme disregard for the vagaries of individual thought, and reduce any particular consciousness to a mere function of themselves.[4]

The theme of the domination of language over human understanding continues in the work of Jacques Lacan, a French psychoanalyst who is classified as a poststructuralist. Lacan applied the tenets of structuralism to his field with emphasis on the ideas of Freud. He argues that Freud has been much misunderstood, that his most important discovery is that the unconscious has structure. To uncover this structure is the job of psychoanalysts, for the unconscious represses its own structure. This structure of the unconscious is like the structure of language, according to Lacan. Individuals, when they acquire speech, adopt the pre-existing structure of the language they learn. Thus the libido becomes organized by the symbolic order of language. To attempt to identify pre-linguistic thought is a waste of time, Lacan argues, for like Saussure, he sees human thought as constituted by language. Thus, the signifier structures not only the signified but the human subject as well.

Lacan calls the state of infancy the Imaginary. Self-awareness begins in the mirror stage, when a reflection of self from others begins the development of an ego. However, true individuality must be surrendered to the Symbolic, which is the symbolic order of language that imposes structure on the Imaginary. As language works through absence (a sign is apart from an object which it claims to represent, and individual signs have meaning only as they are distinct from other signs), a child learns about absence and difference simultaneously through language and sexuality, becoming absent from the mother's body and learning sexual difference from distinction between mother, father, and child. Thus is a child inducted into the preexisting linguistic and sexual symbolic orders. The concept of *absence* has some similarities to Kenneth Burke's concept of the *negative*, which is discussed in chapter one. Absence is what is left out by the sign; it is that which is *not* (that which is *not* signified and that which is *not* present).[5]

Lacan notes the primacy of the signifier over the signified, which is created thereby. He inscribes this relationship as "S/s."[6] Thus, the object of both linguists and psychoanalysts, who are attempting to understand the unconscious, is signifiers, for the unconscious becomes "visible and audible in speech."[7] Chains of signifiers create and recreate both signifieds and subject. The domain in which this perpetual restructuring takes place is the Symbolic order. Signifiers have associations from a variety of contexts. In conscious discourse, this shifting and sliding variety is excluded and controlled in order that meaning remains somewhat coherent. For example, when we use a name ("my friend Ian") to refer to a person, we create a stable reference which does not reveal the change in our feelings for and understanding of that person over time.

The unconscious has various signifiers whose meaning is unclear either because it is repressed or because the shifting and sliding of multiple signifieds is not controlled; thus meaning fades and

evaporates, never yielding itself to conscious understanding.[8] That
which is barred or repressed in consciousness remains in the
unconscious; it is the *Other*, which is one of Lacan's most central and
elusive terms. The Symbolic creates linguistic and sexual "Others"—
those which are absent when signifiers create particular immediate
signifieds. (The *Other* is a concept also used by some feminist theorists
and in discussion of "signifyin[g]" in Black English, which are reviewed
in chapter twelve.) Thus, to understand the repressed meanings of the
unconscious, the psychoanalyst should study signifiers; he or she must
be, as Malcolm Bowie suggests, a student of rhetoric:

> The analyst who knows about rhetoric is more likely than a
> colleague who does not to remain alert both to those inflections
> of normal usage which comprise the "style" and the singularity
> of an individual patient's discourse and to the specific characters
> of the unconscious discourse which the spoken word allows the
> analyst to reconstrue.[9]

Roland Barthes, a Frenchman, applied structuralism to literary
criticism. He notes the tendency of signs to appear natural; that is,
signifiers present signifieds as if they had some real rather than
arbitrary existence. Thus, signs create a hidden ideology that becomes
accepted, that becomes *doxa*—the popular opinion to which Plato was
so antagonistic (see chapters three and seven). Eagleton explains,
"Ideology seeks to convert culture into Nature, and the 'natural' sign
is one of its weapons. Saluting a flag, or agreeing that Western
democracy represents the true meaning of the word 'freedom[,'] become
the most obvious, spontaneous responses in the world."[10] Barthes'
message is that the "real" is nothing more than "the 'already written'"
(or the already stated).[11]

Barthes demonstrates the ideological effects of *doxa* in mass
communication. In his book *Mythologies*, for example, he uses
Saussure's ideas to uncover the underlying structure in aspects of
popular culture, ranging from advertisements to wrestling matches,
and the ideology or particular value they conceal. In Barthes' criticism,
he does not concern himself with the author of discourse or the author's
intent. He argues that "[t]o give a text an Author is to impose a limit
on that text, to furnish it with a final signified."[12] No person, he argues,
is the voice of a text. Indeed, Barthes looks only at the language or code
itself, and he treats the language not as determinate and with single
meaning but as indeterminate, with as many meanings as possible,
no one preferable to the other.[13] Structural criticism, according to
Barthes, is an activity whereby one makes intelligible the objects of
human understanding. As he describes this activity, it is "to
reconstruct an 'object' in such a way as to manifest thereby the rules

of functioning (the 'functions') of this object."[14]

Each of these scholars gives insight into the school of thought known as structuralism, a school that focuses on systems of signification and prepares the way for understanding Foucault's poststructuralism. Other common threads run through them. As Sturrock explains:

> All these thinkers are against authority, and against metaphysics. They do not wish to transcend what they see, in pursuit of some hidden, ultimate meaning which would "explain" everything; they do not believe that everything can be explained. Nor do they hold with teleological interpretations of history. They are against the singular and for the plural, preferring whole galaxies of meanings to emerge from a limited set of phenomena to the notion that it must hold one, unifying, dominant meaning.[15]

At the same time, they elevate the signifier above the signified, and frequently they ignore diachronic issues including history and social change. A structuralist perspective is different than a traditional rhetorical perspective. Whereas the latter concerns the communicative function of language, the former examines the conditions whereby meaning arises.[16]

Structuralism is the pathway to two writers who have had a profound effect upon most humanities and social-science disciplines in the late twentieth century. Michel Foucault suggests a study of language as discursive formations, which create not only objects but humans within them. Jacques Derrida sets forth a project which has come to be known as deconstruction, a poststructural movement that seeks to uncover assumptions and biases within Western writing and to propose a method for reading and rereading texts. The works of these two authors exemplifies Eagleton's description of poststructuralism's aims: "Unable to break the structures of state power [in the 1968 student uprisings all over Europe], post-structuralism found it possible instead to subvert the structures of language."[17]

## Michel Foucault

Foucault was a French scholar of philosophy, psychology, and psychiatry. Although his ideas clearly have roots in structuralism, he moves beyond language structure to consider both power and history. One of Foucault's central theses is that language systems are far more important than individuals in understanding human nature. Some of his work is devoted to understanding the historical development of knowledge and the effects of linguistic knowledge systems upon social and intellectual activity. He also studied discourse on the margins of society, including the history and social practices of imprisonment and the history of conceptions of sexuality.

Coming from the structuralist perspective, Foucault does not view discourse as a means of conveying information, and he rejects or ignores the possibility of a reality that preexists discourse. Further, he discounts the importance of individual senders or authors of communication, arguing that discourse is not merely expression of a "thinking, knowing, speaking subject."[18] Instead, for Foucault, discourse is the total linguistic network not only of things stated but potentiality to state things that delimit and define the human world. In other words, individual human subjects are born into a system of discourse; those discursive structures or "discursive formations" form the human being and give sense and order to (that is, "create") the world of human experience. Thus, discourses are "practices that systematically form the objects of which they speak."[19] An important result of such a view is that truth is a function of language rather than something natural or extralinguistic.[20]

## Statement

Foucault's atom of discursive analysis is the statement, that which is not reducible to other linguistic elements.[21] He distinguishes statements from propositions, sentences, speech acts, objects, and structures. Statements are, for Foucault, the necessary elements of language, without which language would not exist. However, no specific statement is indispensable to language. Unlike sentences and propositions, a statement always is bordered by other statements; individual statements exist only in relation to a whole verbal network, that is, an *enunciative* or *associated field*, which involves all the formulations to which the statement refers and all the formulations whose status the statement in question shares:

> there is no statement in general, no free, neutral, independent statement; but a statement always belongs to a series or a whole, always plays a role among other statements, deriving support from them and distinguishing itself from them: it is always part of a network of statements, in which it has a role, however minimal it may be, to play.[22]

Two identical sentences could be different statements, and different sentences could be the same statement. Thus the sentence *I love you* may be, at different times and in different enunciations, a very different statement. Although the actual speaking, the enunciation, of a statement is an unrepeatable event, a statement is not reducible to its enunciation. In other words, a statement is repeatable; it may be "reinscripted" as well as "transcripted." Foucault explains:

> Instead of being something said once and for all—and lost in the past like the result of a battle, a geological catastrophe, or the death of a king—the statement, as it emerges in its materiality, appears with a status, enters various networks and various fields of use, is subjected to transferences or modifications, is integrated into operations and strategies in which its identity is maintained or effaced.[23]

One role of statements is to create objects by defining and delimiting possibilities of their appearance.

## Formation of Objects of Discourse

In *The Archaeology of Knowledge*, Foucault analyzes how objects of discourse, that is, the "things" about which one can talk, are created through discourse. That humans see individual objects when they view "reality" is, according to Foucault, a function of discourse rather than reality. "[I]t is not enough," he argues, "for us to open our eyes, to pay attention, or to be aware, for new objects suddenly to light up and emerge out of the ground."[24] In other words, reality as we understand it does not lay waiting to be discovered; instead, objects are formed because of the linguistic or discursive practices of society. Part of Foucault's work is to describe the forces that result in the formation of the objects of discourse.

First, discourse creates the *surfaces or planes of the emergence* of objects. The language and the society into which an individual is born have an enormous number of conceptual codes, theories, rationalizations, and linguistic agreements that limit discourse and give certain pattern to sensation. These codes create objects (for example, *democracy* or *sport*), making them "manifest, nameable, and describable."[25] A second way in which objects of discourse are created is by *authorities of delimitation*. Within a society, all sorts of authoritative institutions—law, church, government, art and literary criticism, and historical texts—create objects by acknowledging them. Thus, poststructuralism became a thing, a concept, because literary and other scholars began to refer to particular works by this name. A third way in which objects are created are the *grids of specification*, which are the linguistic schemes of classification, the categories of the language. Genderizing nouns in languages such as Spanish (*la mesa, el abrazo*) gives to those objects a certain nature.

To illustrate the creation of objects, one easily can imagine a society in which race is not a concept. The humans in the society are classified by gender and may display a whole array of skin tones, but race is not a concept; it is not an object in that society. The concept *race* exists in Western society only because of the patterns of discourse and authority, the conceptual codes and categories, the authoritative institutions, and the linguistic schemes of classification which have given it existence.

However, these structures of language, notes Foucault, are inadequate to describe completely how objects arise in a society. In addition, certain historical conditions are necessary for the appearance of an object. Also, particular discursive relations must exist between institutions, social processes, norms, behavioral patterns, and so on, that allow the object to appear. Foucault explains these relations:

> Discursive relations are not, as we can see, internal to discourse: they do not connect concepts or words with one another; they do not establish a deductive or rhetorical structure between propositions or sentences. Yet they are not relations exterior to discourse, relations that might limit it, or impose certain forms upon it, or force it, in certain circumstances, to state certain things. They are, in a sense, at the limit of discourse: they offer it objects of which it can speak, or rather (for this image of offering presupposes that objects are formed independently of discourse), they determine the group of relations that discourse must establish in order to speak of this or that object. . . . These relations characterize not the language (*langue*) used by discourse or the circumstances in which it is deployed, but discourse itself as a practice.[26]

Among the discursive relations that cause objects to arise are questions of roles and sites of authoritative discourse.

Some roles in society are accorded importance; presumption of truth attaches to what individuals occupying these roles say. Scientists, particularly well-known scientists at large research institutions, determine what scientific objects exist and what scientific theories are true. Doctors have status to diagnose or identify disease. The Supreme Court has the status to interpret the Constitution. A person in a soup-kitchen line may stand on a chair and make a startling scientific pronouncement. However, that discourse has no power to define objects or create truth. Intellectuals in society are in a role to define objects. However, intellectuals are not important as individuals but only in these roles, which include class, conditions of life and work, and the politics of truth of the society.[27] In this, Foucault parts company with some structuralists and poststructuralists who ignore the author. Although he personally discounts the importance of *individual* authors or speakers, he acknowledges the significance given not only to the *role* of the originator of discourse but also to the "author function," which is one of the central discursive functions that has historical as well as theoretical importance. He argues that the importance of the author in industrial society relates to the discursive practices of the time; he predicts a future in which authors no longer are important, in which discourses "would then develop in the anonymity of a murmur."[28]

Part of the legitimacy of discourse comes from its site. Material that appears in professional journals carries an imprimatur of truth. To be taken seriously, to be accorded the status of knowledge, legal information has to appear at an authoritative site. Academic writing is valued according to its form; articles in major, national journals are given status above articles in state journals or articles that never are published. Further, discourse that frequently is cited as authority is given more authority than discourse which is ignored by the academic community.

The discursive practices, historical conditions, and the discursive relations, including the role from which the discourse emanates and the site of the discourse, affect the formation of objects. This discursive or linguistic creation of human understanding affects Foucault's view of truth.

## Truth

For Foucault, truth has no independent existence. Instead, truth is a product of discourse and of power relations, which themselves stem from discursive practices. In a very illuminating discussion, Foucault describes his notion:

> truth isn't outside power, or lacking in power: contrary to a myth whose history and functions would repay further study, truth isn't the reward of free spirits, the child of protracted solitude, or the privilege of those who have succeeded in liberating themselves. Truth is a thing of this world: it is produced only by virtue of multiple forms of constraint. And it induces regular effects of power. Each society has its régime of truth, its "general politics" of truth: that is, the types of discourse which it accepts and makes function as true; the mechanisms and instances which enable one to distinguish true and false statements, the means by which each is sanctioned; the techniques and procedures accorded value in the acquisition of truth; the status of those who are charged with saying what counts as true.[29]

The régime of truth, then, includes the procedures whereby statements are produced, distributed, ordered, regulated, and so forth—the manner in which statements are identified as true and false. This régime involves "the form of scientific discourse and the institutions which produce it." Further, truth is subject to "economic and political incitement," that is, to the "demand for truth." Truth also is diffused and consumed by educational and informational apparatuses whose role in society is to announce truth. In addition, truth is produced under the control of a few powerful institutions, such as universities, mass media, the government, and the military, and it is the subject of "political debate and social confrontation," by which Foucault means that truth becomes the subject of ideological struggle.[30]

## Political Agenda

This view of truth may indicate Foucault's political agenda. An intellectual should not struggle with the issue of what counts as true and false; instead, the entire régime of truth must be challenged. The battle for truth is not " 'on behalf' of the truth" but "about the status of truth."[31] In a sense, Foucault's only political agenda is change. As Allan Megill notes, Foucault attacks order—not only the existing order but any order. Because all language and discourse enslave and all order oppresses, one is "justified in opposing these orders."[32]

Foucault also appears to want to break the bonds of power to give voice to those not in powerful roles, those who are silenced. In "The Order of Discourse," he discusses how discourse is ordered and, thereby, controlled. Among the procedures he describes are methods of exclusion exterior to discourse and those interior to it.

Exterior methods of excluding discourse include forbidding speech, labeling it as madness, and the will to truth. Some speech simply is taboo (forbidden) in the society, such as certain sexual discourse. One is not allowed to express certain desires or thoughts, which must be repressed. Another type of exclusion lies in the distinction between reason and madness. If discourse is labeled rational, it is included; however, the discourse of the insane is ignored. A third type of exclusion occurs in the distinction between truth and falsity. If discourse is labeled false according to the prevailing mechanics of truth, it is discounted. For example, the discourse of creationists is excluded from serious consideration by modern society. Foucault, like Nietzsche, calls this the "will to truth": "This will to truth, like the other systems of exclusion, rests on an institutional support: it is both reinforced and renewed by whole strata of practices, such as pedagogy, of course; and the system of books, publishing, libraries; learned societies in the past and laboratories now."[33]

Foucault also identifies internal procedures, procedures within discourse, that act to order and control truth. Such controls include the major narratives of a society, the notion of an author, and the control of disciplines over discourse. The narratives accepted and retold by the society act to limit what else can be said. In the United States, the Constitution and the Bill of Rights operate as controlling narratives. That language is repeated, again and again, to justify and prohibit discourse. The Bible also operates as such a text, just as the major text of any religious group operates as a narrative of control.

Another internal means of control, according to Foucault, is the author function, by which he means not necessarily the individual who created a certain text but the role of author. Presently, scientific and academic texts have no standing if not attributed to an author; further, the standing is relative to the distinction of the author. Thus, certain discourse can come only from doctors, from lawyers, from judges, or from religious leaders. When it comes from anyone else, it is discounted.

The notion of a discipline also acts as a controlling factor. For discourse to belong to a particular discipline, it has to fulfill certain conditions, address certain objects, and meet certain standards of expression. Laboratory controls, sampling techniques, statistical procedures, and other conditions must be met in empirical research or the discourse is discounted. Certain objects are pushed beyond disciplinary boundaries, as medicine pushes acupuncture, spiritual healing, and chiropractic outside its boundaries. As Foucault says: "It is always possible that one might speak the truth in the space of a wild exteriority, but one is 'in the true' only by obeying the rules of a discursive 'policing' which one has to reactivate in each of one's discourses."[34]

A final means of controlling discourse is limiting access. This limiting occurs by societal rituals, by the existence of particular societies of discourse, by doctrine, and by the educational system. Societal rituals that limit who can access particular discourse include the "gestures, behaviour, circumstances, and the whole set of signs which must accompany discourse."[35] For example, the law does not acknowledge promises to sell land that are not expressed in writing. Further, marriage vows are not acknowledged unless accompanied by particular legal and/or religious gestures and expressions. In some cultures, couples are divorced if the husband says, three times, "I divorce you." Such discourse, unaccompanied by legal documents and pronouncements, would be discounted in the West. A second way of limiting access to discourse is the "societies of discourse" charged with preserving or producing particular discourse. For example, discourse not published in certain ways is discounted. Therefore, the publishing houses operate as societies of discourse by choosing what to publish; mass media also limit access to discourse. Further, doctrine can operate to limit access to discourse. If individuals subscribe to certain doctrines, they are, in essence, blind to other types of discourse. As Foucault notes: "Doctrine brings about a double subjection: of the speaking subjects to discourses, and of discourses to the (at least virtual) group of speaking individuals."[36] Further, the educational system operates to limit access to discourse. Education creates social distances and struggles, which prevents or allows access to certain discourse. The educational system operates to ritualize speech, fixing roles for speaking subjects, creating doctrine, and appropriating status to particular discourse.

Although Western society may seem to respect discourse and be liberated from constraints, Foucault finds hidden fears, prohibitions, and limits—a "logophobia" that seeks to remove from the richness of discourse "the most dangerous part," to prevent "the surging-up of all these statements, against all that could be violent, discontinuous, pugnacious, disorderly," and to control "this great incessant and disordered buzzing of discourse." To open ourselves to this disordered but rich potential and to better understand our fear of discourse, not only must we lose the will to truth, but we must restore discourse to "its character as event" and "throw off the sovereignty of the signifier."[37]

## Importance of the Human Subject

Foucault calls the great intellectual periods of history, which can be characterized by the set of relations that unite all discursive practices, *epistemes*. The modern *episteme*, which began in the late 1800s and continues currently, "was bound up with the disappearance of Discourse." Western reason and science led to objective knowledge about nature, language, and humans themselves. The objective gained superiority over the subjective and over language. The referent was privileged over signifier and signified.

Foucault suggests that the increasing importance currently given to language may signal the next historical *episteme*, which will have language as its central organizing principle ("the imperious unity of Discourse"). This leads to one of his most well-known statements, the claim that understanding humans as language-using animals makes them creatures created by discourse. Thus, language, not humans, becomes of central importance. Foucault asks, is "this not the sign that the whole of this configuration is now about to topple, and that man is in the process of perishing as the being of language continues to shine ever brighter upon our horizon."[38] By this, Foucault means that a future set of discursive formations will not feature the individual as centrally as do the discursive practices of capitalistic, industrial, Western democratic societies. Just as the author function will disappear, so, he argues, will the human as the central organizing principle of knowledge. Our present conception of the human being is, he argues, relatively recent: "Strangely enough, man—the study of whom is supposed by the naïve to be the oldest investigation since Socrates—is probably no more than a kind of rift in the order of things. . . . [The human] is only a recent invention . . . a new wrinkle in our knowledge . . . [who] will disappear again as soon as that knowledge has discovered a new form."[39]

Foucault's project is to identify the operation of discursive practices whereby objects and knowledge are created in order to allow challenge to those operations. The disappearance of the human being which he forecasts and the challenge to the constraints of a given discursive formation are well underway in the methods of deconstruction.

## Jacques Derrida

Deconstruction begins with Derrida, who was born in Algiers and studied in France. His method is a close reading of texts, concentrating on seemingly marginal elements that, when emphasized, point out internal contradictions between the logic of the text and its message. However, to call his reading a "method" is, as Megill notes, "an act of violence," for Derrida himself claims that his writings are meaningless. Megill continues: "Imagine Derrida as a modern Penelope, unraveling by night what he weaves by day—or rather raveling and unraveling at the same time."[40] Thus, to attempt some understanding of deconstruction is a daunting task. Central to Derrida's purpose are the related notions of *logocentrism* ("the blindly logical orientation of Western thought")[41] and the *metaphysics of presence* (fundamental assumptions of truth and existence which are the foundations of Western reason).

## Logocentrism

According to Derrida, European languages are caught up in assumptions of Western logic. Thus, when criticizing Western reason, one of necessity is firmly within its grasp. In an essay critical of Foucault, he writes: "The unsurpassable, unique, and imperial grandeur of the order of reason, that which makes it not just another actual order or structure (a determined historical structure, one structure among other possible ones), is that one cannot speak out against it except by being for it, that one can protest it only from within it; and within its domain."[42] Deconstruction is Derrida's strategy not for criticizing reason but rather for challenging the logocentric bias in language.

Derrida argues that language is not referential, that there is nothing outside the text.[43] By this he agrees with Foucault that knowledge is created by discourse. One cannot reach the signified by dispensing with the signifier; concepts do not preexist their expression. A key difficulty with logocentrism is that it assumes a transcendental signified, an existence outside of and prior to language. However, Derrida suggests that even those who recognize that knowledge is created by discourse (such as Foucault) fall prey, in their writings, to logocentrism by their very intention to communicate. Derrida explains:

> Communication presupposes subjects (whose identity and presence are constituted before the signifying operation) and objects (signified concepts, a thought meaning that the passage of communication will have neither to constitute, nor, by all rights, to transform). *A* communicates *B* to *C*. Through the sign the emitter communicates something to a receptor, etc.[44]

Writing, however, suffers less in this regard than does speech. Derrida argues that Western tradition elevates speech over language, which he describes as logocentrism in the form of phonocentrism. We understand speech to represent something beyond speech—some external reality; writing represents speech. Writing is, then, a representation of a representation. Distanced one step further from the assumed transcendental signified, writing exists in absence of an author: "For a writing to be a writing, it must continue to 'act' and to be readable even when what is called the author of the writing no longer answers for what he has written." Writing is freed of context and semantic moorings, thus is somewhat less tied to the metaphysics of presence.[45]

## Metaphysics of Presence

The metaphysics of presence sees the signifier, sees speech (and, at one step removed, text), as mere dressing of the signified, or perhaps of the referent. Speech is about something; it is representative. It makes something present in discourse, as Chaim Perelman and Lucie Olbrechts-Tyteca suggest (see chapter nine). This assumption of existence and fundamental principles from which everything else flows (this "metaphysics"), underlies all Western thought, which focuses on that which is present, that which *is*, that which is exterior to and named by discourse. Descartes' *cogito* ("I think, therefore I am") falls prey to the metaphysics of presence, identifying the *I*, the thinking self, as that which is present and cannot be doubted. Objects are accorded the same sort of presence, because of their existence through time. As Jonathan Culler explains, "Reality is thus made up of a series of present states" which are "basic, the elementary constituents which are given and on which our account of the universe depends. This view is powerful and persuasive."[46]

Derrida's project is to challenge logocentrism and the metaphysics of presence; this is, he suggests, a project formulated but not achieved by Foucault.[47] Derrida argues that no one or thing can be fully present because language, which creates and is a part of any and everything, works by absences, by the difference between the concept accorded presence and that which is not present. In other words, language works by difference not by presence; it operates by being different and deferred. As access to "reality" is through language; the shifting, relative web of language that creates nonidentical meanings by means of differences and absences denies the possibility of presence. Derrida's point is that the law of identity (discussed in chapter nine) is wrong. A does not equal A, for meaning cannot be fixed from moment to moment. Meaning is always the sign of a sign, as C. K. Ogden and I. A. Richards' semantic triangle (discussed in chapter four) indicates; humans using signs are caught in a logic of difference and supplementarity.

> The play of differences supposes, in effect, syntheses and referrals which forbid at any moment, or in any sense, that a simple element be *present* in and of itself, referring only to itself. Whether in the order of spoken or written discourse, no element can function as a sign without referring to another element which itself is not simply present. This interweaving results in each "element"—phoneme or grapheme—being constituted on the basis of the trace within it of the other elements of the chain or system. This interweaving, this textile, is the *text* produced only in the transformation of another text. Nothing, neither among the elements nor within the system, is anywhere ever simply present or absent. There are only, everywhere, differences and traces of traces.[48]

Derrida, then, deconstructs written texts, reading them in such a way as to attempt to reverse hierarchies, to break the structures of reason, to display the differences and traces that deny presence, and thereby to avoid logocentric bias.

Derrida, in an attempt to resist what he criticizes in others, tries to avoid indicating a presence or truth behind his own discourse. As a result, his statements attempt to deconstruct but not construct. He uses metaphor, ambiguity, and a special vocabulary, which he refuses to define, to avoid reference to, reliance on, or implication of an existence prior to language. Among Derrida's specialized vocabulary is the term *differance*; he also places words under erasure.

**Differance**.    The spelling of this word is designed to suggest how meaning cannot be pinned down or fixed. Although the word is pronounced "difference," the adoption of the *a* indicates that the meaning does not preexist the word. Although *differance* should not be defined, Derrida says:

> Differance is the systematic play of differences, of the traces of differences, of the *spacing* by means of which elements are related to each other. This spacing is the simultaneously active and passive (the *a* of differance indicates this indecision as concerns activity and passivity, that which cannot be governed by or distributed between the terms of this opposition) production of the intervals without which the "full" terms would not signify, would not function.[49]

Not only is meaning a part of the web within which a statement appears, as Foucault indicates, but also meaning is not *present* in language; some slippage always exists. As Christopher Norris notes, to attempt to define *differance* is to wrench it from Derrida's text, where it operates rather than exists, and give to it the very permanence of meaning which he denies exists.[50]

**Sous Rature**.    Another of Derrida's strategies is to place terms "under erasure." That is, the terms are used on a page for a tactical reason but, by putting a slash through them, he indicates that they do not have the semantic stability that writing would seem to give them. A sign always implies something excluded, something absent, leaving a trace of what is excluded. This trace is under erasure. We may be able better to understand the "in-between" if we are aware of both presence and absence. Gayatri Spivak explains this erasure: "Derrida, then, gives the name 'trace' to the part played by the radically other within the structure of difference that is the sign. . . . Derrida's trace is the mark of the absence of a presence, an always already absent present, of the lack at the origin that is the condition of thought and experience."[51] Even the notion of writing, which is a part of the history of metaphysics, must be used *sous rature*, under erasure. "*The (pure) trace is differance.*"[52]

## Deconstruction

Deconstruction challenges the ideas and beliefs that implicitly serve as basic premises of texts, calling into question those things that legitimize current forms of knowledge. These texts, whether literary or philosophical, are seen as "rhetorical constructs." Deconstruction is an activity which involves the reading of texts in a manner that questions both the "metaphysical prejudice," which supposes that concepts exist outside language, and the idea of logical consistency.[53] As Spivak describes deconstruction, it attempts "[t]o locate the promising marginal text, to disclose the undecidable moment, to pry it loose with the positive lever of the signifier; to reverse the resident hierarchy, only to displace it; to dismantle the order to reconstitute what is always already inscribed."[54]

Derrida says there is no substitute for the hard work of reading and rereading texts. One must do an internal distancing to prevent the metaphysics of presence in concepts from becoming routine habits of thought. One does this by reading texts to dismantle conceptual oppositions, binary opposites, and hierarchical systems of thought. In this activity, Derrida demonstrates the existence of the metaphysics of presence as well as internal inconsistency in texts: "the writer writes *in* a language and *in* a logic" which dominates the discourse.[55] Deconstruction seeks out blind spots of self-contradiction between what is written and the logic of what is written, between what the author means to say and what the logic of the language constrains it to mean. Says Derrida:

> There is no concept that is metaphysical in itself. There is a labor—metaphysical or not—performed on conceptual systems. Deconstruction does not consist in moving from one concept to another, but in reversing and displacing a conceptual order as well as the nonconceptual order with which it is articulated.[56]

Derrida unearths these blind spots in a text, exposing the "law of its composition and the rules of its game,"[57] by reading the margins of the text—the minor terms and unregarded details such as footnotes, metaphors, allusions, and incidental phrases—and by showing how they threaten to unravel the whole. What he seeks are the binary opposites, like true/false, good/bad, speech/writing, and so on, central to Western logic. As Eagleton explains:

> Structuralism was generally satisfied if it could carve up a text into binary oppositions (high/low, light/dark, Nature/Culture and so on) and expose the logic of their working. Deconstruction tries to show how such oppositions, in order to hold themselves in place, are sometimes betrayed into inverting or collapsing

themselves, or need to banish to the text's margins certain niggling details which can be made to return and plague them.[58]

The result of deconstructing a text is not exposing a new truth or presence hidden within but merely giving it a new reading. The activity of reading a text becomes, in a sense, a rewriting of the text, as "reading and writing are one."[59] Readers and writers "create" texts on the basis of all the texts they have encountered. As David Harvey explains

> Cultural life is then viewed as a series of texts intersecting with other texts, producing more texts . . . This intertextual weaving has a life of its own. . . . It is vain to try and master a text because the perpetual interweaving of texts and meanings is beyond our control. Language works through us. Recognizing that, the deconstructionist impulse is to look inside one text for another, dissolve one text into another, or build one text into another.[60]

Derrida does not put forth a theory of language; indeed, his ideas deny theories and other forms and structures of permanence. Instead, he reads and writes about texts, deconstructing them. Only those who follow him attempt to create a system out of what Derrida refuses to make systematic.[61] Every writer who attempts to explain Derrida, then, is caught in this conundrum of attempting to do with Derrida that which Derrida says must not be done. Norris uses the Wittgensteinian way out, arguing that his own introduction to Derrida is like the ladder that, once climbed, should be "unceremoniously kicked away" after serving its purpose.[62] As Culler notes, however, systematizing of Derrida is inevitable.[63] As his works are read, interpreted, and discussed, his method is extracted and systematized, and his writing is combed for theoretical bases. Derrida himself is adamant that deconstruction is *not* "primarily a matter of philosophical contents, themes or theses . . . but especially and inseparably [of] meaningful frames, institutional structures, pedagogical or rhetorical norms, the possibilities of law, of authority, of representation in terms of its very market." As Christopher Norris notes, in this statement, "Derrida effectively repudiates just about everything that has been carried on in the name of 'deconstruction' by his various exegetes and disciples."[64] Perhaps the best that can be done to understand Derrida is to maintain the realization that "the exercise of language and thought involves us in intractable paradoxes, which we can not escape but only repress."[65] Further, by deconstructing first principles, identifying that which the texts exclude and by which they are defined, and revealing binary opposites, readers are less controlled by the metaphysics of presence.

Derrida has been criticized as a modern-day sophist bent on reducing every discipline to a species of rhetorical play, as having no regard for reason or truth. Rumors of the "death" of deconstruction are rife. At this time, however, it is still impossible to tell what will become of deconstruction, whether it will be a passing fad, the end of philosophy, or the beginning of revolutionary models of understanding.

## Summary

Ihab Hassan argues that poststructural theory, "though full of brio and bravura, can only taunt our desire to make sense. It can only tease us into further thought, not anchor our meanings."[66] The challenge to the rational paradigm created by poststructuralism as well as deconstruction not only denies the possibility of truth and progress but challenges Western views of logic and common-sense understandings. As Jon Snyder notes, "everything we encounter in our experience of the world is no more and no less than an *interpretation* . . . and thus *the only world that can ever be known is a world of difference* (that is, a world of interpretations)."[67]

This "world of interpretations" is illustrated in Christopher Sergel's dramatization of *Black Elk Speaks*. Black Elk attempts to explain the tragedy of Wounded Knee by reviewing the history of the Indian and white culture. As a part of that review, the following statements are made to the audience by actors portraying Black Elk and Andrew Jackson:

Black Elk . . .

(Again to the audience)

A prominent Indian killer has been elected your president— the man you call Andrew Jackson. . . . The man we call Sharp Knife.

Jackson

To prevent racial incidents between citizens of Georgia and the Cherokee, I suggest the propriety of removing the Indians to an area west of the Mississippi where they'll have the protection of a permanent Indian frontier, which I promise—

(To BLACK ELK, who is starting away)

for as long as grass grows or water runs.

Black Elk

(After Jackson)
It won't be the grass or the water that forgets. . . .

Jackson

(Prodded by anger into frankness)

It's vain to charge us with results that grow out of the inevitable march of human events. . . . It's our manifest destiny to possess this land. . . .

Black Elk . . .

When you steal land you call it Manifest Destiny. When an Indian tries to defend himself, you call him a hostile. Even after destroying us with guns, whisky and smallpox, you find your word to describe what happened. You say we've Vanished.[68]

The difference in interpretation is described but not evaluated by many poststructural theories. Poststructuralism identifies all human understanding as a construct of discursive formations and relations, and deconstruction concentrates on dismantling all metaphysical truth-claims and systems of logic; both, at the same time, deny the possibility of a new truth or a new reason to take the place of that which has been destroyed. This leaves humans in the late twentieth century in what has been called "the postmodern condition," which is described in chapter eleven.

## Endnotes

1. John Sturrock, "Introduction," *Structuralism and Since: From Lévi-Strauss to Derrida*, ed. John Sturrock (1979; rpt. New York: Oxford UP, 1981) 5.
2. Sturrock 6.
3. Terry Eagleton, *Literary Theory: An Introduction* (Minneapolis: U of Minnesota P, 1983) 97.
4. Eagleton 104.
5. See Kenneth Burke, *The Rhetoric of Religion: Studies in Logology* (Berkeley: U of California P, 1970) 18–22; *A Grammar of Motives* (Berkeley: U of California P, 1969) 294–97; and *Language as Symbolic Action: Essays on Life, Literature, and Method* (Berkeley: U of California P, 1966) 419–21.
6. Jacques Lacan, "The Insistence of the Letter in the Unconscious," trans. Jan Miel, *Modern Criticism and Theory: A Reader*, ed. David Lodge (New York: Longman, 1988) 83.
7. Malcolm Bowie, "Jacques Lacan," *Structuralism and Since: From Lévi-Strauss to Derrida*, ed. John Sturrock (1979; rpt. New York: Oxford UP, 1981) 131.
8. Eagleton 169.
9. Bowie 139.
10. Eagleton 135.
11. John Sturrock, "Roland Barthes," *Structuralism and Since: From Lévi-Strauss to Derrida*, ed. John Sturrock (1979; rpt. New York: Oxford UP, 1981) 74.
12. Roland Barthes, "The Death of the Author," trans. Geoff Bennington, *Modern*

*Criticism and Theory: A Reader*, ed. David Lodge (New York: Longman, 1988) 171.

13. "[T]he birth of the reader must be at the cost of the death of the Author." Barthes 172.

14. Roland Barthes, "The Structuralist Activity," trans. Richard Howard, *Contemporary Literary Criticism: Literary and Cultural Studies*, ed. Robert Con Davis and Ronald Schleifer, 2nd ed. (New York: Longman, 1989) 171.

15. Sturrock, "Introduction" 15.

16. Robert Con Davis and Ronald Schleifer, "Structuralism and Semiotics," *Contemporary Literary Criticism: Literary and Cultural Studies*, ed. Robert Con Davis and Ronald Schleifer, 2nd ed. (New York: Longman, 1989) 143.

17. Eagleton 142.

18. Michel Foucault, *The Archaeology of Knowledge and the Discourse on Language*, trans. A. M. Sheridan Smith (1972; rpt. New York: Pantheon, 1982) 55.

19. Foucault 49.

20. For a review of Foucault's works, see Sonja K. Foss, Karen A. Foss, and Robert Trapp, *Contemporary Perspectives on Rhetoric*, 2nd ed. (Prospect Heights, IL: Waveland, 1991) 209–39.

21. Carole Blair argues that the concept is central to Foucault's critical posture. "The Statement: Foundation of Foucault's Historical Criticism," *Western Journal of Speech Communication* 51 (1987): 364–83.

22. Foucault 99.

23. Foucault 105.

24. Foucault 44–45.

25. Foucault 41.

26. Foucault 46.

27. Michel Foucault, *Power/Knowledge: Selected Interviews and Other Writings 1972–1977*, ed. Colin Gordon, trans. Colin Gordon, Leo Marshall, John Mepham, Kate Soper (New York: Pantheon, 1980) 132.

28. Michel Foucault, "What Is an Author?," trans. Josué V. Harari, *The Foucault Reader*, ed. Paul Rabinow (New York: Pantheon, 1984) 119.

29. Foucault, *Power/Knowledge* 131. For a discussion of Foucault's views on power, see Barbara Biesecker, "Michel Foucault and the Question of Rhetoric," *Philosophy and Rhetoric* 25 (1992): 351–64.

30. Foucault, *Power/Knowledge* 131–32.

31. Foucault, *Power/Knowledge* 132.

32. Allan Megill, *Prophets of Extremity: Nietzsche, Heidegger, Foucault, Derrida* (1985; rpt. Berkeley: U of California P, 1987) 197–98.

33. Michel Foucault, "The Order of Discourse," *Untying the Text: A Post-Structuralist Reader*, ed. Robert Young (Boston: Routledge & Kegan Paul, 1981) 55. See also, Friedrich Nietzsche, *The Will to Power*, trans. Walter Kaufmann and R. J. Hollingdale, ed. Water Kaufmann (1967; rpt. New York: Vintage, 1968).

34. Foucault, "The Order of Discourse" 61.

35. Foucault, "The Order of Discourse" 62.

36. Foucault, "The Order of Discourse" 64.

37. Foucault, "The Order of Discourse" 66.

38. Michel Foucault, *The Order of Things: An Archaeology of the Human Sciences* (New York: Vintage, 1973) 385–86.

39. Foucault, *The Order of Things* xxiii.

40. Megill 259.

41. Megill 215.

42. Jacques Derrida, *Writing and Difference*, trans. Alan Bass (Chicago: U of Chicago P, 1978) 36.

43. Jacques Derrida, *Of Grammatology*, trans. Gayatri Chakravorty Spivak (Baltimore: Johns Hopkins UP, 1976) 158.

44. Jacques Derrida, *Positions*, trans. Alan Bass (1981; rpt. Chicago: U of Chicago P, 1982) 23–24.

45. Jacques Derrida, "Signature Event Context," trans. Samuel Weber and Jeffrey Mehlman, *The Rhetorical Tradition: Readings from Classical Times to the Present.* ed. Patricia Bizzell and Bruce Herzberg (Boston: Bedford, 1990) 1174.

46. Jonathan Culler, "Jacques Derrida," *Structuralism and Since: From Lévi-Strauss to Derrida*, ed. John Sturrock (1979; rpt. New York: Oxford UP, 1981) 162.

47. Derrida, *Writing and Difference* 36.

48. Derrida, *Positions* 26.

49. Derrida, *Positions* 27.

50. Christopher Norris, *Derrida* (Cambridge: Harvard UP, 1987) 15.

51. Gayatri Chakravorty Spivak, "Translator's Preface," *Of Grammatology*, (Baltimore: Johns Hopkins UP, 1976) xvii.

52. Derrida, *Of Grammatology* 60–62.

53. Christopher Norris, *The Deconstructive Turn: Essays in the Rhetoric of Philosophy* (New York: Methuen, 1983) 5–6.

54. Spivak lxxvii.

55. Derrida, *Of Grammatology* 158.

56. Derrida, "Signature Event Context" 1184.

57. Jacques Derrida, "Plato's Pharmacy," *Dissemination*, trans. Barbara Johnson (Chicago: U of Chicago P, 1981) 63.

58. Eagleton 133.

59. Derrida, "Plato's Pharmacy" 63.

60. David Harvey, *The Condition of Postmodernity: An Enquiry into the Origins of Cultural Change* (1990; rpt. Cambridge, MA: Basil Blackwell, 1992) 49–50.

61. Edward W. Said criticizes Derrida for creating something "as inadvertently systematizing as logocentrism itself." "Opponents, Audiences, Constituencies and Community," *The Anti-Aesthetic: Essays on Postmodern Culture*, ed. Hal Foster (Port Townsend, WA: Bay, 1983) 143.

62. Norris 17. Wittgenstein said: "My propositions are elucidatory in this way: he who understands me finally recognizes them as senseless, when he has climbed out through them, on them, over them. (He must so to speak throw away the ladder, after he has climbed upon it.) He must surmount these propositions; then he sees the world rightly." Ludwig Wittgenstein, *Tractatus Logico-Philosophicus*, trans. C. K. Ogden (1922; rpt. Boston: Routledge & Kegan Paul 1985) 6.54.

63. Culler 156.

64. Norris 14.

65. Culler 156.

66. Ihab Hassan, *The Postmodern Turn: Essays in Postmodern Theory and Culture* (Columbus, OH: Ohio State UP, 1987) 202.

67. Jon R. Snyder, "Translator's Introduction," Gianni Vattimo, *The End of Modernity: Nihilism and Hermeneutics in Postmodern Culture* (Baltimore: Johns Hopkins UP, 1988) xiii.

68. Christopher Sergel, *Black Elk Speaks* (Chicago: Dramatic Publishing Co. 1976) 19–21. This dramatization is based on the book by John G. Neihardt.

# Chapter Eleven

# Postmodernism

Postmodernism is a cultural phenomenon that began somewhere in the 1960s or early 1970s.[1] It coincides with and embraces aspects of poststructuralism, deconstruction, post-Marxism, and feminism, and it reacts to Western reason, the notion of technological progress, and the exalted status of science. Whereas structuralism championed the role of the signifier over the signified, postmodernism furthers the poststructural and deconstructive challenge to the signifier— suggesting that, just as the "objects" created by language use have no "real" existence, neither do particular texts, which are changed with every reading, viewing, or listening and which cannot be judged by independent standards. Among the aims of postmodern theorists, writers, and artists seem to be dismantling Aristotelian logic and Enlightenment metaphysics, challenging assumptions of a scientifically certifiable truth, denying individualism, and dismissing monolithic views of culture and the social order, thereby preserving cultural diversity. In this chapter, definitions of postmodernism are reviewed and major themes are discussed. In addition, the views of some critics of postmodernism are detailed, with particular attention to the defense of modernity offered by Jürgen Habermas.

## Definitions

Definitions of *postmodernism* are not abundant, for most writers note the impossibility of defining the term. Thus, they spend chapters if not entire books discussing postmodern cultural activities and critiques and leave that discussion to speak for the term. A key difficulty with the term, in addition to the definitional problems, is its awkwardness. As Ihab Hassan notes, the term is "uncouth," for it "contains its enemy [*modernism*] within."[2] Among the statements made about postmodernism, the following illustrate both the general sense and the indeterminacy of the term:

- "Postmodernism is a rhapsodic, elusive, exhilarating concept, used with license, because the hopes and fears—anxious ambitions?—of theorists are riding on it. . . . [T]he term . . . is deliberately kept flexible and enchanting—so rich with connotations that it dissolves on direct contact with reality."[3]

- "It is safest to grasp the concept of the postmodern as an attempt to think the present historically in an age that has forgotten how to think historically in the first place."[4]

- "[Postmodernism is] incredulity toward metanarratives."[5]

- "Postmodernism is what you have when the modernization process is complete and nature is gone for good."[6]

- "Postmodernism is not as such a new style of creating artworks, of synthesizing novel self-expressions, and of justifying theoretically its aesthetic practices. Postmodernism does not open up a new field of artistic, philosophical, cultural, or even institutional activities. Its very significance is to marginalize, delimit, disseminate, and decenter the primary (and often secondary) works of modernist and premodernist cultural inscriptions."[7]

Perhaps the main thrust of the term lies in this last definition, for, in some sense, postmodernism is a reaction to the modern. The term is widely used in such fields as the arts, architecture, literary criticism, theology, sciences, rhetoric, and psychoanalysis. Further, what sometimes passes for the postmodern is a complex collection of cultural activities, ranging from art to music to writing. Postmodernism may be the next *episteme*;[8] on the other hand, it may be a term that, in its very popularity and faddishness, amounts to nothing. As both its definitions and the very term itself indicate something apart from modernism, a return to that concept will ground the discussion in this chapter.

## Modernism

The beginning of the modern period is identified variously, ranging from as early as the 15th century, with Gutenberg's invention of the movable type, to as late as the end of the 19th, when Freud published his psychoanalytic theories. Frequently, scholars place the starting date as the 17th century, finding in Descartes and the beginnings of modern science the foundations of modernity. Stephen Toulmin, however, identifies an earlier beginning, in the 16th century; he suggests that Renaissance humanism, discussed in chapter three and chapter eight, serves as context for understanding 17th-century innovations in philosophy and science not as "revolutionary advances" but rather "a defensive counter-revolution."[9] Philosophers in the 17th century were reacting to the skepticism of the 16th century, in which humanist tolerance of religious differences and emphasis on pluralism had led not to peaceful coexistence but to religious warfare.[10] Thus, the project of the 17th century was to provide certain foundations for belief, as "*un*certainty had become *un*acceptable."[11]

In the attempt to understand postmodernism, no description of modernism is more helpful than that given by Toulmin. He argues that philosophers in the 17th century, in this quest for certainty upon which to base belief, shifted understandings of knowledge to the written from the oral, to the universal from the particular, to the general from the local, and to the timeless from the timely.[12] Seen in this light, the 17th century's quest for certainty was an attempt to decontextualize philosophy and science:

> [T]he Cartesian program for philosophy swept aside the "reasonable" uncertainties and hesitations of 16th-century skeptics, in favor of new, mathematical kinds of "rational" certainty and proof. . . . [T]hat change of attitude—the devaluation of the oral, the particular, the local, the timely, and the concrete—appeared a small price to pay for a formally "rational" theory grounded on abstract, universal, timeless concepts.[13]

Postmodernism, then, is partially a reaction to the modernism grounded in 17th-century rationalism. Chief among postmodernism's characteristics is the disavowal of the major tenets of this modernism.

## Characteristics of Postmodernism

Hassan, who both characterizes and criticizes postmodernism, presents the contrasts between modernism and postmodernism as polarizations:

| Modernism | Postmodernism |
|-----------|---------------|
| Purpose | Play |
| Design | Chance |
| Hierarchy | Anarchy |
| Finished Work | Process |
| Presence | Absence |
| Centering | Dispersal |
| Semantics | Rhetoric |
| Signified | Signifier[14] |

Not everyone agrees with this tactic; David Harvey argues that it is "dangerous . . . to depict complex relations as simple polarization," but he cites Hassan's list as a useful starting point for understanding postmodernism.[15] This starting point leads to other characteristics, including postmodernism's disavowal of truth and certain knowledge.

## Truth and Knowledge

Postmodernism in its many forms disavows truth, which is the aim of traditional metaphysical thought and rationality. When the search for truth in the West did not lead to absolutes and when science multiplied rather than narrowed the range of possible "answers," the result was profound skepticism and, even more fundamental, a challenge to the notion of a metanarrative. Science and much of modern Western culture are "governed by the demand for legitimation."[16] Any knowledge-producing activity such as science legitimates itself by reference to a discourse that is an accepted statement of truth. That discourse operates as a "metanarrative"; such a narrative is at the foundation of all sciences, including the study of humans.

These metanarratives allow society to define criteria for competence and to make evaluations according to those criteria; therefore, the metanarrative controls "what is performed or can be performed within it."[17] For example, a scientific statement is verified through argumentation and proof, but what counts as proof and what qualifies as a good argument are determined by standards outside science. Those standards are part of a metanarrative which is accepted as true. (Much of Part Three of this text describes the modern Western metanarrative.) According to Lyotard, science cannot operate without this metanarrative, which is ironic, as the metanarrative is, by definition, unscientific; it is unavailable for testing and not subject to proof.

> Scientific knowledge cannot know and make known that it is
> the true knowledge without resorting to the other, narrative,
> kind of knowledge, which from its point of view is no knowledge

at all. Without such recourse it would be in the position of presupposing its own validity and would be stooping to what it condemns: begging the question, proceeding on prejudice. But does it not fall into the same trap by using narrative as its authority?[18]

The postmodern condition involves, according to Lyotard, "incredulity toward metanarratives." The "grand narrative," upon which science and other knowledge-producing activities are based, "has lost its credibility."[19] To be incredulous toward metanarratives is to disbelieve in those absolute truths from which science derives its legitimacy. Thus, in the postmodern period, all forms of knowledge, even modern science, become discourses which are based on narratives that cannot claim any particular validity because no credence is given to the metanarrative or accepted truth that might legitimize them. Science no longer is the path to truth but merely one type of discourse. Thus, knowledge has no permanent, fixed, or privileged status; it is singular, relative, and individual. It also is shifting, fragmented, and indeterminant. This view of knowledge reflects the postmodern challenge to modern conceptions of rationality.

The replacement of metanarratives with a plurality of systems for legitimizing truths requires a reconceptualization of the notion of reason. If any system or narrative can serve as the basis upon which to judge the truth of denotative statements, then no standard for truth exists. Indeed, postmodernism attacks one of the most fundamental principles of Western logic—the law of noncontradiction. This law, which suggests that an object cannot be both A and not A, has long served as a basic premise of Western logic, as discussed in chapter nine. However, postmodernists see the law of noncontradiction as little more than an instrument useful for asserting control. Postmodernism not only refuses to control or authorize but seeks to undermine such authority. The law of noncontradiction operates to exclude contents that would be included in the chaotic whole of experience existing prior to the ordering and delimiting work of reason. John McGowan notes that postmodernists "often proclaim their allegiance to this more inclusive whole, one that avoids the hierarchical differentiations and exclusions that mark the more ordered and less complete, integral wholes created by reason."[20]

## History and Subject

The postmodernist distrust of any ordering or integration results in the disconnection and fragmentation of that which the modern paradigm attempts to order and define. Unlike modernism, postmodernism does not try to transcend or control the chaotic elements of existence; instead, it "swims, even wallows, in the . . . chaotic currents of change as if that is all there is."[21] That change, however, has no order, for the postmodern project also eschews history; humans exist in fragmented current moments. The modern historian attempts to make sense of the past, to find causes and to define periods or epochs. Harvey suggests that the only role for the postmodern historian may be as the Foucaultian archaeologist, digging up remnants from the past and setting them beside current artifacts with no explanation or attempt to order. "There is, in postmodernism, little overt attempt to sustain continuity of values, beliefs, or even disbeliefs."[22] Gianni Vattimo explains the relationship of postmodernism to history somewhat differently. He suggests that the postmodern is the "end of history" because rather than supplanting the modern, postmodernism dissolves the category of the *new*. Also dissolved is the modern notion of progress. No longer do the victors control history, preserving only stories which legitimate their power.[23]

The "death of the subject" also is found in postmodernism.[24] In a discussion sounding somewhat like Foucault, Lyotard describes how each self exists in a complex and everchanging "fabric" of social relations, which are founded upon language games. Individuals occupy a position within one or more language games; they are points on "specific communication circuits" in games in which each player has some power over messages. In these games, any individual may be the sender, the receiver, or the referent.[25] In this constantly moving web of language games, the subject dissolves.[26] Legitimation of the self, much like legitimation of science, can come only from linguistic practice and communicative interaction. By acknowledging that the self is socially and linguistically constructed, postmodernism denies autonomy and individualism.[27] Jameson notes the existence of a "more radical" position, one which he calls poststructural—that the individual subject always was a myth; it never existed. Instead the self is merely a construct, a "philosophical and cultural mystification which sought to persuade people that they 'had' individual subjects and possessed this unique personal identity."[28] Thus, the postmodernist artist or writer has no privileged status; the subject is in the margin and the art or the text are what "counts."

## Postmodern Cultural Activities

Postmodernism may have affected the arts even more than it has philosophy. Postmodern artistic expression claims to be playful, chaotic, and without authority. The elimination of distinctions makes the conception of postmodern art almost an oxymoron. Jameson's description of the postmodern demonstrates this parallel—"everything has become 'cultural' in some sense. A whole new house of mirrors of visual replication and of textual reproduction has replaced the older stability of reference and of the non-cultural 'real' " (that is, replaced the transcendental signifier and reality apart from and prior to both language and art).[29] Therefore, the artistic images (the signifiers) are that which is "real"—no object or event precedes them as the original or the thing which art represents. Instead, the focus is on "sheer, insistent immanence."[30] Art, says Hassan, "pretends to abolish itself" or becomes "indistinguishable from life."[31] Thus, adopting the language of Jacques Derrida, texts, both linguistic and artistic, rather than nature, are that which is *present* for the postmodern human.

The variety in postmodern cultural activity challenges modern distinctions of any sort but particularly those between literature and other types of discourse and between artist and critic, as such distinctions allow privileging of one side of the pair. This privileging, and even the existence of the distinction, is laid to the flawed nature of Western reason. In rejecting that reason, postmodernism celebrates heterogeneity.[32]

Another distinction rejected by postmodernism is that between high and popular culture. Frequently postmodern artists embrace the latter:

> The postmodernists have, in fact, been fascinated precisely by this whole "degraded" landscape of schlock and kitsch, of TV series and *Reader's Digest* culture, of advertising and motels, of the late show and the grade-B Hollywood film, of so-called paraliterature, with its airport paperback categories of the gothic and the romance, the popular biography, the murder mystery, and the science fiction or fantasy novel: materials they no longer simply "quote," as a Joyce or a Mahler might have done, but incorporate into their very substance."[33]

Thus, popular culture is integrated with all other culture, becoming art. This eclectic activity presents bits and pieces of the past and the present mixed together, as in E. L. Doctorow's novel, *Ragtime*, which features stereotypes about the past in a sort of "pop history." Among other examples of postmodern cultural activities are Andy Warhol's pop art; John Cage's music; punk and new wave rock music; David Lynch's films and films like *Wings of Desire* and *Blade Runner*; break dancing and dancing in musical-group videos; and the writing of James Joyce, William Burroughs, and Thomas Pynchon. Frequently, this art is sexually explicit, rebellious, and critical of both political and social norms. It also is schizophrenic and disorderly. Much postmodern art fits Lyotard's description of the postmodern writer who "is in the position of a philosopher: the text he writes, the work he produces are not in principle governed by preestablished rules, and they cannot be judged according to a determining judgment, by applying familiar categories to the text or to the work."[34]

Postmodern architecture, rather than seeking to be a monument that stands apart from the other buildings and from the commercial existence of the surrounding city, becomes part of it. As Jameson explains, such buildings seek to speak the language of the "commercial sign system of the surrounding city," using "its lexicon and syntax as that has been emblematically 'learned from Las Vegas.'"[35] Space is shaped to aesthetic rather than social purposes.

The driving force of postmodern cultural activities becomes consumerism, which, as Harvey notes, "is the primary language of communication in our society." The "reality" of art is demonstrated as architecture begins to "mimic media images." Harvey cites Baltimore's Harbor Place, a waterfront development, as an example of the architecture of urban "spectacles, with its sense of surface glitter and transitory participatory pleasure." Although modern urban spectacles of the 1960s grew out of political movements (riots, anti-war demonstrations) and counter-cultural events (rock concerts, "love-ins"), postmodern urban spectacles involve the institutionalization of commercial and recreational indulgences. Further, many such spectacles are nearly identical, such as South Street Seaport in New York, Quincy Market in Boston, and Harbor Place in Baltimore.[36] Thus, argues Jameson, the emergence of postmodernism is related to consumerism or "multinational capitalism,"[37] which includes such familiar characteristics as planned obsolescence, rapidly changing fads in clothing and style, penetration of society by advertising through various media, the rapid growth of transportation (resulting in McLuhan's global village, as discussed in chapter seven), and the standardization of consumption due to multinational corporate ownership.

## Political Goals

Postmodern knowledge, notes Lyotard, "refines our sensitivity to differences and reinforces our ability to tolerate the incommensurable."[38] The resulting pluralism embraces the notion of cultural diversity. Ranging from Foucault's elevation of the discourse of marginal groups and individuals, as discussed in chapter ten, to giving voice to women and ethnic minorities, which is discussed in chapter twelve, postmodernism allows all groups an "authentic and legitimate" voice.[39] The political goal of postmodernism, according to McGowan, is to disrupt the social hierarchy by empowering suppressed groups. The disruption is not of economic practices or political institutions but of "culture's signifying patterns," that is, of the symbolic order.[40] The individualism and autonomy that are central to the modern worldview become, for the postmodern condition, oppressive to women and minorities; further, Western hierarchical order is a threat to the "egalitarian distribution of power."[41] Once Western reason and its accompanying assumptions are diffused, society can, according to Richard Rorty, "substitute Freedom for Truth as the goal of thinking and of social progress."[42]

## The Role of Rhetoric

The role of rhetoric in postmodernism is significant. This role is illustrated by the ideas of Thomas Kuhn, a theorist upon which postmodernists frequently rely. Kuhn suggests that science does not happen in a bias-free arena within which absolute truths are the reward of careful and exacting method. Instead, science is guided by accepted paradigms of understanding. From time to time, so-called scientific revolutions cause a shift in paradigms, such as that caused by Copernicus' determination that the Earth revolved around the sun. The ensuing science then operates within the confines of this new paradigm.[43] The aspect of Kuhn's argument which appeals to postmodernists is, as Jon Snyder notes, that the choice among paradigms ultimately is made "on the basis of the *persuasive* power, and hence the rhetorical efficacy, of a given paradigm: a paradigm imposes itself on a given society or social group through its powers of conviction rather than of scientific demonstration." Thus, in this shifting of paradigms, the history of science and the history of art "display the same essentially rhetorical traits."[44]

The same role for rhetoric may not exist in modernism, at least that which is grounded in 17th-century rationalism. For a society in search of timeless, abstract, and universal truths, rhetoric is "subordinate to logic: the validity and truth of 'rational' arguments is independent of *who* presents them, *to whom*, or *in what context*—such rhetorical questions can contribute nothing to the impartial establishment of human knowledge. [In the 17th century, f]or the first time since Aristotle, logical analysis was separated from, and elevated far above, the study of rhetoric, discourse and argumentation."[45] With postmodernism, the reversals Toulmin found in the 17th century are themselves reversed.

## Critics of the Postmodern

Postmodernism is an easy target for critics, although such criticism frequently is dismissed by postmodernists as being informed by outmoded narratives of logic and metaphysics. Critics claim that postmodernism deprives humans of some constant whereby they can understand the meaning of their texts. If all language is immanent, if no distinction can be made between literature and other types of discourse, and if the author no longer exists, then the questionable result of the tremendous freedom of postmodernism is an inability to make "sense" of texts. Similarly, the meaning of human existence is left to individuals.[46]

The most telling criticism, however, is that postmodernism cannot save itself from relativism. With the denial of metanarratives comes the inability to make judgments, be they aesthetic, scientific, or moral. Thus, a postmodern society is one with no sense of individual responsibility, with no means for determining any sorts of truth, and with increased rather than decreased "likelihood of irrational or 'terroristic' actions committed without regard for other individuals or their social contexts."[47] The celebration of pluralism is one thing; abject relativism is another, particularly if it allows for the complete breakdown of society and the retribalization of the global village. Without access to metanarratives, our need for moral guidance can be filled only by that which is before us. If there is nothing outside language, then "[i]t is our history, our community, our hope that is abandoned."[48]

Even Harvey agrees that postmodernism "takes matters too far." Although postmodernist philosophers urge that we take delight in the "cacophony of voices through which the dilemmas of the modern world are understood," by deconstructing and delegitimating everything they encounter, postmodern individuals "can end only in condemning their own validity claims to the point where nothing remains of any basis for reasoned action." Indeed, postmodernism may harm the very groups it seems to serve. While creating possibilities for previously marginalized voices, "postmodernist thinking immediately shuts off those other voices from access to more universal sources of power by ghettoizing them" and disempowering them with the same broad brush that it disempowers all voices.[49] Thus, some see postmodernist discourse as "futile, self-righteous rage signalling nothing but its own preaching thunder."[50] This becomes an argument for metanarratives of some sort, in which may lie the only hope for empowering currently marginalized voices.

One solution to the relativism that seems to be an inevitable result of postmodernism is the pragmatism that Hassan suggests, which allows some unshifting existence to arise from discourse—some presence. "What makes statements true (in lower case) is use, context, what I call benevolent consequence in particular circumstance. For human beings possess no mirror to reflect the immutable face of reality. And though judgments about consequences are themselves debatable, still they remain subject to quotidian mediations, negotiations; they are part of our endless 'conversation,'" which "takes the place of knowledge"; it is the social justification of belief.[51] This social justification of belief is the foundation of Jürgen Habermas' defense of modernity.

## Jürgen Habermas

Habermas responds to the chaotic incoherence of postmodernism by attempting to salvage modernism and the aims of the Enlightenment. Without arguing in favor of particular metanarratives, he suggests that in language and in the dialogue between senders and receivers arises a reason born of consensus.

Habermas' ideas are based upon John Austin's and John Searle's concept of speech acts, discussed in chapter four. Habermas focuses on the illocutionary act, whereby the speaker performs an action, such as a statement, a command, or a promise. Habermas' central term is *communicative action*, by which he means "those linguistically mediated interactions in which all participants pursue illocutionary aims . . . with their mediating acts of communication." In his ideal communication situation, all individuals "harmonize their individual plans of action with one another," thus pursuing their illocutionary aims.[52] The result of such activity is consensus; all participants to the linguistically mediated interaction arrive at an agreement, which serves as the basis for individual plans of action.

Some agreements are tacit. In conversation, "participants rightly count on world conditions being what is understood in their linguistic community as 'normal.'" Without these assumptions, no communicative action is possible. If participants in a conversation do not share certain background assumptions, they may have to discuss and agree upon suppositions in order for the conversation to come to fruition.[53] Their arrival at agreement is helped by the "pressure for decisions proper to the communicative practice of everyday life," for they cannot coordinate communicative action in absence of consensus about fundamental rules and principles.[54] As Habermas explains, "[f]undamental to the paradigm of mutual understanding is, rather, the performative attitude of participants in interaction, who coordinate their plans for action by coming to an understanding about something in the world."[55]

In this process of building consensus about basic assumptions, Habermas finds a modernist reason that avoids both the problems of the 17th-century absolute metanarratives and the relativism of postmodernism's incredulity toward any metanarratives.[56] Central to his argument is the notion of *lifeworld*, a complex term based on the notion of a socially constructed reality.[57] A community of speaking subjects holds particular understandings and beliefs about the objective world; indeed, these beliefs are necessary if they are to reach understandings with each other. Beliefs about reality operate as an "intersubjectively shared lifeworld."[58] This lifeworld is presented to the present community of speakers by preceding generations; in any communicative activity it is "presupposed by participants as unproblematic."[59] The lifeworld forms a context and serves as resource for discussion.[60]

The reason which Habermas champions is "incarnated" in the "contexts of communicative action" and in the "structures of the lifeworld"; that is, it becomes part of the tacit agreement within linguistic or social communities and is, thereby, a part of the assumed metanarrative for that group.[61] These assumptions, however, do not become part of a discursive formation that cannot be challenged. Instead, they are continually reaffirmed and in some cases may change as a result of intersubjective communicative experience and action, for they are "communicatively structured."[62] Habermas' reason is, therefore, a "communicative rationality" which

> recalls older ideas of logos, inasmuch as it brings along with it the connotations of a noncoercively unifying, consensus-building force of a discourse in which the participants overcome their at first subjectively biased views in favor of a rationally motivated agreement. Communicative reason is expressed in a decentered understanding of the world.[63]

Everyday communication and the lifeworld, thus, are intertwined and affect each other. In a sense, this is a revisited marketplace of ideas, depending not upon a single metanarrative nor leading to one absolute truth but rather one which creates consensual truths that become the operative metanarratives of everyday life.

Habermas also levels a particular challenge to postmodernism through the works of Foucault and Derrida as well as others. Among his criticisms are that these theories remove the distinction among types of discourse—particularly literature, science, and philosophy—by declaring the "primacy of rhetoric over logic" and by subjecting all discourse to literary criticism.[64] Habermas argues that keeping distinctions among types of discourse can help to salvage the notion of modern reason. As noted above, when humans are engaged in speech acts, they are using language as if it had illocutionary force; fiction, on the other hand, may not have illocutionary force or that force may be mimetic. Thus, literary discourses are freed from the arena of everyday discourse, "empowering them for the playful creation of new worlds."[65] Thus, Habermas suggests two general types of discourse—that with "capacities for world-disclosure," which includes art and literature, and that with "problem-solving capacities," which includes morality, science and law.[66]

Lyotard challenges the consensus that is central to Habermas' system because it is based on the validity of a "narrative of emancipation," and postmodernism challenges all such metanarratives. Further, Habermas' position assumes that speakers can come to agreement on rules that have universal validity for language games; however, argues Lyotard, not only are individual language games unlike each other, so are the rules that govern them. Finally, Lyotard claims that the consensus for which Habermas' system calls is never reached: "If all messages could circulate freely among all individuals, the quantity of the information that would have to be taken into account before making the correct choice would delay decisions considerably." With the emphasis in contemporary Western society on performance and speed, which frequently are related to power, the time necessary for consensus will not be available. Lyotard also argues that consensus is not the goal of most discussion. Indeed, he suggests that consensus is an outmoded value; instead, he prefers the postmodern paradigm, in which individuals create their own rules each time they participate in conversation, free from any metanarratives, consensual or absolute.[67]

Lyotard illustrates his criticism of a consensual reason by noting that countless scientists have their contributions, that is, their "moves" in the language game of science, ignored or repressed "because it too abruptly destabilized the accepted positions" in the university and the field of science. "The stronger the 'move,' the more likely it is to be denied the minimum consensus, precisely because it changes the rules of the game upon which consensus had been based."[68] This story illustrates Hassan's explanation of the differences between the two: For Lyotard, language is "conflictual," and consensus is merely one phase of discourse; for Habermas, language is largely communicative, and consensus is the ultimate goal of discourse.[69] Thus, postmodernism challenges all notions of reason, as they are based upon metanarratives of one sort or another.

## Summary

The debate about postmodernism is a debate about the direction of Western culture. The very notion of postmodernism is that modern Western ways of seeing, knowing, and representing, as discussed in Part Three of this text, are being significantly altered. The challenge to the rational paradigm occurs on many levels. At its foundation, the absence of any truth, even the consensual truth described by Habermas, denies the possibility of rationality. Dissolution of the notions of progress and history apparently eliminate the need for rationality. Elevation of language above the subject makes the rules of the language game, rather than rational choice of the subject, the only option for action.

In John Kennedy Toole's novel, *A Confederacy of Dunces*, the main character, Ignatius Reilly, an enormous, fussy, waspish, thunderous, flatulent, absurd, self-pronounced genius of a character who always wears a green hunting cap with earflaps and a plaid shirt, believes his life to be spun out of his control by Fortuna, causing him to be fired from jobs, get drunk, fall in with amazing and comic characters, and tangle with the law and proper society. Fortuna sees to it that nothing good befalls Ignatius, and he staggers from one absurd situation to the next—such as being forced at fork-point to go to work as a vendor of hot dogs from a cart (in the shape of a hot dog) in the French Quarter after he could not pay for the hot dogs he consumes in order to overcome his depression, which is the result of being fired from his job as a janitor at Levy Pants. Ignatius' life, which he claims to be beyond his control, is one postmodern experience after another.

John O'Neill offers this description of the postmodern world:

> We must recognize that words and things have come unstuck. Thus we are all schizophrenics without logos; the flesh writhes, shouts, screams, or sinks into speechlessness. Or perhaps women, hitherto excluded from language, will resuture words and things for us, if there is still time left for such gynesis. For it now looks as though European men have declared themselves as much out of style as have Hollywood men.[70]

Whether women can "resuture words and things" is unclear. The new voices of women and African Americans are discussed in chapter twelve.

## Endnotes

1. David Harvey claims it was between 1968 and 1972. *The Condition of Postmodernity: An Enquiry into the Origins of Cultural Change* (1989; rpt. Cambridge, MA: Basil Blackwell, 1992) 38. John McGowan dates postmodernism from "about 1975." *Postmodernism and Its Critics* (Ithaca, NY: Cornell UP,

1991) ix. Fredric Jameson cites the late 1950s or early 1960s. *Postmodernism, or, the Cultural Logic of Late Capitalism* (Durham, NC: Duke UP, 1991) 1. Ihab Hassan, on the other hand, scoffs at noting a beginning or even a period because postmodernism "requires *both* historical *and* theoretical definition." *The Postmodern Turn: Essays in Postmodern Theory and Culture* (Columbus, OH: Ohio State UP, 1987) 88.

2. He recognizes, however, that we have no better term, unless it be the "Age of Indetermanence." Hassan 87.

3. Donald Kuspit, "The Contradictory Character of Postmodernism," *Postmodernism—Philosophy and the Arts*, ed. Hugh J. Silverman, Continental Philosophy III (New York: Routledge, 1990) 54.

4. Jameson ix.

5. Jean-François Lyotard, *The Postmodern Condition: A Report on Knowledge*, trans. Geoff Bennington and Brian Massumi, Theory and History of Literature, Vol. 10 (1984; rpt. Minneapolis: U of Minnesota P, 1988) xxiv.

6. Jameson ix.

7. Hugh J. Silverman, "Introduction: The Philosophy of Postmodernism," *Postmodernism—Philosophy and the Arts*, ed. Hugh J. Silverman, Continental Philosophy III (New York: Routledge, 1990) 1.

8. Hassan 165. As discussed in chapter ten, Michel Foucault identifies several historical periods categorizable by their epistemological characteristics, that is, by the possibilities for knowledge to be created and delimited. He identifies particular epistemological characteristics of the Classical age (based upon representation and language) as well as the modern period (based upon objectivity, historicity, and the human subject—the *cogito*). Foucault forecasts a new episteme in which the human being will revert to epistemological insignificance. Michel Foucault, *The Order of Things: An Archaeology of the Human Sciences* (1970; rpt. New York: Vintage, 1973) xxiii, 386.

9. Stephen Toulmin, *Cosmopolis: The Hidden Agenda of Modernity* (New York: Free Press, 1990) 17.

10. The assassination of the French king, Henry of Navarre, led to the Thirty Years' War.

11. Toulmin 55.

12. Toulmin 30–33.

13. Toulmin 75.

14. Items excerpted from list in Hassan 91–92.

15. Harvey 42.

16. Lyotard 27.

17. Lyotard 20.

18. Lyotard 29.

19. Lyotard xxiv, 37.

20. McGowan 19.

21. Harvey 44. See also, Hassan 168.

22. Harvey 56. Harvey's reference is to Michel Foucault, *The Archeology of Knowledge and the Discourse on Language*, trans. A. M. Sheridan Smith (1972; rpt. New York: Pantheon, 1982).

23. Gianni Vattimo, *The End of Modernity: Nihilism and Hermeneutics in Postmodern Culture*, trans. Jon R. Snyder (Baltimore: Johns Hopkins UP, 1988) 4–9.

24. Margaret A. Rose, *The Post-modern and the Post-industrial: A Critical Analysis* (New York: Cambridge UP, 1991) 71. See chapter ten for a discussion of the

role of the subject in structuralism, poststructuralism, and deconstruction.

25. Lyotard 15.
26. Lyotard 40.
27. McGowan 20.
28. Fredric Jameson, "Postmodernism and Consumer Society," *The Anti-Aesthetic: Essays on Postmodern Culture*, ed. Hal Foster (Port Townsend, WA: Bay, 1983) 115. See also, Jameson, *The Cultural Logic* 15.
29. Fredric Jameson, "Hans Haacke and the Cultural Logic of Postmodernism," *Hans Haacke: Unfinished Business*, ed. Brian Wallis (Cambridge: Massachusetts Institute of Technology P, 1987) 42.
30. Brian G. Caraher, "A Modernist Allegory of Narration: Joseph Conrad's 'Youth' and the Ideology of the Image," *Image and Ideology in Modern/PostModern Discourse*, ed. David B. Downing and Susan Bazargan (Albany: State U of New York P, 1991) 63.
31. Hassan 39.
32. McGowan 19–20.
33. Jameson, *Postmodernism* 2–3.
34. Lyotard 81.
35. Jameson, *Postmodernism* 39.
36. Harvey 77, 85–91, 295.
37. Jameson, "Postmodernism and Consumer Society" 124–25.
38. Lyotard xxv.
39. Harvey 48.
40. McGowan 17.
41. McGowan 21.
42. Richard Rorty. *Contingency, Irony, and Solidarity* (Cambridge: Cambridge UP, 1989) xiii.
43. Thomas S. Kuhn, *The Structure of Scientific Revolutions*, 2nd ed., Foundations of the Unity of Science, vol. II, no. 2 (1970; rpt. Chicago: U of Chicago P, 1974).
44. Jon R. Snyder, "Translator's Introduction," in Gianni Vattimo, *The End of Modernity: Nihilism and Hermeneutics in Postmodern Culture*, trans. Jon R. Snyder (Baltimore: Johns Hopkins UP, 1988) xxxv. Hassan argues that, when "[a]pplied to the humanities, Kuhn's ideas probably need a rest." Hassan 120.
45. Toulmin 75.
46. Hassan 201.
47. Rose 58.
48. John O'Neill, "Postmodernism and (Post)Marxism," *Postmodernism—The Philosophy and the Arts*, ed. Hugh J. Silverman, Continental Philosophy III (New York: Routledge, 1990) 74.
49. Harvey 116–17.
50. Kuspit 58.
51. Hassan 204–05. Hassan cites Richard Rorty, *Philosophy and the Mirror of Nature* (Princeton, NJ: Princeton UP, 1979).
52. Jürgen Habermas, *The Theory of Communicative Action: Reason and the Rationalization of Society*, vol. 1, trans. Thomas McCarthy (Boston: Beacon Press, 1984) 295, 294.
53. Jürgen Habermas, *The Philosophical Discourse of Modernity: Twelve Lecturers*, trans. Frederick Lawrence (Cambridge, MA: Massachusetts Institute of Technology P, 1987) 197.
54. Habermas, *Philosophical Discourse* 198.
55. Habermas, *Philosophical Discourse* 296.

56. Habermas also suggests that a "paradigm-change" from "subject-centered to communicative reason" would alleviate certain dilemmas in Foucault's analysis. Habermas, *Philosophical Discourse* 301.
57. Jürgen Habermas, *Legitimation Crisis*, trans. Thomas McCarthy (Boston: Beacon, 1975) 4. Habermas cites, in his explanation, Peter L. Berger and Thomas Luckmann, *The Social Construction of Reality: A Treatise in the Sociology of Knowledge* (1966; rpt. Garden City, NY: Anchor, 1967).
58. Habermas, *Communicative Action* 13 (emphasis omitted).
59. Habermas, *Communicative Action* 70.
60. Habermas, *Philosophical Discourse* 298.
61. Habermas, *Philosophical Discourse* 322 (emphasis omitted).
62. Habermas, *Philosophical Discourse* 299.
63. Habermas, *Philosophical Discourse* 315.
64. Habermas, *Philosophical Discourse* 185, 190–92. Indeed, Habermas suggests this is the reason Derrida has received so much attention in the United States. In this analysis, Habermas indicates his rather limited definition for rhetoric, which is opposed to logic.
65. Habermas, *Philosophical Discourse* 201.
66. Habermas, *Philosophical Discourse* 207 (emphasis omitted).
67. Lyotard 60–66.
68. Lyotard 63.
69. Hassan 199.
70. O'Neill 78.

# Chapter Twelve

# Voice

In the United States, the language of women and slaves was not valued, and in some cases it was outlawed. For example, a 1740 South Carolina statute made it illegal to teach slaves to write.[1] The historical effort to keep particular groups from reading and writing is understandable, given the power of discourse. If individuals can be limited to the oral dissemination of messages, and if those messages are accorded no value by the dominant culture, then the group will remain in the margins of society—those individuals will be powerless. The banishment of women and ethnic minorities to the political margins of society is not merely a historical phenomenon; the dominant culture in the United States continues to be that of the white male.

Some contemporary theories of discourse acknowledge the diversity in society, focus on the political and other societal forces that keep some discourse in the margins, and promote development of strategies for reversal of hierarchies and for privileging that which is absent.[2] If society is to embrace and to value all of its members, it must break the silence of women, ethnic minorities, and others in the margins of society. We must learn to listen to all the voices, and individuals must find an authentic voice of their own.

## Women

"If silence is golden, it costs too much," claims Nancy Gray. "Women have been paying the price for a very long time."[3] In a society in which males are privileged, in a *patriarchy*,[4] woman is the "Other." Giving women a voice is one of the major goals of those feminists writing in the last half of the twentieth century. Indeed, most feminist theories of rhetoric seek to identify the societal and linguistic structures that silence women's voices, to disrupt those structures, and to encourage women to talk and to write in ways that will empower them. Some of the early scholarship focuses on particularities of female language and its reception by the patriarchy. Other scholarship argues that women should not try to fit themselves or their language within the structures of patriarchal society. Instead, women should adopt their own, particularly female language, empowering themselves rather than seeking acknowledgment from the patriarchy that its criteria for powerful speech are met.

## Women's Language and Language about Women

The issue of sexist language has become tiresome for some. Those tired of new forms such as *chairperson* or *her/his* (which are used to avoid sexist reference) make claims such as, "*man* is a generic noun." This claim certainly has much historical backing, as a review of many of the quotations in this text illustrates. *Man* is used as synonymous with *human* by a significant number of the theorists cited herein. Elizabeth Minnich, however, effectively refutes that viewpoint:

> We hit absurdity fairly fast on this level. Consider the famous syllogism: "Man is mortal. Socrates is a man. Therefore, Socrates is mortal." Try it with a woman: "Man is mortal. Alice is _____" what? A man? No one says that, not even philosophers. "Man," the supposedly generic term, does not allow us to say, "Alice is a man." So we say, "Alice is a woman." Then what are we to deduce? . . . Is Alice, who is female and hence not in a category that is either neutral or masculine, then *immortal*? . . . We can think of Socrates as a man without derailing the syllogism; we cannot think of Alice as a woman. Reason flounders; the center holds, with Man in it, but it is an exclusive, not a universal or neutral, center. Alice disappears through the looking glass.[5]

Other language issues include the loss of a female's surname at marriage, adjectives commonly used to describe each gender, and gender-specific pronouns used for generic reference.[6] As debate concerning language about women continues, more recent focus is on women's language.

Among the classic texts discussing female language and "woman's place" in society is that of Robin Lakoff. She argues that women are socialized to use particular language, language which is trivial and uncertain. As a result, women are "denied access to power, on the grounds that they are not capable of holding it as demonstrated by their linguistic behavior."[7] The sort of linguistic behavior she describes—"talking like a lady"—includes making precise color discriminations ("mauve"), using weaker expletives ("oh dear"), using particular empty adjectives ("adorable" or "divine"), adding polite tags to commands ("Won't you close the door?"), and using a questioning tone when answering questions (in response to "When will dinner be ready?" answering, "Oh . . . around six o'clock?"). These, in addition to linguistic inequalities used to describe women ("lady doctor" and "spinster" versus "bachelor") reflect, according to Lakoff, inequalities in society. Thus, women are caught in a double bind—they are viewed as unfeminine if they don't learn to speak women's language; if they do, they are not taken seriously. Lakoff argues that women's overly polite language is "stifling, exclusive and oppressive," and she urges women to change their linguistic habits.[8]

Following Lakoff, numerous researchers attempted to identify language differences between males and females in a variety of situations. The assumption of these studies was that women, either naturally or because of socialization, use language differently than men and are marginalized by that language. Researchers looked for women's language to be softer and less dogmatic and to involve more questions and hedges. Other scholars sought to challenge her; indeed, the research done in an effort to refute Lakoff may be among the most important results of her work.[9] Marilyn French, on the other hand, argues that the question which should be asked as a result of Lakoff's research is not how the language of women and men differ or how those differences lead to inequalities but "[w]hat does it create?" French suggests that "general women's language aims for harmony with others rather than an expression of control over them," and "the former seems preferable to the latter as a societal standard."[10]

The differences between harmony and control are reflected in Carol Gilligan's work, which suggests that women's logic and methods of moral judgment are distinct from that of men. She suggests that women's logic is based on responsibility and relationships; it is a psychological logic, leading to an "ethic of care." Women's methods of moral judgment are based on this ethic, while male moral judgments adhere from an ethic of rights, based on fairness, equality, and reciprocity.[11]

More recently, feminist scholars have sought to break the silence of women and to elevate female language and the values reflected therein. This approach to female language is quite different from Lakoff's, for rather than changing female language so that women will be viewed as more powerful, these writers argue that women should empower themselves by creating and using their own language, by writing and speaking in their own voices. This is a shift to "woman as subject."[12]

## L'écriture Feminine

A chorus of voices has called for a feminine but powerful way of using language. This call is for a feminine writing—a language of women's own. One such voice is that of Hélène Cixous, whose ideas are grounded in but go well beyond those of Jacques Derrida and Jacques Lacan. Cixous argues that only one gender, the male, is present in history and writing. Although speech (*parole*) allows one to "traverse and experience," it also is caught up in the dominant system of discourse. Cixous believes there is no experience prior to its enunciation in and through language. Existing patriarchal systems of language create a social reality in which women occupy a negative place: Woman is the gap, the silence. Man is presence; woman is trace.

Furthermore, if nothing is outside language, the body, like everything else, is a product of discourse. Thus, Cixous advocates that a female "write her self." By writing herself, the woman puts herself into the world and into history. This writing, which Cixous calls *l'écriture feminine*, debuted in "Laugh of the Medusa," which is Cixous' attempt to deconstruct male-centered understanding, that is, *phallocentrism*.[13]

The history of writing, Cixous argues, is confounded with the history of reason. Only an occasional poet (because poetry taps the unconscious, which is the place where the repressed survives) has escaped the phallocentric tradition. By seizing the occasion to speak, women forge for themselves what Cixous calls the "antilogos weapon"; they can overcome the boundaries created by phallocentric language and initiate new understandings.[14]

Cixous refuses to describe the women's writing she advocates, as to do so falls prey to theorizing, which belongs to the patriarchal order. Instead, she envisions a multiplicity of discourses, for the "[w]omen's imaginary is inexhaustible." These women's texts will "invent the impregnable language that will wreck partitions, classes, and rhetorics, regulations and codes." Such language will "fly"; a "feminine text cannot fail to be more than subversive. It is volcanic; as it is written it brings about an upheaval of the old property crust, carrier of masculine investments; there's no other way."[15] This women's writing will be writing of non-repression, writing which *gives*, thus passing on to others the break with structure and form. Women's texts will be unpredictable and unknowable; they will take risks; they will be wandering and excessive.[16]

Cixous's own writing indicates what one form of *l'écriture feminine* might look like. Her writing involves metaphors, puns, and word play. What she encourages is what she feels is natural in women—soft and tactile writing: "Let's look not at syntax but at fantasy, at the unconscious: all the feminine texts I've read are very close to the voice, very close to the flesh of language, much more so than masculine texts . . . . There's *tactility* in the feminine text, there's touch, and this touch passes through the ear."[17] Cixous proposes metaphor as one means to release the feminine from bonds of phallocentric language. Metaphor breaks down semantic hierarchy and reason, releases the unconscious: "[M]etaphor breaks free; all that belongs to the realm of fantasmatic production . . . , all that belongs to the imaginary and smashes language from all sides represents a force that cannot be controlled. Metaphors are what drives language mad."[18]

Cixous argues that men and women exist only in language, which dictates to both its rules and order, laying down models of behavior and interaction. What the woman must do is to speak, ignoring what she is taught in school (to listen and to believe). Cixous argues for elimination of the systems of censorship that limit the speech of the feminine. When women "venture to speak," they "will of necessity bring about a shift in metalanguage," in the hidden assumptions, rules, and orders that are the inherent structures of language.[19]

## Creating a Language of the Feminine

Luce Irigaray also urges women to adopt a language of the feminine, one that rejects the patriarchy. Without such a language, women are condemned to silence. To make possible women's language requires nothing less, claims Irigaray, than destroying the existing discursive mechanism. To do that requires, as a first step, a rereading of patriarchal texts: "What is called for instead is an examination of the *operation of the 'grammar'* of each figure of discourse, its syntactic laws or requirements, its imaginary configurations, its metaphoric networks, and also, of course, what it does not articulate at the level of utterance: *its silences.*"[20]

Once the patriarchal discourse is understood, Irigaray argues that it must be discarded. Women must "pry out" of the discourse what it has borrowed from the feminine and make it " 'render up' and give back" what it owes to the feminine. Woman as Other is the logical product of this discourse; more than the male, it is language that rules as woman's master. Thus, women should identify the oppositions of patriarchal texts. Women should challenge every dichotomy: "Nothing is ever to be *posited* that is not also reversed and caught up again in the *supplementarity of this reversal.*"[21] Woman is a threat to patriarchal language, as she threatens to disrupt its logic and its order.

Perhaps no one has gone farther in creating and promoting a feminine language than Mary Daly, who teaches feminist ethics at Boston College. According to Daly, because language is in service of the patriarchy, all naming, describing, and theorizing about values and about the good comes to women through a "maze/haze of deception."[22] The images presented by and the perceptions imbedded in language operate to keep women the Other. Daly's solution for breaking the mental bonds of patriarchy is to change the language. Although she develops this new language over the course of all her writings, her strategies are described in *Websters' First New Intergalactic Wickedary of the English Language*, authored "in cahoots with" Jane Caputi. In the book, she weaves a web of words, giving new or sometimes liberating old meanings of words, some of which currently have negative connotations, such as *hag* and *crone*. In creating this women's language, Daly challenges conventions of style, spelling, grammar, pronouncing, syntax, and scholarship. She describes the work of the *Wickedary* as "freeing words from the cages and prisons of patriarchal patterns," and she attempts to "unwind the bindings of mummified/numbified words." Daly challenges women to exercise their "Elemental Communication Powers," which have been "tied down by the spiritbindings of sadospiritual fixers." Those who understand, who are "Elemental Mediums," "Howl to silenced Soothsayers to shout down the lies of 'authorities.' They call to housebound/housebroken Gossips to get off the phone, get away from the phoneys, and once again Gossip Wisdom from the stars."[23]

**Capitalization**.   Many more words are capitalized in Daly's prose than in patriarchal prose. She uses capitals to indicate background words, to distinguish from standard usage, or to create emphasis. Thus, she refers to women confronted by "Biggest Lies," to "Naming" and "Metabeing," and to the "female Elemental Race" which has "Stamina."[24]

**Spelling**.   Daly also changes the spelling of words to free their meanings. Some words are hyphenated, such as "Dis-cover" and "Be-muse." Other words are used in different contexts, such as "Busy Beeing." Further, she "spins off" words by weaving around them other words, to demonstrate new understandings, such as the book title, "Websters' Wickedary," to indicate that it is a dictionary for wicked women. Another example is "Nag-nostic."

Daly also emphasizes the importance of the oral, citing the role of rhyme and rhythm in brain activity and oral traditions.[25] "Spelling/

Be-Spelling," she argues, should be "Out Loud." Talking out loud creates "Living Words," which have different patterns and orders, "vital vibrations," which change reality, overcoming the negative vibrations of phallocentric language, of the "incessant droning of the mass media," of "academented sadoscholarship" which challenges nothing, can "Name Nothing," and has the "aura of styrofoam and the texture of plastic."[26]

**Grammar**.   Daly seeks to "unfix the fixations" of the grammar of phallocentric language. She argues that grammar operates to control, allowing language to be an instrument of oppression. Adopting a feminist syntactics ("Sin-Tactics") allows women to break taboos and communicate "Glamourie," which is the state of mind of witches, in which they see apparitions and visions. Words are placed in different order to break the pattern of consciousness that phallocentric language creates. Daly champions present tense and active voice.[27]

**Names and Terms**.   Certain words in phallocentric language operate to distort reality, according to Daly. This distortion creates artificiality and "bespoils" nature with technology and all its poisonous by-products. The terms of which she complains are terms that stop thinking. For example, she objects to using *plant* to refer to a nuclear facility or *bug* to an electronic device that invades the privacy and homes of individuals. She argues that instruments of destruction should not be allowed to have names that have positive connotations— such as *breeder reactor, air-breathing missile*, or *mushroom cloud*.

Daly also objects to what she calls *archetypal elementary* terms, terms like *civilization, mystery, custom, forefathers, history,* and *revelation*, which are used by teachers ("schoolmasters, who are the pillars of pedantocracy"), in the mass media, and by politicians. The role of such terms, she argues, is "to mummify minds and memories." These words pretend to tell you something about that which they speak. Instead, they are ideological words that stop thought and judgment: "These boring old priestly terms are not only the building blobs of archetypal civilization; they are also the silly putty that holds it together, that is, apart."[28]

Daly has other difficulties with terms. She challenges degrading terms and labels, such as *chick, bitch, dog, pig*. She explains how words work to reverse thinking processes, such as a line of makeup called "The Natural Look," or to create false dichotomies, such as the term *forcible rape*, which implies existence of a benign rape.[29]

Daly not only suggests a change of language, she adopts it. A characteristic example of her prose demonstrates many of these elements:

> This Life-Lusty atmosphere has several noteworthy qualities by which it can immediately be identified. It is marked by Haggard Humor—the Lusty Laughter of Leaping Women who Laugh Out Loud at cockaludicrous loutishness. It is characterized also by explosions of Righteous Rage on behalf of all Elemental sisters. This Metapatriarchal atmosphere vibrates with Virtuous Disgust at the dreariness of daddyland, with its deceptive dickspeak and dis-spiriting, dryasdust dogmas and daddygods.[30]

In another example, she says:

> Since the bafflers attempt to interpret the Crones' Chorus by the rules of the going logic, they remain baffled. Since they can hear only sounds but cannot hear hearing, they cannot break the code of the Gyn/Ecologists' Un-Convention, whose participants are hearing ever more deeply into the secret chambers of the labyrinth. Since the bafflers are only gamesters, they are unable to perceive the high creativity of Crones, which is playful celebration.[31]

Daly, by challenging the structure of phallocentric language and adopting a female language, is able to transcend the "trickery" and "illusions/deceptions" of patriarchal language and break out of the understandings of the dominant paradigm. "[W]ords, having been stolen, are coming home."[32]

## Other Feminine Voices

Julia Kristeva, "one of the most brilliant and versatile of the French intellectual figures of the last two decades,"[33] seeks to correct phallocentric theories of language. However, she is antagonistic to the ideas of Irigaray, Daly, and other feminists who deny all aspects of male language and social order. Kristeva argues that, by creating the type of feminine language they suggest, women fall back into mysticism while remaining within the same metaphysical enclosure they currently inhabit. Such feminism, she claims, necessarily will yield an alternate master discourse, not a discourse that is master-free.[34]

In addition to the voice resulting from adoption of a female language, some feminist scholars note other avenues of expression. Sonja Foss and Karen Foss suggest that women "have an eloquence of their own, manifest in a variety of contexts and forms, that creates worlds of immense richness for them and those around them."[35] They identify and illustrate the eloquence in such means of expression as baking, dance, motherhood, jewelry design, architecture, and shopping.

## Political Goals

Although the call for a feminine language is widespread, the political goals of feminists are quite diverse. Cixous argues that the transformation of subjectivity must precede social transformations. She rejects feminism as a movement because it merely imitates the phallocentric search for power. Irigaray and Daly would have women withdraw not only from phallocentric language but society as well. Irigaray argues that merely attempting to change the distribution of power in society is to resubject women to what is a phallocentric order and logic. Only by denying the order can women become present. Thus her argument becomes not only an argument for a feminine language but a sexuality that is uniquely feminine. Similarly, Mary Daly's solution to the patriarchal control of language and knowledge is to carve a life, and a language, that is outside the patriarchy, that is feminine.

Daly claims that male-dominated society uses four methods of mystification, what she calls "games of the father." The first is *erasure*, in which women have no presence and no place in the scholarship of the patriarchy. The second method of mystification is *reversal*, in which the order of things is presented backwards, to privilege males. Thus, Adam gives "birth" to Eve. The third method is *false polarization*, in which the patriarchy creates definitions which set up false dichotomies, such as feminism against sexism. The final method is *divide and conquer*. Daly argues that women, in order to develop their fullest feminine selves, must stick together as they attempt to make their way in professional life and in the life of the mind. Thus, she discards both phallocentric society and the men that it privileges. She urges women to band together, to seek the "fire" of female friendship. Inclusion into patriarchal institutions, she claims, is tokenism that is destructive to sisterhood and to the emancipation and "enspiriting" of the female self. "Crones kindle the Fury of our own kind against the godfathers who burned our foremothers. The uprising of Cinderellas from the cinders/ashes of our mothers is the righteous Renaissance." This fury creates "Fire" in light of which males will be forced to see their history and their treatment of women.[36]

Kristeva argues that women should not withdraw into their own societies, as Irigaray and Daly urge them to do. Kristeva calls their position second-generation feminism and argues for a third generation, one which will seek to reunite society. The first generation of feminists were the suffragettes, who aspired to gain a place in linear time. These women wanted equal work for equal pay and an equal footing with men in the political and economic world; this first generation of feminists wanted to be inserted into history. The second generation of feminists, according to Kristeva, discount the importance of joining the men's world, of gaining a place in linear time. Instead, they seek to regain what is repressed in women, to champion and exalt that which is feminine. As Kristeva explains, they "seek to give a language to the intrasubjective and corporeal experiences left mute by culture in the past."[37] The second generation involves a radical refusal to join history. Certainly Irigaray and Daly fit into this category. The third generation of feminists must determine, says Kristeva, what their place is in the symbolic order. The new feminist ideology comes from being left out of the "sociosymbolic contract" and left out "of language as the fundamental social bond." The project to be completed by third-generation feminists is research designed to "break the code, to shatter language, to find a specific discourse closer to the body and emotions." However, Kristeva makes clear that she is not talking about a feminine language, which is "highly problematical."[38] She wants changes in the language that both sexes speak; she wants women to use their feminine nature in ways that shatter the sociosymbolic contract of Western society, a contract based in violence and war.

In an attack on second-generation feminists, Kristeva argues that this third generation, which seeks to change society from within, is superior to the second generation, which denies the male, thereby making the same mistakes as those made by patriarchal society. Female-only societies are based on expulsion and scapegoating of men. Such a strategy results in the same marginalization that feminism opposes. Thus, she argues, second-generation feminists fall prey to an "inverted sexism" and follow the very logic they claim to repudiate. Rather than sulking in isolation, female innovation must be based on better understandings between maternity and female creativity.[39] True dissidence, she argues, comes in thought—a thought that works through rather than ignores differences. The third generation must embrace what is feminine without denying the masculine, embracing the "*community* of language" which can equalize, acknowledging the singularity of each individual as well as individual multiplicity.[40]

However, despite her rejection of second-generation feminism, Kristeva does credit its role. Although such women may be reduced to "naïve whining" or "market-place romanticism," and "no matter how dubious the results of these recent productions by women," says Kristeva, "the symptom is there—women are writing, and the air is heavy with expectation."[41]

## Logic

Andrea Nye reviews the history of Western logic from a feminist perspective and finds it wanting. First, she notes that such a history is not of *logic* but of logics, each situated historically—a product of the man who created it and of its time. For example, the logics of Plato and Aristotle are situated in language. Plato's logic arises from interaction between speakers and involves a superior who leads a passive inferior to truth, and Aristotle's begins (in the *Prior Analytics*) in disputation, although it creates a system of rules that takes precedence over any discussion. By the *Posterior Analytics*, according to Nye, the need for discussion has disappeared. This logic "insulates the speaker's words from anything anyone else might say."[42] In the logic of the Stoics comes the move beyond any particular language, as a logic appropriate for Athenian Greeks was no longer adequate after Alexander ruled not only Athens but most of the West and Near East (see chapter eight for further discussion). After the Stoics, logic "had established an alternative meta-universe of discourse, neither psychological nor physical, in which truth could be reliably established." The truth of propositions in Stoic logic depended upon correspondence to "facts," which were neither linguistically nor perceptually affected. As Nye explains, "[l]ogic provided . . . a language that constructed its own world of entities and structures to correspond to its own truths."[43]

Much later in this history, Gottlob Frege's logic finally moved beyond language entirely to the realm of mathematics. He saw the reliance on words as an impediment to logic; thus, in Frege's logic, proper thought becomes mathematical. This logic has created the most damage, according to Nye, who argues that it makes talk powerless—"Fragmented, private opinions, a matter of feelings, sensations that can change from one day to the next"—these things are unimportant to a logic "divorced from reality and from the life force of a living community." Thus, logic is separate from feelings, from lived reality, from experience. "A logical language is a language without style, a language purged of the coloring, nuance, rhythm, metaphor, rhetoric that mark an individual voice."[44]

In concluding, Nye announces that she finds "no 'logic' in the history of logic," and no progress toward a universal rationality in the history of logics. She challenges that history and its separation of truth and logic from subjectivity, passion, and intent. Logic brings truths "independent of contingent human affairs and of natural language's role in concrete human experiences of interaction and intercourse." She counters that "words themselves, no matter how cleverly arranged, cannot tell the truth; they must have meaning and to have meaning they must be spoken by someone somewhere on some occasion."[45] Thus, the antidote to logic is language itself but not, she is careful to point out, a women's language. Instead, women must *respond* to logic, as Nye has, by pointing out that "logic is not thought at all but the denial of any challenge that might stimulate thought"; women must challenge logic's claim to be "reason and truth and knowledge." Women also must use skills of reading, including "attention, listening, understanding, [and] responding" skills, which are antithetical to the methods of logic, according to Nye.[46]

## Knowledge

The feminist attack on the patriarchy does not end with language or other forms of discourse. Scholars argue that the problem lies with the very conception of knowledge. The issue is what counts as knowledge, the importance of the concept *knowledge* to human understanding, and the nature of rationality itself. The work of Mary Field Belenky, Blythe McVicker Clinchy, Nancy Rule Goldberger and Jill Mattuck Tarule suggests that current "models of intellectual development" are patterned after the male experience. "The mental processes that are involved in considering the abstract and the impersonal have been labeled 'thinking' and are attributed primarily to men, while those that deal with the personal and interpersonal fall under the rubric of 'emotions' and are largely relegated to women."[47]

In the research of Belenky, Clinchy, Goldberger, and Tarule, they found that women know in a variety of ways, which can be categorized as developmental stages. Some women are *received knowers* who listen in order to learn and who feel that all knowledge is outside the self. Received knowers have a dualistic, right/wrong perspective on truth. The next stage of knowing is subjective. *Subjective knowers* listen to an inner voice and trust their own intuitions. According to women who have reached it, this stage moves beyond received knowing because women "become their own authorities" and feel stronger and more self-sufficient. However, "[i]n a world that emphasizes rationalism and scientific thought," subjective knowers pay "personal and social costs."[48] The subjective stage of knowledge involves listening to and watching others as a means of gathering observations. "During the period of subjective knowing, women lay down procedures for systematically learning and analyzing experience. But what seems distinctive in these women is that their strategies for knowing grow out of their very embeddedness in human relationships and their alertness to the details of everyday life."[49] The third stage of knowledge is procedural knowledge, which involves "conscious, deliberate, systematic analysis."[50] For *procedural knowers*, the issue is not the morality or rightness of the conclusion but the thoroughness of the procedure of thinking and deciding. The authors cite a term coined by Mary Daly—*methodolatry*—to describe this stage.[51] As a result of their skill in obtaining and communicating knowledge, procedural knowers feel in control. Their knowledge is more objective than that of subjective knowers. Procedural knowers can be either *separate knowers* (knowers whose orientation is toward impersonal rules that an outside authority has set and which one must master to win the game) or *connected knowers* (knowers whose orientation is toward relationship, so that the quest for knowledge is a quest to understand the other). Procedural knowers of either type "can criticize a system, but only in the system's terms, only according to the system's standards."[52] The final stage of female knowledge is constructed knowledge, in which women go outside the dominant structures and create their own system. *Connected knowers* "learn to speak in a unique and authentic voice."[53] At this level of knowing, women can take from the outside that which they want, integrate it with their subjective knowledge, and weave a new whole that includes both the rational and the emotional. Connected knowers realize that all knowledge is constructed and the knower is a part of that which is known.[54] This knower is a passionate knower, one who makes maximum use of Jürgen Habermas' communicative action in an ideal speech situation.[55] Moral judgment for these women is contextual and includes consideration of the broader community and their own commitments.

Minnich argues that women can understand both the knowledge of the dominant paradigm and women's ways of knowing. To throw out the entire patriarchal system of discourse and knowledge, she cautions, will void the voices of women who spoke within that system and in spite of it. Further, "we run the risk of finding ourselves in no-time, with no place that is our own to stand, and with no tongue to speak that does not entrap us the minute we open our mouths."[56] Thus, for Minnich, no intellectual stance exists that is outside the dominant tradition. To understand knowledge, women must be able to think within, about, and beyond the dominant tradition. She notes:

> Fortunately, humans are creatures of translation, transitive creatures able to understand more than one language and to move between languages without losing either what is unique to each or what is common enough to make translation possible. We are able to apprehend more than can be spoken in any one language, and can stretch that language in ways that change and enrich it. There are many ways to be both within and without our own cultures.[57]

Women are searching for a voice because they feel that patriarchal society attempts to silence them. Other groups whose voices are not heard also challenge the dominant language. One such group is African Americans.

## African Americans

Although finding an authentic voice is imperative to all persons in the margins of society, particularly ethnic minorities, no other group has the history of marginality in U.S. society that African Americans have. The search for individual voices by African Americans is ongoing; however, a complex, unique, and fascinating African-American language and style have existed since the early days of slavery and serve today as an African-American voice. Geneva Smitherman notes:

> Black Dialect is an Africanized form of English reflecting Black America's linguistic-cultural African heritage and the conditions of servitude, oppression and life in America. Black Language is Euro-American speech with an Afro-American meaning, nuance, tone, and gesture. The Black Idiom is used by 80 to 90 percent of American blacks, at least some of the time. It has allowed blacks to create a culture of survival in an alien land, and as a by-product has served to enrich the language of all Americans.[58]

### Influence of West Africa

The native language of an African slave might have been Ibo, Hausa, Yoruba, or any other West African language. When Africans were brought to the United States, they quickly developed pidgin and later creole languages in order to speak to each other and to English-speaking whites. (See chapter two for discussion of pidgins and creoles). Over time, as they learned English and combined that language with aspects of native African languages and with their experience and lifestyle in the United States, they developed the particulars of the African-American dialect.[59]

   The oral traditions of West Africa also shaped the African-American dialect. Smitherman notes that the "preslavery background was one in which the concept of Nommo, the magic power of the Word, was believed necessary to actualize life and give man mastery over things."[60] Thus, the style of the African-American dialect is the style of the oral traditions—rhyming and rhythmic—and oral performance is a significant part of the communication.

### Signifyin(g)

In addition to the effects of West African languages, the conditions of slavery and discrimination affected the development of the African-American dialect. Although slaves were forced to communicate in a form of English, they also needed a coded or disguised form of that language for speaking to each other. The result was perhaps the most fascinating characteristic of African-American "black speech." Frequently, statements had double or even multiple meanings. Thus, a statement which sounded innocuous to a white audience might carry a hidden meaning to other African Americans. This was true not only of speech but songs as well. Smitherman illustrates:

> [S]lave song lyrics and spirituals had a double-edged meaning. For instance, note the following stanza from an old black song:
>
> > You mought be Carroll from Carrollton
> > Arrive here night afo' Lawd made creation
> > But you can't keep the World from moverin' around
> > And not turn her back from the gaining ground.
>
> The phrase "not turn her" in the last line is a concealed reference to preacher-revolutionary Nat Turner.[61]

This coded language continued beyond the institution of slavery and is still a part of some "black talk." John Baugh counts among his earliest childhood memories being able to tell whether his mother, who held a doctorate, "was talking [on the phone] to someone black or someone white, based on her speech alone."[62] She used different dialects when talking to individuals of different groups. Certainly, not all contemporary African Americans use the same dialect. However, the so-called "street speech" that harkens back to the days of slavery is, for some African Americans, essential to their cultural identity, and they use a form of that dialect when talking to each other. This dialect is governed by complicated rules of grammar, semantics, and syntax and demonstrates the fascinating voice created by an oppressed and oral people.

The rules of this dialect have been studied and variously named. Henry Louis Gates groups all semantic characteristics under the heading "signifyin(g)." Signifyin(g) includes all the various strategies in the present-day African-American elaboration of the coded and disguised language of the slaves. Gates finds the exemplar of signifyin(g) (and its trope) in the Signifying Monkey, tales of whom originated in the oral traditions of slavery. The Signifying Monkey is, according to Gates, an oxymoron—an "ironic reversal of a received racist image in the Western imagination of the black as simianlike."[63] The Signifying Monkey survives by his wits; his gift for fluid, fancy, and fast speech; his verbal trickery; and his superior intelligence. In many of the stories, the Monkey saves himself from the Lion by signifying—by using his fancy, coded, and involved speech that confuses the Lion into believing that the Elephant had done him wrong. When the Lion goes after the Elephant, the larger beast inevitably wins the contest. Then, the enraged Lion returns to hunt the Monkey who, once again, by his facile and tricky speech, saves himself from the Lion. Hundreds of stories about the Signifying Monkey have been recorded. Gates suggests that they begin, and end, formulaicly, as do many oral traditions. He gives the following illustrations:

> Deep down in the jungle so they say
> There's a signifying monkey down the way
> There hadn't been no disturbin' in the jungle for quite a bit,
> For up jumped the monkey in the tree one day and laughed
> "I guess I'll start some shit."

* * *

> "Monkey," said the Lion,
> Beat to his unbooted knees,
> "You and your signifying children
> Better stay up in the trees."
> Which is why today
> Monkey does his signifying
> A-*way-up* out of the way.[64]

Like the Signifying Monkey, signifyin[g] involves complicated and tricky speech that has multiple levels of meaning. The surface level is understandable to all speakers of English; beneath that are hidden one or more meanings that are understandable to others who understand signifyin[g]. Thus, *bad* can mean good or beautiful. The multiple meanings are created through a variety of verbal arts. These arts are variously named and include such things as *capping*, *testifying*, *playing the dozens*, and *toasting*. Smitherman organizes these verbal arts into call response, signification, tonal semantics and narrative sequencing.

**Call Response**.   *Call response* is the verbal and nonverbal interaction between the speaker and the audience that happens spontaneously. The audience response in many African-American churches illustrates this aspect of black talk ("Amen," "Hallelujah, brother," "Oh, yessuh," "Lord ha mercy"). Call response erases distinctions between performer and audience, creates a sense of solidarity and cooperation, and makes speech participatory and spontaneous.[65]

**Signifying**.   *Signifying* is the art of verbal insult and put down and of verbal indirection.[66] For example, *Playing the Dozens* is insulting a person by signifying on a relative, particularly the mother. The retort, "Yo momma," is an example of the Dozens. The Dozens can become very sophisticated, as verbal insults are exchanged back and forth. According to Baugh, the Dozens most frequently is "reserved for situations that are almost always exclusive to black males who are intimates.''[67] The first person to get angry loses the game. Other acts of verbal misdirection and multiple meaning are meant to communicate within the black speech community but not outside of it. These acts sometimes are called *shuckin'* and *jivin.'* *Loud-talking* is directing remarks to a third person by speaking to a second in a tone just loud enough for the third person, at whom the remark really is directed, to hear. The various forms of signifying can involve irony, puns, humor, metaphor, and other figures of speech. Gates notes an enormous number of names for forms of signifying, including

> talking shit, woofing, spouting, muckty muck, boogerbang, beating your gums, talking smart, putting down, putting on, playing, sounding, telling lies, shag-lag, marking, shucking, jiving, jitterbugging, bugging, mounting, charging, cracking, harping, rapping, bookooing, low-rating, hoorawing, sweet-talking, smart-talking . . .[68]

Signifying, then, is all of these forms of verbal misdirection. It is a mode of persuasive communication unique to the black community that involves various sophisticated rhetorical strategies that give multiple and metaphoric meaning to words. As Gates notes, complicated figures of speech including metonymy, metaphor, allegory, and the like are found in ''the rapping of black kids on street corners, who recite and thereby preserve the classical black rhetorical structures.''[69]

**Tonal Semantics**. This aspect of ''black talking'' refers to the vocal inflection and voice rhythms of the speech. Although *tonal semantics* cannot be reproduced in print, they can be heard in rap music, in the speeches of Jesse Jackson and Martin Luther King, Jr., in the talk of H. Rap Brown, and in the comedy routines of Richard Pryor. Smitherman argues that the ''key to understanding black tonal semantics is to recognize that the sound of what is being said is just as important as 'sense.'''[70] Rhyme also is a part of tonal semantics.

**Narrative Sequencing**. The last mode of discourse identified by Smitherman is *narrative sequencing* or storytelling. The stories are designed to be persuasive, but are long and take considerable time to get to the point. Smitherman describes them thusly: ''This meandering away from the 'point' takes the listener on episodic journeys and over tributary rhetorical routes, but like the flow of nature's rivers and streams, it all eventually leads back to the source.''[71]

Various forms of narrative sequencing exist, including *testifying* and *Toasts*. Testifying involves telling the truth by means of a story, which might include visions, testimony about religious experience, and the like. The Toast is a story in which the hero is rebellious and boastful about his sexuality, badness, and fighting ability. It is filled with profanities and sexual allusions, is in the first person, and is "a tribute—that is, a 'toast'—to this superbad, omnipotent black hustler, pimp, player, killer who is mean to the max."[72]

By these methods—call response, signifying, tonal semantics, and narrative sequencing—black speech becomes "a functional dynamic that is simultaneously a mechanism for learning about life and the world and a vehicle for achieving group approval and recognition."[73] If an African-American child is brought up in a signifyin(g) family, a part of the familial socialization is instruction in this verbal art, instruction in this dialect and voice. In a very real sense, many African Americans are nearly bilingual, for they can switch dialects, as Baugh's mother switched, depending upon whom she was talking to at the time. Signifyin[g] is a second language which is shared among African Americans.[74]

Signifyin[g] also is a very controversial issue. For African Americans to be upwardly mobile in this society, they must adopt the linguistic structures of the dominant culture. Indeed, so-called Black English often is seen as incorrect, lazy, and without rules. Black dialect, however, is not without rules; its rules are different than other English dialects. Its rules derive from the oral traditions, while other dialects derive from European print culture. To characterize one as "correct" and one as "incorrect" is to give uncritical acceptance to the same dominant paradigm that feminists challenge. Indeed, Smitherman chastises those who seek "correct" language. Instead, she argues that we should ask, "What is dynamic and vivid language? . . . What is contextually appropriate language? . . . What is truthful language?"[75] The way in which we use language, the voice we adopt, will affect our human understanding.

## Summary

The metaphor *voice* is widely adopted as a way for groups and for individuals to express their search for identity, for connection to others and to a shared past, for their own particular worldview, and for their place not in the margins but in the center of a society. Ntozake Shange, in her "choreopoem," *for colored girls who have considered suicide/when the rainbow is enuf*, has the "lady in brown" say:

> somebody/anybody
> sing a black girl's song
> bring her out

to know yourself
to know you
but sing her rhythms
carin/struggle/hard times
sing her song of life
she's been dead so long
closed in silence so long
she doesn't know the sound
of her own voice.[76]

To speak in one's voice frequently is a challenge to the rational paradigm. Standards of language and logic and the rationality privileged in the dominant culture are discounted when individuals marginalized by that culture assert their own ways of thinking and talking and understanding.

Although the two groups discussed in this chapter, as well as other groups, differ in their voices, each advocate or practice a reworking of the dominant language—or its supplementation with a unique and fascinating language of one's own. This rethinking of language, of the ways in which categories create realities and stereotypes, the ways in which use of particular words changes thinking, the ways in which discourse omits certain people, is perhaps the most valuable lesson feminist language and signifyin(g) offer. Western society and language should recognize the existence of a variety of voices. To marginalize this variety is to deny society that which would strengthen it most. Perhaps that point is made best by Hannah Nelson, an elderly African-American domestic worker: "I have grown to womanhood in a world where the saner you are, the madder you are made to appear."[77]

## Endnotes

1. Henry Louis Gates, Jr., *Figures in Black: Words, Signs, and the "Racial" Self* (New York: Oxford UP, 1987) 17.
2. This is not true for all theories and may not be true of postmodernism. Owens notes: "[I]f one of the most salient aspects of our postmodern culture is the presence of an insistent feminist voice . . . , theories of postmodernism have tended either to neglect or to repress that voice." Craig Owens, "The Discourse of Others: Feminists and Postmodernism," *The Anti-Aesthetic: Essays on Postmodern Culture*, ed. Hal Foster (Port Townsend, WA: Bay, 1983) 61.
3. Nancy Gray, *Language Unbound: On Experimental Writing by Women* (Urbana, IL: U of Illinois P, 1992) 1.
4. For a description of the creation of the patriarchy, see Marilyn French, *Beyond Power: On Women, Men, and Morals* (1985; rpt. New York: Ballantine, 1986) 65–122.
5. Elizabeth Kamarck Minnich, *Transforming Knowledge* (Philadelphia: Temple UP, 1990) 39. See also Wendy Martyna, "Beyond the He/Man Approach: The

Case for Nonsexist Language," *Language, Gender and Society*, ed. Barrie Thorne, Cheris Kramarae, and Nancy Henley (Rowley, MA: Newbury House, 1983) 25–37.

6. See, for example, Casey Miller and Kate Swift, *Words and Women: New Language in New Times* (1976; rpt. Garden City, NY: Anchor, 1977).

7. Robin Lakoff, *Language and Woman's Place* (New York: Harper & Row, 1975) 7. This is a revision and republication of her article by the same name in *Language and Society* 2 (1973): 45–79.

8. Lakoff 8–19, 23–32, 43, 83.

9. Barbara Bate, *Communication and the Sexes* (Prospect Heights, IL: Waveland, 1988) 105 n. 21.

10. French 477–78.

11. Carol Gilligan, *In a Different Voice: Psychological Theory and Women's Development* (Cambridge, MA: Harvard UP, 1982) 73.

12. Barrie Thorne, Cheris Kramarae, and Nancy Henley, "Language, Gender and Society: Opening a Second Decade of Research," *Language, Gender and Society*, ed. Barrie Thorne, Cheris Kramarae, and Nancy Henley (Rowley, MA: Newbury House, 1983) 17.

13. Hélène Cixous, "The Laugh of the Medusa," trans. Keith Cohen and Paula Cohen, *Signs* 1 (1976): 875.

14. Cixous, "The Laugh of the Medusa" 879–80.

15. Cixous, "The Laugh of the Medusa" 876, 886, 888.

16. Hélène Cixous, "Castration or Decapitation?," trans. Annette Kuhn, *Signs* 7 (1981): 53.

17. Cixous, "Castration or Decapitation?" 54.

18. Hélène Cixous, "Rethinking Differences," *Homosexualities and French Literature: Cultural Contexts/Critical Texts*, ed. George Stambolian and Elaine Marks (Ithaca, NY: Cornell UP, 1979) 71.

19. Cixous, "Castration or Decapitation?" 51.

20. Luce Irigaray, *The Sex Which Is Not One*, trans. Catherine Porter (1985; rpt. Ithaca, NY: Cornell UP, 1988) 75.

21. Irigaray 74, 79–80.

22. Mary Daly, *Gyn/Ecology: The Metaethics of Radical Feminism* (Boston: Beacon, 1978) 2.

23. Mary Daly and Jane Caputi, *Websters' First New Intergalactic Wickedary of the English Language* (Boston: Beacon, 1987) 3, 9, 11.

24. Mary Daly, *Pure Lust: Elemental Feminist Philosophy* (Boston: Beacon, 1984) 56, 87.

25. Specifically, she cites Julian Jaynes, *The Origin of Consciousness in the Breakdown of the Bicameral Mind* (1976; rpt. Boston: Houghton Mifflin, 1990), which is discussed in chapter seven.

26. Daly and Caputi 19–21.

27. Daly and Caputi 23–32; Daly, *Gyn/Ecology* 324–29.

28. Daly and Caputi 239–44.

29. Daly and Caputi 248–60.

30. Daly and Caputi 17.

31. Daly, *Gyn/Ecology* 414.

32. Daly, *Pure Lust* 113, 120.

33. David Lodge, ed., *Modern Criticism and Theory: A Reader* (New York: Longman, 1988) 229.

34. Julia Kristeva, "Women's Time," trans. Alice Jardine and Harry Blake, *The Kristeva Reader*, ed. Toril Moi (New York: Columbia UP, 1986) 203.

35. Karen A. Foss and Sonja K. Foss, *Women Speak: The Eloquence of Women's Lives* (Prospect Heights, IL: Waveland, 1991) 2.
36. Daly, *Gyn/Ecology* 8, 384.
37. Kristeva, "Women's Time" 194.
38. Kristeva, "Women's Time" 200.
39. Julia Kristeva, "A New Type of Intellectual: The Dissident," trans. Séan Hand, *The Kristeva Reader*, ed. Toril Moi (New York: Columbia UP, 1986) 298.
40. Kristeva, "Women's Time" 210.
41. Kristeva, "Women's Time" 207.
42. Andrea Nye, *Words of Power: A Feminist Reading of the History of Logic* (New York: Routledge, 1990) 59.
43. Nye 67, 79.
44. Nye 151, 154.
45. Nye 173–75.
46. Nye 179–83.
47. Mary Field Belenky, Blythe McVicker Clinchy, Nancy Rule Goldberger, and Jill Mattuck Tarule, *Women's Ways of Knowing: The Development of Self, Voice, and Mind* (n.p.: Basic, 1986) 7.
48. Belenky, Clinchy, Goldberger, and Tarule 54–55.
49. Belenky, Clinchy, Goldberger, and Tarule 85.
50. Belenky, Clinchy, Goldberger, and Tarule 93.
51. Belenky, Clinchy, Goldberger, and Tarule 95. See Mary Daly, *Beyond God the Father: Toward a Philosophy of Women's Liberation* (Boston: Beacon, 1973) 11.
52. Belenky, Clinchy, Goldberger, and Tarule 127.
53. Belenky, Clinchy, Goldberger, and Tarule 134.
54. Belenky, Clinchy, Goldberger, and Tarule 137.
55. Belenky, Clinchy, Goldberger, and Tarule 145. See the discussion of Jürgen Habermas in chapter eleven.
56. Minnich 9.
57. Minnich 29.
58. Geneva Smitherman, *Talkin and Testifyin: The Language of Black America* (Boston: Houghton Mifflin, 1977) 2–3.
59. For a description of this development and an explanation of the grammar and structure rules of West African languages, see Smitherman 3–15.
60. Smitherman 78.
61. Smitherman 47–48.
62. John Baugh, *Black Street Speech: Its History, Structure, and Survival* (1983; rpt. Austin: U of Texas P, 1985) ix.
63. Gates 235–36. The Signifying Monkey itself finds root in the sacred Yoruba trickster, Esu-Elegbara.
64. Henry Louis Gates, Jr., *The Signifying Monkey: A Theory of Afro-American Literary Criticism* (New York: Oxford UP, 1988) 179–83.
65. Smitherman 104–18.
66. Smitherman 118–34.
67. Baugh 26.
68. Gates, *The Signifying Monkey* 77–78 (emphasis omitted).
69. Gates, *The Signifying Monkey* 88.
70. Smitherman 135.
71. Smitherman 148.
72. Smitherman 157.
73. Smitherman 80.
74. Gates, *The Signifying Monkey* 76.

75. Smitherman 186.
76. Ntozake Shange, *for colored girls who have considered suicide/ when the rainbow is enuf* (New York: MacMillan, 1977) 2.
77. John Langston Gwaltney, *Drylongso: A Self-Portrait of Black America* (New York: Random House, 1980) 7.

# Conclusion

The purpose of this book has been to introduce you to various aspects of rhetoric—from the signs that are its constituent parts to the various theories about rhetoric and its relationship to human understanding. No matter how you define rhetoric, human beings are rhetorical creatures who live within and spin a web of words, see the world through terministic screens, or are thrust unwittingly into and created by a discursive formation. To understand rhetoric is to understand ourselves.

The book began with a challenge to you to engage in a dialogue with scholars who have studied rhetoric. If you accepted that challenge, you thought about various ideas as you read this text—developing refutations against some and adopting others. In short, you joined the conversation concerning rhetoric. This is a conversation that should continue beyond this text and beyond any class you presently are taking, for understanding rhetoric (as well as understanding yourself) is a never-ending process of personal growth.

The final chapter of this text is the beginning of that lifelong conversation about rhetoric. It offers you a second challenge—to develop your own rhetorical point of view.

# Chapter Thirteen

# A Rhetorical Point of View

To take a rhetorical point of view is to understand some of the issues surrounding rhetoric and to choose particular positions, or at least to understand the positions implied by your beliefs and attitudes. The first section of this chapter attempts to categorize some of these issues. To take a rhetorical point of view also involves a consciousness of the operation of rhetoric in your life. Thus, this chapter offers a challenge to you—to be aware of the rhetorical processes of human existence and to take an active role in understanding and, where possible, managing them.

## Issues in Rhetoric

Centuries of theorizing about rhetoric and about its constituent parts have resolved few questions. Issues still range from the appropriate definition for rhetoric to its scope and province. Which position you adopt on any of these issues is less important than understanding the options and making a conscious and critical decision. Of the many issues surrounding rhetoric, this chapter reviews the possible relationships between signs and reality, the nature of rhetoric, and the possible perspectives from which rhetoric can be viewed.

### Relationship of Signs to Reality

Nearly every theory about rhetoric, either explicitly or implicitly, is based on a philosophical position regarding the relationship of linguistic signs to reality. These positions roughly fall into three main categories: 1) language represents reality; 2) language affects perceptions of reality; and 3) language creates reality.

**Language Represents Reality**.   One philosophical position taken by rhetoricians is essentially the realist position—that the natural world exists, is knowable, and is represented either well or poorly by particular language. This position is illustrated by the General Semanticists. Although the basic philosophical tenets of the movement were laid out by Alexander Bryan Johnson,[1] credit as founder is given to Alfred Korzybski, whose text, *Science and Sanity*,[2] details the principles of General Semantics. Korzybski refers to his system as "non-Aristotelian," by which he means that it is not based on Aristotle's logic, which he characterizes as a two-valued, either/or system. Korzybski argues that the laws of thought (identity, noncontradiction, and excluded middle, which are discussed in chapter nine) implicit in Western thinking create false dichotomies, such as right/wrong, saved/damned, black/white. Rather than two-valued, reality is multi-valued, according to Korzybski. Our language and our logic thus should be expanded to recognize the various items that lie between such bipolar distinctions. His point is that no circle is perfectly round; some humans do not have two legs; and many shades of gray can be identified. Korzybski also identifies a related problem he calls *elementalism*, which is the problem of separating in language what is not separated in nature. Examples of this false separation, according to Korzybski, include space/time and heredity/environment.

Although other scholars wrote about General Semantics, only S. I. Hayakawa, with his very readable text, *Language in Thought and Action*,[3] reached the same level of popularity as Korzybski. To remind language users that reality is multifaceted and ever changing while language is more static, Hayakawa proposes the use of index numbers. These index numbers are of two sorts. The first indicate dates as a reminder that things and people change over time, as *Ronald Reagan*$_{1945}$ is not the same as *Ronald Reagan*$_{1984}$. Most individuals would like others to acknowledge that they change and should not be held forever to account for things they did or were in the past. Other index numbers are to operate as reminders that individuals in a class are not all the same, as *college student*$_1$ is not identical to *college student*$_2$. Failure to make this latter distinction, which Hayakawa refers to as "confused levels of abstraction," allows assumptions about a class to affect perceptions about individuals in that class. Examples of this problem abound. If a woman is treated poorly by one man, she might decide that all men are bad. The same thinking causes people to condemn a race or a religious group because one member of the group caused them difficulties.

Hayakawa also develops what he calls the three rules of General Semantics. The first rule is *the word is not the thing*, by which he means that language and reality are distinct. People who read a ghost story, then have difficulty falling asleep because of the fear they experience, are, according to Hayakawa, confusing words and things. He calls such confusion a "semantic reaction." His second rule is *the word is not all the thing*. By this he means that one never can say all there is to say about something. You can describe an object in many, many ways; however, something always remains to be said. To describe his first two rules further, Hayakawa uses the analogy of a map. A map represents a certain territory just as, he suggests, a word represents a certain thing. However, the map and the territory are different (rule one), and the map can never show all the territory (rule two). His final rule is *language is self-reflexive*; that is, we must use language when we talk about language. This makes the study of language somewhat more complex than the study of other things.

Hayakawa also distinguished among types of statements humans make about the world. Reports, which he prefers, are verifiable statements. Inferences, on the other hand, are statements about the unknown made on the basis of the known. If you make a statement about someone's economic status based on the type of car she drives or the house in which he lives, you are not reporting but are using language to infer, according to Hayakawa. Finally, judgments, which Hayakawa likes least of all, are statements of approval or disapproval, such as "Beka is a wonderful person." Hayakawa claims that some statements masquerading as reports really are judgments, such as "Jim is a thief" or "Annika is an over-achiever." What you can *report* is that Jim was convicted by a jury of stealing a car in July of 1992 or that Annika is president of the student body, works twenty hours a week, gets a 4.0 grade point average, and volunteers at the local nursing home.

As these ideas of Korzybski and Hayakawa illustrate, General Semantics is based on the premise that reality is separate from language but knowable by humans and that it can be represented in language. This common sense philosophical position likely is implicit in other rhetorical theories as well.

**Language Affects Perceptions of Reality**.   A very popular position with contemporary rhetoricians is that, although reality exists apart from humans, language affects how we view reality. I. A. Richards is among the rhetoricians who hold this view. He acknowledges reality as one point in his semantic triangle, which is discussed in chapter four.

However, that reality is very much colored by our language—"so far from being a solid matter of fact," it is instead "a fabric of conventions."[4]

Two other rhetorical theorists discussed in chapter three hold this view. Richard Weaver, in a vitriolic attack on General Semanticists, argues that "the word is a sort of deliverance from the shifting world of appearances."[5] Words, according to Weaver, have the power to define physical reality for us or to compel particular views of that reality. Further, language use by a community results in meanings that could not be reached by a single language user. He notes:

> I am inclined to agree with W. M. Urban, in his *Language and Reality*, that the situation is the reverse of what is usually conceived. It is not that things give meaning to words; it is that meaning makes things "things." It does not make things in their subsistence; but it does make things in their discreetness for the understanding. . . . To know a thing is not to arrive finally at some direct perception of a property, as Locke suggests, but to form some ideal construct of it, in which meaning and value are closely bound. Theories of meaning that include only the symbol and the thing symbolized leave out of account the interpreter.[6]

Kenneth Burke acknowledges that language affects reality by pointing out "how fantastically much of our 'Reality' could not exist for us, were it not for our profound and inveterate involvement in symbol systems."[7]

Mary Daly and others advocating a women's language understand that language affects perceptions of reality; to change language is to change understanding. In seeking to cast off patriarchal reality, Daly writes: "We eject, banish, depose the possessing language—spoken and written words, body language, architectural language, technological language, the language of symbols and of institutional structures. . . ."[8] She urges women to rename reality: "Our Naming/analysis becomes ever more direct and urgent as we confront the advanced stages of nuclearism, Nagging women to Realize our own biophilic reality. . . . The work of such complex Naming is an invocation of Other reality." Daly argues that words spin and weave "tapestries of Elemental creation."[9]

**Language Creates Reality**.   The final version of this relationship is akin to the philosophy of radical idealism—that language actually creates reality. Something close to this position is espoused by several postmodern writers who decry metaphysics and simply ignore questions about the existence of a reality beyond the one posited by language.

Michel Foucault seems to take this position. He argues that the historical claim that discourse is the covering on preexisting meanings is wrong; he calls it the "will to truth." We have this will to truth, according to Foucault, because we feel that individuals create discourse and that the natural world is the source of discourse. In this view, we use language to exchange knowledge but not to create it. Foucault, as noted in chapter ten, argues that discourse creates the world rather than reflects it:

> The conditions necessary for the appearance of an object of discourse . . . are many and imposing. Which means that one cannot speak of anything at any time; it is not easy to say something new. . . . [T]he object does not await in limbo the order that will free it and enable it to become embodied in a visible and prolix objectivity; it does not pre-exist itself, held back by some obstacle at the first edges of light.[10]

For Foucault, discourses "systematically form the objects of which they speak."[11]

Jacques Derrida's project, also discussed in chapter ten, has been accused by many critics of suggesting that nothing "real" exists outside the written text. Although he has gone to great lengths to deny this, most critics remain unconvinced. As Christopher Norris points out, these arguments are "ingenious but finally unconvincing. As a matter of record they have not done much to dispel the idea among Derrida's opponents" that he is unconcerned about reality beyond the text.[12] Certainly statements such as *"il n' y a pas de hors-texte"* (there is nothing outside the text)[13] feed this categorization of Derrida.

One of these perspectives on the relationship of signs to reality is a part of every rhetorical point of view. Likely, few people live their lives based upon the latter assumption, as defining speeding trucks out of existence is difficult when one is crossing a busy street. Although postmodern views seem to adopt this position, some obvious limits to its applicability are apparent. However, most contemporary theories of rhetoric proceed from the assumption that much if not all of what humans know as reality is rhetorically constructed. This leads to a second issue—what is the nature of rhetoric?

## Nature of Rhetoric

The classical view of rhetoric is that it constitutes persuasive public discourse—oratory intended to affect policy in the legislature, to determine facts in the courts, or to assign praise or blame in the public arena. In this view, rhetoric involves the invention and arrangement of arguments, stylistic choice of words, and the presentational aspects of the speech. In a later view, rhetoric was only the stylistic aspects of discourse—with emphasis on ornament and presentation.

Some contemporary views of rhetoric assign to the concept all intentional uses of signs. In this view, any discourse, as it affects both the participants and those who encounter it, is rhetorical. Indeed, for some theorists, any intentional use of any sign system whatsoever becomes rhetoric; they point out that visual (as well as, one suspects, auditory) nonlinguistic signs are used to create meaning for human beings. Other theorists conceptualize rhetoric even more broadly—for they dispense with the need for intention. Thus any signs that create meaning become rhetoric.

All of these perspectives see rhetoric as the use of signs, as a human action leading to a discursive or other sign-created event. However, rhetoric also can be conceived as an ability, as in George Kennedy's translation of Aristotle's definition of rhetoric, noted in chapter three: "Let rhetoric be [defined as] an ability, in each [particular] case, to see the available means of persuasion."[14] Kennedy has since suggested his own conception of rhetoric, which is perhaps the broadest of all. He defines rhetoric as an energy that is prior to speech, an energy that compels communication. His definition opens up the possibility of nonhuman rhetoric, as this rhetorical energy is "manifest in all animal life and existed long before the evolution of human beings."[15]

The conceptions of rhetoric as the human use of signs can be distinguished by the outcome, in some cases intended and in others not, of such use. These conceptions range from persuasion to the creation of meaning or human understanding. Related to these various conceptions about the nature of rhetoric is the perspective from which rhetoric is viewed.

## Perspective on Rhetoric

Some scholars view rhetoric from the perspective of the rhetor. In this perspective, a subject creates rhetoric by giving a speech, writing an essay, or managing signs in some fashion. If rhetoric is viewed from the point of view of the rhetor, scholars are concerned with the actions of the rhetor. Critics evaluate rhetorical actions, and the rhetor makes use of various prescriptive theories about rhetoric in making choices, ranging from choices about words to patterns of arrangement to types of argument, based on his or her knowledge of the audience and of the situation.

Other scholars view rhetoric from the perspective of the audience. If rhetoric is viewed from the point of view of the audience, scholars are concerned largely with the effects of rhetoric. How are we persuaded? How is meaning created? Do we, as audience, play an active or a passive role? Is persuasion something over which we have choice, or does discourse work its magic while we remain enchanted and unaware? Does rhetoric control us or do we remain free agents capable of choice? Can we deconstruct a text to expose its circularities and its contradictions?

Still other scholars view rhetoric from an omniscient perspective. If rhetoric is viewed from an omniscient point of view, new issues arise. What is truth and is it created by or is it prior to rhetoric? If created, is truth the product of a consensus born of discussion, debate, or communicative action? If prior to rhetoric, how do humans access it? Do the concepts of *speaker* or *author* add anything to our understanding of rhetoric?

Related to these issues is the role of the individual in a rhetorical perspective. As noted above, the individual may be seen as the subject or author of rhetorical activities. In this light, some scholars see the individual as an actor in a drama; others add to this conception a dimension of ethical choice. Other scholars see the individual as part of the audience or as reader. This may be a passive role, or the reader/listener may create, with each interaction, a new text. Further, the individual may be the result of discourse or may be relegated, as the result of dominant discourse, to the role of Other. In short, an individual may be constructed, created, or controlled by rhetorical action.

The position you adopt on these and other issues[16] regarding rhetoric will affect your rhetorical point of view. Whatever choices you make, you should strive to heighten your awareness of the operation of rhetoric in your life. To encourage you to become more aware of rhetoric, one particular rhetorical point of view (the author's) is presented in the section below. This point of view should serve merely as an illustration; in no way is it presented as a model to be adopted or emulated.

## One Rhetorical Point of View

Human beings experience reality only through their various systems of signs and as it is presented to them by the society within which they live and the groups of which they are a part. Thus, reality is, in human terms, socially constructed by rhetorical means. Although the author does not knowingly step in front of speeding automobiles, what she understands of them, as well as how she interprets the rest of her experience, has little if anything to do with a reality apart from language and human conversations. Further, having once stepped in front of and been hit by a speeding automobile, she now understands busy streets and approaches crossing any street in a fashion very much affected by her rhetorical experience of this prior event. In other words, she understands rhetorically not purely objectively.

One means for understanding rhetorical experience is by analogy to oral societies. To view oral societies as primitive is to miss the lessons they teach about the rhetorical nature of contemporary human existence. Among these lessons is a deeper understanding of the constituent parts of rhetoric—words, language, narratives, and conversations.

Words are magic in our contemporary existence just as they were for oral peoples. By naming, we create objects. We cull objects from the disorder of sensation and, by giving them a name, make something of them. Much of this naming was done prior to any one human's entrance into society. Thus the human project is not so much naming but learning how reality is named and ordered. This is the process of being socialized into the discursive formation that surrounds us. Individuals may do some naming of reality during their lives; more likely, they are part of the unconscious but ongoing changing of language that Ferdinand de Saussure describes as its mutability (see chapter two).

The language we speak also has magical attributes. The magic of language—which lies both in its potential and in its use—is described well by Nancy Gray:

> Language is as complex and loaded as a spell. It carries intention and consequence, anticipated and not, yet is alive with its own energy. Like a spell, it takes shape both as itself and for a purpose; its being and its purpose are not separate and not one. Spells, like language, are always a bit tricky to handle; one can never be sure they will do one's bidding. Spells take action. Given form in language and by concentration of the will, they are of and interact with the experience of the speaker to become the experience of the listener. Once, it has been said, words cast as spells were considered a form of action in the world as real as any other. Now that action is regarded as superstition, a delusion borne of primitive ignorance and irrationality.[17]

Gray argues that Western rationality discounts this magic of language; however, from a rhetorical point of view, these discursive spells are prior to and more fundamental than rationality. They are the source and definer of all other human action, and they operate as the metanarratives of human existence.

Contemporary humans live by our narratives much as oral peoples lived by theirs. Contemporary Western narratives include our histories; our stories about art, science, and philosophy; our logics; and our religions. By means of these narratives, we order the flux, just as primal human beings made sense of their surroundings by means of their oral traditions. At a more fundamental level are the metanarratives of human existence, the paradigms of human thought and understanding, which are by their very nature rhetorical. Although the postmodern project claims to dispense with metanarratives, by that claim, it merely succeeds in substituting a different metanarrative.

To view the narratives and metanarratives of contemporary Western society as a chosen means for ordering the flux rather than a never-changing truth is to see the world as possibility rather than fact. The result is not, however, a relativist world in which no judgments about good or bad can be made. Rather, it is a world created by discourse, by human consensus that is a product of debate and of conversation.

Rhetoric is found in more than texts, that is, in speeches and essays; rhetoric also occurs in conversation, in discourse. Each conversation, each linguistic exchange, creates something new. This is the process of interpretation that makes something out of the flux. At the end of Lawrence Durrell's first novel in the Alexandria Quartet, *Justine*, the male narrator decides not to answer a letter from Clea, an old friend who proposes a relationship, allowing her to make what she will of his silence. He muses, "Does not everything depend on our interpretation of the silence around us?"[18] The result of our many conversations is precisely that—to interpret the silence around us, to make sense of our existence.

All of these constituent parts of rhetoric are understood best when viewed from an omniscient perspective—where one sees truth as the product of conversations. The end result of the sum of conversations is a consensus, ranging from strong to uneasy, about various things within various groups. The results of consensus are the metanarratives, the values, and the codes of our various cultures. These rhetorical agreements, by which we measure our lives and our actions, are that which keep us from the dark abyss of relativity. Understanding that they are agreements rather than absolute truths keeps us, on the other hand, from becoming dogmatic, self-righteous, oppressive, or worse.

Although all sorts of sign systems are important and rhetorical, language is central. Further, all language users are important to the rhetorical process. Texts are not created without authors; subjects are important because subjects make choices that have consequences. Although constrained by the discursive formation, by the consensus of one's group and society, by the language that one speaks, and by the texts one has encountered—individuals still make choices within these various constraints, and such choices have consequences. Tell a child something, and the child will believe it. Thus, humans have responsibilities for what they say to children, and for what they say to each other. As discussed in chapter three, Weaver suggests we are all preachers, in our private and in our public lives. Every time we speak, we urge a particular view of the world on those who hear us. By our choices, our speeches, our writings, our conversations, and even our actions, we affect one another and the world around us. Thus, to ignore the subject is to ignore a critical constituent component of rhetorical action.

The audience is also important, however, and not just as an entity to be analyzed or one to which the rhetor must adapt. The audience is central to the creation of the texts of our lives. Indeed, in a significant sense, new texts are created each time someone reads an essay, as she brings to that text all the other texts that have affected her. Even oral texts become different things to different people. Human understanding comes as a result of this interaction of subject, audience, and other texts, not merely as a result of an orator or an author persuading an audience.

As Elizabeth Minnich argues, over the course of our lives, we are affected much less by written texts than by conversations.[19] Indeed, it is within conversations that our rhetorical point of view is developed—as we grow to understand by creating a framework from our many and various conversations. From this rhetorical point of view, listening is as rhetorical an action as is speaking or writing. When we speak or write, we often are seduced by the sound of our single voice. When we listen, we realize the cacophony. As Gray describes it, the cacophony is "vibrant, one in which no assumption of knowledge is stable but depends on a continual process of experience, of language as experience, as action and enactment, using everything. To hear this language we must pay attention."[20] This cacophony of discourse can push language past the boundaries of its consciousness—to new experience.

This rhetorical point of view does not discount everything in the Western tradition, as some postmodern theories seem to do. We can learn from the logics of Western rationality just as we can learn from their critics. Indeed, the very structure of the English language (as well as texts in English which purport to criticize or decry logic and argumentation) rely on some basic principles of Western reasoning. However, one sees more broadly when one realizes that Western reason is only one of several ways of thinking, that discussions of reason are not adequate to describe many operations of the human mind, including intuition, passion, and emotion. Exploring other ways of understanding leads not to the irrational but to a deeper understanding of human possibility. It falls not to persuaders, who operate within the constraints of Western rationality, but to poets to challenge the paradigms of language. Henry Louis Gates, in describing particular African-American poetry, says, "the poet not only has accepted his or her role as the point of consciousness of the language but has pushed that language to express that which is untranslatable.''[21] In everyday discourse, metaphor operates much like poetry; that is, poetry and metaphor create and recreate meaning.

This rhetorical point of view is not, in the final analysis, postmodern, at least not insofar as that term means without metanarratives. To understand the postmodern is important; to try to live it as a rhetorical being may be impossible. Katherine Hayles describes a component of postmodernism as ''the denaturing of language'':

> The sense that language is constantly unraveling, even as one weaves it into a design; that any utterance can be deconstructed to show that it already presupposes what it would say and hence has no prior ground on which to rest; that all texts are penetrated by infinite numbers of intertexts so that contextual horizons are always constructions rather than givens; in short, that signification is a construction rather than a natural result of speaking or writing—all this was implied by the denaturing process as it applies to language. Denatured language is language regarded as ground painted under our feet while we hang suspended in a void. We cannot dispense with the illusion of ground, because we need a place from which to speak. But it is bracketed by our knowledge that it is only a painting, not natural ground.[22]

From a rhetorical point of view, that ''it is only a painting'' is of no special concern, for everything is painting; that is, everything human is rhetorical. Humans are not suspended in a void; they have always lived comfortably within their painted—their rhetorical—reality. Oral humans lived within their narratives; so do we. The world oral humans saw was painted by their stories; so is ours. If any distinction can be made between early oral and contemporary literate individuals, perhaps we have become more self-conscious—which includes consciousness of the rhetorical aspects of our lives. That self-consciousness should be cause for celebration not despair. It should be cause for conversation.

## Summary

Our world is a world of words. In ''A River Runs through It,'' Norman Maclean describes his early family life, which centered around the rivers of Montana on which his father, a Presbyterian minister, taught Maclean and his brother to become expert fly fishermen. (''In our family, there was no clear line between religion and fly fishing,'' he begins his story.) When Maclean has told the story of his family and is left, an old man, the only one still alive, fly fishing in the waning summer light of Montana, he says:

> Eventually, all things merge into one, and a river runs through it. The river was cut by the world's great flood and runs over rocks from the basement of time. On some of the rocks are timeless raindrops. Under the rocks are the words, and some of the words are theirs.
>
> I am haunted by waters.[23]

And by words.

## Endnotes

1. Although his ideas originally were published in 1828, Alexander Bryan Johnson was not widely known until republication in *A Treatise On Language*, ed. David Rynin (Berkeley: University of California P, 1947). Even then, he remained in the shadow of Korzybski.

2. Alfred Korzybski, *Science and Sanity: An Introduction to Non-Aristotelian Systems and General Semantics* (1933; rpt. Lakeville, CT.: International Non-Aristotelian, 1958).

3. S. I. Hayakawa, *Language in Thought and Action*, 4th ed. (New York: Harcourt Brace Jovanovich, 1978).

4. I. A. Richards, *The Philosophy of Rhetoric* (1936; rpt. New York: Oxford UP, 1965) 41.

5. Richard Weaver, "The Power of the Word," *Language is Sermonic: Richard M. Weaver on the Nature of Rhetoric*, eds. Richard L. Johannesen, Rennard Strickland, and Ralph T. Eubanks (Baton Rouge: Louisiana State UP, 1970) 35.

6. Richard M. Weaver, "Relativism and the Use of Language," in *Language is Sermonic: Richard M. Weaver on the Nature of Rhetoric*, eds. Richard L. Johannesen, Rennard Strickland, and Ralph T. Eubanks (Baton Rouge: Louisiana State UP, 1970) 121.

7. Kenneth Burke, *Language as Symbolic Action: Essays on Life, Literature, and Method* (Berkeley: University of California P, 1966) 48.

8. Mary Daly, *Gyn/Ecology: The Metaethics of Radical Feminism* (Boston: Beacon, 1978) 345.

9. Mary Daly, *Pure Lust: Elemental Feminist Philosophy* (Boston: Beacon, 1984) xii.

10. Michel Foucault, *The Archaeology of Knowledge and the Discourse on Language*, trans. A. M. Sheridan Smith (New York: Pantheon, 1972) 44–45.

11. Foucault 49.

12. Christopher Norris, *Derrida* (Cambridge: Harvard UP, 1987) 144.

13. Jacques Derrida, *Of Grammatology*, trans. Gayatri Chakravorty Spivak (Baltimore: Johns Hopkins UP, 1976) 158.

14. Aristotle, *On Rhetoric: A Theory of Civic Discourse*, trans. George A. Kennedy (New York: Oxford UP, 1991) I 1355 36–37.

15. George A. Kennedy, "A Hoot in the Dark: The Evolution of General Rhetoric," *Philosophy and Rhetoric* 25 (1992): 4.

16. For a discussion of other issues, see Sonja K. Foss, Karen A. Foss, and Robert Trapp, *Contemporary Perspectives on Rhetoric*, 2nd ed. (Prospect Heights, IL: Waveland, 1991) 316–35.

17. Nancy Gray, *Language Unbound: On Experimental Writing by Women* (Urbana: University of Illinois P, 1992) 133.
18. Lawrence Durrell, *Justine* (1957; rpt. New York: Simon & Schuster, 1969) 222.
19. Elizabeth Kamark Minnich, *Transforming Knowledge* (Philadelphia: Temple UP, 1990) xiii.
20. Gray 132.
21. Henry Louis Gates, Jr., *Figures in Black: Words, Signs, and the "Racial" Self* (New York: Oxford UP, 1987) 195.
22. N. Katherine Hayles, *Chaos Bound: Orderly Disorder in Contemporary Literature and Science* (Ithaca, NY: Cornell UP, 1990) 268–69.
23. Norman Maclean, *A River Runs through It and Other Stories* (1976; rpt. New York: Simon & Schuster, 1992) 113.

# Index